Southern Tales

Southern Tales

A Treasury of Stories from Virginia, North Carolina, South Carolina, Georgia, Florida, Alabama, Kentucky, Tennessee, and Mississippi

Webb Garrison

GALAHAD BOOKS
NEW YORK

First Galahad Books edition published in 1997.

Galahad Books
A division of BBS Publishing Corporation
386 Park Avenue South
New York, NY 10016

Galahad Books is a registered trademark of BBS Publishing Corporation.

Published by arrangement with Rutledge Hill Press.

Library of Congress Catalog Card Number: 97-73425

ISBN: 0-88365-963-8

Printed in the United States of America.

Contents

Part One: Virginia

1. Alexander Spotswood Put an End to Piracy .. 3
2. Captain Sally Healed More Than One
   Thousand Wounded Men 9
3. "Let Lee's Mansion Be First to Fall" 15
4. Daniel Boone Never, Never Gave Up 23
5. George Washington's Longest Battle Was with
   His Own Countrymen.................. 29
6. Little Books of William McGuffey Shaped the
   Mind of Nineteenth-Century America 35
7. Booker T. Washington Took His Own
   Medicine: "Let Your Buckets Down Where
   You Are"........................... 41
8. Puzzled but Obedient, Hill Lamon Left
   Lincoln Unguarded 47

Part Two: North Carolina

9. Sherman's Plan Would Have Avoided
   Reconstruction...................... 55
10. Gunmaker Said He'd Put an End to War 59
11. Wright Brothers Started Over En Route to
    Kitty Hawk 63
12. They Called Elizabeth Blackwell "Mad or
    Bad"............................. 67
13. Jackson County M.D. Pioneered in Organ
    Transplants 71

14. "Poorest of the Vanderbilts" Built Largest
Mansion . . . .　75
15. Dorothea Dix Shook Up the Lawmakers . . . . .　79
16. Tsali Gave His Life for Fellow Tribesmen . . . .　83
17. Benjamin Hawkins Smoked the Peace Pipe . .　87
18. Dan Morgan Masterminded "Most Imitated
Battle" . . . .　91
19. The Battle That Changed Naval Warfare
Forever . . . .　95
20. "Sherman in Gray" Burned a Wide Swath
Around the World . . . .　99
21. Boy Hero of the Waxhaws Defied the British .　103
22. Original Siamese Twins Reared Families in
Carolina . . . .　107

Part Three: South Carolina
23. Every Voyage of the *Hunley* Was a Suicide
Mission . . . .　113
24. Charlestonian Added Twenty-Eight Million
Acres to the Nation . . . .　117
25. No One Ever Wielded a Cane Like Preston
Brooks . . . .　121
26. Joel Poinsett's "Ghost" Is Here Every
Christmas . . . .　125
27. William Moultrie Was First to Fight
the British . . . .　129
28. Penelope Barker Led Nation's First Women's
Protest . . . .　133
29. Angelina Grimke Defied Charleston Tradition .　137
30. Gibson's General Store Shook and Swayed . . .　141
31. Showdown in Charleston Harbor . . . .　145
32. Sharpshooter Who Spared George Washington
Lies at Kings Mountain . . . .　149
33. Flag of Truce Was Osceola's Undoing . . . . . .　153
34. Sergeant Jasper Saved the Flag! . . . .　157
35. Calhoun Sowed Seeds That Led to War . . . . .　161
36. Charleston Invalid Saved Mount Vernon for
the Nation . . . .　165

Part Four: Georgia

37. Perilous Voyage to an Unknown Destination . 171
38. Shotgun Totin' Dentist Was Pivotal at the
    O K Corral 175
39. Beautiful Widow's Problems Led to the
    Cotton Gin 179
40. Runaway Thomas Sims Helped Shape the
    Nation's Destiny 183
41. Vice-President Aaron Burr Hid from the Law
    on St. Simons 187
42. Dueling Grounds Saw Blue Blood Flow Like
    Water 191
43. Claiming Innocence, Swiss Doctor Died for
    War Crimes 195
44. Manhunt Netted President Jefferson Davis . . . 199
45. First Land Pirate Was an Indian Princess 203
46. Heisman Guided Yellow Jackets to All-Time
    Record 207
47. "Blind Tom" Bethune Awed Crowned Heads
    of Europe 211
48. Oglethorpe's "Indian Ways" Stopped Spain
    Cold 215
49. Slave Girl Triggered First Big North/South
    Split 219

Part Five: Florida

50. Juan Ponce de León Was One of Spain's Most
    Splendid Failures 225
51. A Fair Swap: All Florida for Havana and
    West Cuba 229
52. Governor Bloxham Negotiated America's
    Biggest Land Deal 233
53. Florida's "Founder" Started with Nine Cents . 239
54. No More Fear of Spain! 243
55. Julia Tuttle Sent Orange Blossoms to Flagler . 249
56. Key West Was Home to Hemingway 255
57. FDR Was Saved by the Wife of a Miami
    Physician 259

58. Colin Kelly Became the First Hero of World
    War II   265
59. America Probes the Universe from Cape
    Canaveral   271
60. Brownie Wise Taught the World How to
    Give a Party   277
61. "Somebody's Grabbing Up an Awful Lot of
    Land"   283

Part Six: Alabama
62. Tomochichi: Early Exile   291
63. Josiah Gorgas: Quick-change Artist   297
64. Junaluska: American Hero   303
65. Abel D. Streight: Race Across the State   311
66. Tecumseh: My Spirit Will Return!   317
67. Emma Sansom: Sunbonnet Heroine   323
68. CSS *Alabama*: 294 Searches   331
69. William C. Gorgas: Fever Fighter   339
70. Jesse Owens: Roller-Coaster Gold   347
71. Joseph Wheeler: 120 Pounds, Soaking Wet . . .   353
72. Tallulah Bankhead: Sque-e-ze Me!   359

Part Seven: Kentucky
73. John James Audubon: Bird Man   369
74. Jefferson Davis: Reluctant President   377
75. Abraham Lincoln: Fate and Cunning   383
76. Robert Anderson: Hero or Turncoat?   389
77. Carry Nation: Hatchet Woman   395
78. Daniel Boone: His Feet Itched   401

Part Eight: Tennessee
79. Quivering Earth: Reelfoot Lake   409
80. Andrew Jackson: Born to Fight!   415
81. Davy Crockett: Top Entertainer   423
82. Sam Houston: Red Heart   431
83. Nathan Bedford Forrest: Wizard of the Saddle   439
84. Andrew Johnson: Margin of One   445

85. Dutchman's Grade: Carnage on the Home
    Front 453

Part Nine: Mississippi
86. Hernando de Soto: Sunset on the River 461
87. Camel Corps: Desert Ships 467
88. Varina Davis: Convoluted Belle 473
89. Vicksburg: Forty-Three Days of Siege 481
90. The *Sultana*: Horror on the River 487
91. Eudora Welty: Listen . . . and Look! 493

PART ONE:
Virginia

Explorer Alexander Spotswood *was knighted for his expedition that reached the Susquehanna River.*

Alexander Spotswood Put an End to Piracy

"Are you game for a good fight, Lieutenant?"

Robert Maynard of the warship *Pearl* bristled and started to rise from his chair.

"Sit down, man, sit down! I meant no harm."

"Perhaps not, Your Excellency, but you know I am an officer of the Royal Navy. I have never shrunk from combat and never will."

Governor Alexander Spotswood nodded understanding, then explained: "If you agree to my undertaking, you will be in no ordinary fight. It is my purpose to put an end to piracy in these waters."

"I thought Virginia's coast was now safe . . . ."

"By no means. Near Cape Charles, buccaneers took over the sloop *Betty* not long ago. Once her hold was empty of Madeira wine, they scuttled her. Now they have taken refuge in North Carolina, a colony that has been out of control since it was given its own governor."

"I take it that you plan to launch an invasion of Carolina, a region over which you have no authority?"

Sir Alexander Spotswood remained silent for a moment, then responded soberly: "I have no choice in the matter. These brigands infest Virginia waters. I have it on good authority that they have even beached their vessels on our coast to clear the hulls of barnacles.

"Bath Town, in North Carolina, has become a haven for pirates. The man called Blackbeard has established his vessels in Ocracoke Inlet, and good intelligence has it that he is preparing to erect fortified works."

"I know very little about the New World," countered Maynard, "but I have been told that officials of the Crown make their residence in Bath Town."

"That they do, man! Governor Robert Eden has established himself just across the river from the town. But he will do nothing. Rumor has it that he profits from depredations of the pirates."

"Is there proof that His Majesty's governor sanctions piracy?"

"No proof," admitted the chief executive of Virginia. "But incriminating documents have come into my hands. They indicate that Tobias Knight is aiding and abetting piracy, in return for a good one-third of all the loot that is seized."

"I don't believe I know that name. Who is Knight?"

"He is secretary of the colony and collector of customs. Also a member of the council, recently made chief justice. He can get whatever supplies are needed to fortify Ocracoke Island, perhaps even cannon.

"I have decided to strike by land and by sea before the place becomes too strong to attack. Will you lead vessels of the expedition?"

"I am willing, Sir Alexander. But I doubt very much that London will give permission for warships stationed in Chesapeake Bay to engage in action within waters of a sister colony."

"Of course not! This is a private enterprise, wholly financed by me and employing rented sloops. All I need from you is a handshake guaranteeing your leadership, along with recruitment of your sailors for three weeks of action that will bring them much prize money."

"You propose, then, to treat captured vessels and their contents as prizes?"

"Certainly! And I think you know that the lion's share of prize money goes to the commander."

Robert Maynard nodded understanding and extended his hand. "I am convinced, Your Excellency. Please detail for me your precise plan of action."

Although he was a newcomer to Virginia, the officer who agreed to lead an attack upon the notorious pirate

Blackbeard had heard a great deal about the man who planned the expedition.

Born in Tangier, Morocco, Alexander Spotswood was the son of a physician who attended British troops stationed there. At age seventeen he became an ensign in a foot regiment and fought throughout the War of the Spanish Succession. Wounded in the battle of Blenheim—and by then a lieutenant colonel—his exchange was personally negotiated by the duke of Marlborough. Shortly afterward, perhaps through the influence of Marlborough, he became lieutenant governor of Virginia.

George Hamilton, earl of Orkney, had no intention of going to the colony of which the king had made him governor. In return for half the salary of his subordinate and agent, he relegated management of the New World venture to Spotswood. Although the title was never formally conferred upon him, the physician's son functioned as governor of Virginia.

Spotswood took office on June 23, 1710, and quickly made friends and enemies. His decision to make effective the writ of habeas corpus, previously withheld from the

King George I, who gave the lucrative governorship to the Earl of Orkney, a man who never set foot in Virginia.

province, was cheered everywhere. However, he soon began to regulate the tobacco trade, demanding inspection of all produced for export or offered as security for legal tender. Furious at this edict, wealthy planters started making plans for his removal.

Spotswood led a band of adventurers, servants, and rangers across the Blue Ridge Mountains in 1716. They found a broad, fertile valley which they explored all the way to a river the governor dubbed the Euphrates (now the Shenandoah). To commemorate the expedition and to foster interest in the West, he gave each member of his group a golden horseshoe.

When word of the first exploration of "the great mountains" reached England, King George I rewarded Spotswood with knighthood and sent him a golden horseshoe set with precious stones. That launched the Order of the Golden Horseshoe, America's first fellowship reminiscent of the age of chivalry.

It pained him, Sir Alexander explained to Lieutenant Maynard, that affairs of state made it impossible for him to lead the planned strike against piracy. Already, he had persuaded Capt. Ellis Brand of the warship *Lyme* to head a body of troops that would proceed by land to Bath Town. Maynard's agreement to strike simultaneously by sea meant that the governor's cherished plan could soon be put to the test.

"I have hired two fine sloops," he explained to Maynard. "There are numerous sand bars and reefs in the vicinity of Ocracoke; a warship could not maneuver in those waters. Despite the fact that the vessels you will command are of light draft, you must send a rowboat ahead of them to take soundings. Otherwise, you will find yourself hard aground and an easy target for guns of the pirates."

Pilots familiar with North Carolina waters were put aboard rented sloops that carried fifty-five fighting men. Members of the Virginia council were not informed because Spotswood feared that if lawmakers learned of his plan, they might demand a halt.

Maynard's vessels left Hampton on November 17, 1718,

Ready to split Maynard's skull, Blackbeard was shot by an English seaman.

and worked their way close to "Blackbeard's Hole." Well before sunrise on November 22, he ordered his men to weigh anchors and move toward the pirate ship *Adventure*, known to carry eight cannon.

Momentarily caught on sandbars despite having used rowboats to take soundings, the attacking vessels were raked by fire from Blackbeard's guns. A single blast left more than half of Maynard's men dead or wounded.

Spotswood had foreseen such a development, and he had given detailed advice to Maynard: "If you are hit hard, send below every man who can walk. With weapons at the ready, wait until pirates board your vessel. Then rush up, take them by surprise, and finish them off!"

Following that plan, sailors below decks heard grappling irons from the pirate ship hit their sloop. At a signal, they rushed to the blood-smeared deck and fired their pistols at the astonished pirates.

Robert Maynard personally engaged Blackbeard and exchanged shots. In the melee, the pirate missed, but Maynard's shot hit home. Wounded, the pirate grabbed his cutlass and quickly broke the blade of Maynard's sword near the hilt. As Blackbeard lifted his weapon to split Maynard's skull, a British seaman seized a weapon from the deck and killed the pirate leader on the spot.

The death of their leader and nearly a dozen of his men ended resistance by the pirates. Captives were clapped in irons, and Blackbeard's severed head was hung from the bowsprit of Maynard's vessel. Meanwhile, in Bath Town, Brand and his men seized immense quantities of tobacco, sugar, cotton, and indigo, part of it hidden under hay in a barn belonging to Tobias Knight.

Alexander Spotswood's successful foray into a colony over which he had no authority effectively ended piracy along the Atlantic coast of British America. Before the captured pirates were hanged in Virginia, however, Maynard learned to his consternation that the governor had not revealed his chief motive for taking action.

Continually at odds with members of his own council, the explorer-adventurer who governed Virginia faced probable recall by the Crown. The receiver general of the colony, William Byrd, was then in London bearing a petition to King George. If the monarch acted favorably, the governor's career would be ended.

Only a truly dramatic achievement could offset the barrage of complaints, Spotswood had calculated. Hence the founder of the Order of the Golden Horseshoe put an end to piracy, not so much for the good of the realm, but in a successful bid to remain in office a few more years.

Captain Sally Healed More Than One Thousand Wounded Men

"President Davis will see you now, but you must be brief."

"Thank you. With a waiting room full of military men, he is kind to take time to hear a woman's petition. Yet I think he will find it to be urgent."

Opening a door, an aide to Jefferson Davis, president of the Confederate States of America, announced: "Sir, this is Miss Sally Louisa Tompkins, of the Robertson Hospital. Mr. James Mason, who does not have an appointment, is also here and wishes to see you as soon as possible."

"Tell Mason that I will make time for him immediately," the chief executive responded. Turning to his visitor, he shook hands and pointed her to a seat.

"I know more about you than you may think," began the former U.S. secretary of war. "You have been residing here for a number of years, but I believe you grew up in Mathews County."

"Yes, sir, I spent my early years in Poplar Grove, Virginia, a delightful hamlet, where my father had extensive holdings. My mother and I thought it best to remove to Richmond soon after his death. But my business here is not personal. It concerns your recent order closing the private hospitals of the city."

Glancing at his memorandum, the president nodded understanding. "You are nursing some of our sick and wounded in the home turned over to you by Judge Robertson, I believe. What experience did you have prior to establishing the hospital?"

"Very little," Miss Tompkins admitted. "Since my father was wealthy, I devoted much of my time to aiding the sick and the destitute of Poplar Grove. But there were not many of them, and none were suffering from anything like battlefield wounds.

"When our brave soldiers began pouring into the city six weeks ago after the battle at Manassas Junction, there were too many for the hospitals of the city. A good friend of mine opened her home as a hospital, and that gave me the idea of doing the same, only I wanted a much bigger residence. It took less than a day to find that Judge John Robertson was willing to give me the use of a splendid house belonging to him and temporarily unoccupied."

"So it was easy to locate suitable quarters," mused the president. "There were sick and wounded men aplenty. But how did you go about securing beds and bandages?"

"When my father's estate was settled, I received an ample inheritance. I used my own money to equip the Robertson Hospital. There was plenty left over for food and other essentials. It was not necessary to employ helpers. The brave and gentle women of this city were eager to serve as volunteers."

"A noble enterprise, indeed, young woman. But we are now a nation at war. I am closing all civilian institutions, because military officers can operate hospitals more efficiently."

"How do you measure efficiency, Mr. President?" Sally Tompkins demanded. "Here . . . I have kept a careful list. Robertson Hospital has been in operation, every bed filled, since the second of August. During four full weeks, we have lost only one man, who arrived with his right arm dangling, poor fellow, and his shoulder and thigh riddled with bullet holes."

"That is splendid," Davis admitted. "But I learned years ago that raw mortality figures mean very little. How many of our soldiers have you actually looked after during this period?"

"I have a list of names, ranks, and regiments. I brought it for you to see," responded the Virginia woman. "Look at the bottom. It shows that our Robertson Hospital has cared for

Instead of a weapon, Captain Sally Tompkins wore a nurse's pouch at her waist [VIRGINIA STATE LIBRARY].

forty-one men. A few have been discharged, but most are still there."

"You plead a splendid case, young woman. I wish I could dare to hope that all of our military hospitals would match that record. In spite of the fact that I know they cannot, my orders have already been issued. I cannot countermand them. Thank you for what you have done for our Second American Revolution . . . and may God bless you."

Rising to indicate that the interview was over, Jefferson Davis extended his hand to his visitor. Tradition says that at this point, Sally Louisa began to sob silently, making no move to get up from her chair.

Opening the door, an aide announced briskly, "Mr. Mason has asked me to tell you that his business is urgent, sir, and he can wait only a few minutes more."

"Bring him in," directed the president.

"You must forgive this young woman, Mr. Mason. She will

regain her composure very shortly, I am sure. She is distraught that I have been forced to close the hospital she operates, along with all the rest run by civilians."

"Yes, I know the matter," nodded the man who in March 1861 had resigned the chairmanship of the U.S. Senate Committee on Foreign Affairs. Having accepted appointment as the Confederate States of America emissary to Great Britain, he had found his proposed voyage threatened by the Federal blockade of southern ports.

"I think I have a solution to my transportation problem," James Mason began. "But before exercising it, I believe I should have your approval. I confess that I am disappointed in having found it impossible to board a Confederate vessel headed straight for London.

"Mr. Slidell has received sure intelligence that the British mail-packet *Trent* will be leaving England soon on its regular run. He has proposed that the two of us book passage on this vessel for the return voyage, enabling us to pass through the Federal blockade.

"If your own faithful horse goes lame," he continued with enthusiasm, "the best thing you can do is to borrow a horse from a friend!"

"You have my approval," responded Jefferson Davis soberly. "I am sorry to have detained you. This young woman"—he pointed to a now-composed Sally Tompkins— "made an appointment two days ago, and I was honor bound to see her. Godspeed, sir, as you 'ride a borrowed horse' on your all-important mission."

Sally Tompkins rose and started to follow Mason from the room.

"Wait a moment, Miss Tompkins," directed Jefferson Davis. "Mr. Mason has given me an idea. How would you like to be an officer in our cavalry, in order to ride a horse of your own?"

"I don't understand, sir."

"It has occurred to me that if I give you a commission as an officer, perhaps as a captain—yes, surely a captain, no less and no more—that will place a military officer in charge of the Robertson Hospital. How would you like that?"

Having conceived a plan by which to circumvent his own

C.S.A. President Jefferson Davis made Tompkins an officer in order to permit her hospital to remain in operation.

order, President Davis acted decisively. On September 9, 1861, he signed the commission by which an idealistic young woman became Captain Tompkins of the Confederate cavalry.

"Captain Sally," as she was known for the rest of her life, regularly drew her salary but returned all of it to the government.

Robertson Hospital remained in operation until June 1865. Because the institution had gained a wide reputation, surgeons preferred to send badly wounded men to it, if possible. In spite of caring for a disproportionate number of soldiers whose condition was critical upon arrival, Captain Sally and her staff recorded only 73 deaths from 1,333 admissions. No other Civil War hospital, North or South, had a comparable record.

Confederate veterans, of all ranks and from several states, showered their "angel of mercy" with postwar offers of marriage. She turned down all of them to devote her time, energy, and financial resources to the work of the Episcopal church.

Financial reverses during Reconstruction years left the one-time philanthropist impoverished. Consequently, she took up residence in Richmond's Home for Confederate Women. Never having worn a uniform, at her death in July 1916, the only woman officer of the C.S.A. was buried with full military honors.

3

"Let Lee's Mansion Be First to Fall"

"Gentlemen, I know you are wondering why I have called you here."

"Not really," responded Samuel P. Heintzelman, a brigadier general of U.S. Volunteers who was serving as acting inspector general of the Department of Washington. "We've been sitting on our hands for more than a month since the secessionists fired on Sumter. Some of us old-time West Pointers have been wondering when we'd get a chance to strike our own first blow. This is it, I presume?"

"I suppose you could say so, in a fashion," nodded his immediate superior, white-maned Gen. Joseph K. F. Mansfield. "But we must not use such language, General. Let it be clearly understood that we have come together to make plans for the defense of Washington and the security of the president, my own primary responsibilities."

Mansfield paused to permit his meaning to sink into the minds of his aides.

"As an engineer," he continued, "as soon as I took command of this department, I realized that the capital—and the president—cannot be secure until we have Arlington Heights in our hands.

"All of you know the region well?" he inquired, clucking with satisfaction as every head nodded assent. "This region is barely two miles from executive offices and other government buildings. Some of the best new artillery—hopefully not yet in the hands of secessionists—will throw shells a good four miles. We must act speedily, before our enemies have a chance to bring guns to bear upon this city.

"Once we have staved off disaster by seizing the region, it

15

Mrs. Robert E. Lee, the former Mary Custis.

will be necessary to throw up defensive earthworks there, an undertaking of such magnitude that it must be launched as soon as possible."

"Excuse me, General," interrupted Gen. C. W. Sandford of the New York Militia. "I know I'm here because my troops are in the city and are itching to fight. But if I understand you correctly, sir, you are talking about invasion of Virginia."

"Not at all," snapped Mansfield. "You know, and I know, and citizens at large know that Mr. Lincoln made a solemn promise to the Virginians who came here to talk peace, unaware that supply ships were already on the way to Fort Sumter. He gave them his word that the soil they hold so sacred will never be invaded."

"Then why waste time talking of throwing up earthworks on Arlington Heights?"

"Because the operation that you and your colleagues are to undertake is a *defensive* exercise, pure and simple. To be sure, it will be executed upon Virginia soil. But—"

"Our commanding general is a native of the Old Dominion," interrupted an aide to Gen. Winfield Scott. "Between us, that is the reason he is not presiding over our meeting. Under extreme pressure from President Lincoln, he has concluded that the term *invasion* must be interpreted to mean a hostile incursion not undertaken for defensive purposes. Since we now propose to include Arlington Heights within the defensive perimeter of this city, seizure of the place will not constitute an invasion in the true sense of that term."

Col. Charles P. Stone of Greenfield, Massachusetts, included in the conference because he was personally charged with preserving the safety of the nation's capital, squirmed restlessly and started to speak. Then he changed his mind. Clearly, the decision to move into Virginia had been made in the White House, regardless of explanations offered by senior officers. That being the case, it would be futile to protest. Stone swallowed his half-formed protest and said nothing.

"What about the town of Alexandria? I believe it holds a considerable number of militia units?" inquired Heintzelman.

"Our troops must by-pass the town. It is not essential to our defensive plans."

"My men are itching to move into action," responded the 1826 graduate of West Point, a descendant of German immigrants. "When do we start across the Potomac?"

"Only when we receive word from the very highest quarters," responded Mansfield. "Virginians will vote on secession in just a few days. It would be appropriate to wait until citizens have endorsed the proclamation issued by their governor on the heels of Fort Sumter."

"If Arlington and only Arlington is our goal," mused Sandford, "I believe we will be charged with taking possession of the estate of Robert E. Lee."

"Right," nodded the presiding officer. "Let Lee's mansion be first to fall! But, mind you, gentlemen, not a word about our plans to anyone except your own key subordinates, and tell them as little as possible. Just make sure that their units are ready to move at an hour's notice."

Various streams of oral tradition preserve fragments of the conference over which Mansfield presided. No one present was willing to admit, then or ever, that it actually was a council of war called to make plans for invasion of the South.

Assignments made up on the afternoon of May 23, 1861, were revised and amplified within hours. As a result, when ten thousand Federal troops began moving out of the capital in bright moonlight, several units were instructed to capture and if necessary reduce Alexandria, Virginia.

Newspaper editors rejoiced when they discovered that rumors, floating about for two or three weeks, were soon to be confirmed. It was appropriate, some of them told their readers, that Virginia, "more than any other state responsible for the great rebellion," should be the first to feel the tread of marching columns of Union soldiers. Besides, they pointed out, "our commanders can move one-fourth of our forces into Virginia in one-fourth of the time it will take secessionists to put their own into that region."

Mrs. Robert E. Lee had inherited Arlington from her father, grandson of Martha Washington. An increasingly limited near-invalid, she was urged by letters from her husband to leave posthaste. However, she reported to him that she was in correspondence with Gen. Winfield Scott and Gen. Irvin McDowell. Happily, McDowell had promised to protect Arlington, so she felt no fear.

About May 14, she learned of the Federal plans. Frightened for the first time, Mrs. Lee left so hurriedly that many Washington relics and other treasures were left behind. Only the silver was safe, having been shipped to Lexington earlier, where it was buried.

Just ten days after the wife of the Confederate commander of Virginia forces fled from the mansion in which she had been born and reared, Federal troops seized it and the surrounding region. General Sandford reported to General Scott on May 26 that he had completed "examination of the roads and woods in the vicinity of Arlington." Already, he wrote, he was building a road that would cut through the woods behind Arlington House.

While the new road was still under construction, Gen. Irvin McDowell selected Arlington House as his headquarters. He found that the mansion, built in 1802, still held many memorabilia, despite forty-eight hours of looting. In the entry there were portraits of Revolutionary leaders painted by George Washington Custis, and three deer heads from animals killed by George Washington adorned the dining room. A splendid likeness of the duke of Wellington was faced by a full-length oil painting of Robert E. Lee's Revolutionary War hero father, "Lighthorse Harry" Lee.

Distressed that many pieces of furniture and numerous small objects had already been taken by soldiers, McDowell decided to safeguard the artifacts that were left and sent them across the Potomac, where they were placed on exhibit at the patent office. *Captured at Arlington* proclaimed the placard above a punch bowl, wash stand, mirror, part of a set of china given by Lafayette to George Washington, a few of Washington's tent poles and pins, and a pair of breeches and waistcoat once worn by the Father of His Country.

After the Civil War ended, Mrs. Abraham Lincoln wrote President Andrew Johnson, asking that the artifacts be returned. He appeared ready to comply with her request, but before he could act, Gen. John A. Logan persuaded a congressional committee to take action. Following secret hearings, the committee decided that any move "to deliver [the Washington relics] to the rebel General Robert E. Lee is an insult to the loyal people of the United States."

Meanwhile, Congress had taken drastic steps that directly involved the estate belonging to Lee's wife. In June 1862 a law was enacted that imposed a direct tax upon real estate "in the insurrectionary districts." Commissioners were selected, then given power to assess and collect taxes. Under the law, default by an owner meant that property could be sold for taxes.

Once they assumed their duties, the commissioners decided not to accept payment of taxes by any person other than the owner in person. This meant that men who were far from home wearing Confederate gray would be helpless to meet the demands of federal agents.

Arlington—not simply the mansion, but also the surrounding estate that included three hundred acres of splendid woodlands—was assessed at just under one hundred dollars. Philip R. Fendall, a cousin of the Custis family, was late in tendering the taxes due. Hence he brought along an

Arlington, with invaders posed on the steps [Photographic History of the Civil War].

additional 50 percent with which to pay a penalty. Because he was not the legal owner, the commissioners refused to accept payment.

Therefore, the estate was sold in January 1864 for delinquent taxes, a transaction that involved a bookkeeping transfer of $26,680 from one federal account to another. Eight months later, a tax-sale title was issued to the United States of America.

Robert E. Lee confided to a friend that the sale of furniture, animals, and trees "should have been sufficient to more than meet the taxes." He thought, correctly, that federal officials believed the estate belonged to him rather than to his wife. Before the new title was issued, they had agreed that Arlington would be used as a cemetery for Union soldiers.

When presidents of the United States failed to restore Arlington to its owner, Mrs. Lee's oldest son and heir, George, eventually retained attorneys and launched a long-drawn-suit aimed at regaining the family tract. In 1882 the U.S. Supreme Court ruled in favor of the plaintiff, but by that time tens of thousands of graves covered much of the estate. Regretfully, Lee accepted $150,000 from Congress for one of Virginia's most valuable plantations.

Arlington House, about which the life of the estate revolved, became the first federally owned historic home. Some of the Washington artifacts and some pieces of furniture—also the property of the United States of America—were eventually returned.

Open to visitors free of charge every day of the year except New Year's Day and Christmas, Arlington House is now administered by the National Park Service. Few who visit the mansion and Arlington National Cemetery learn that it was all taken from Martha Washington's descendant for nonpayment of $92.07 in delinquent taxes, which the owner had tried to pay and the government had refused to accept.

4

Daniel Boone Never, Never Gave Up

"Shel-to-wee! Shel-to-wee!"

Inside the stockade at Boonesboro in Virginia's Kentucky country, Flanders Callaway warned his father-in-law, "Don't answer to your Shawnee name. We got plenty of trouble already."

"Gotta answer," responded Daniel Boone. "This time it is Black Fish, himself. I'm goin' out. If they grab me, I want you boys to slam the gate and start firin'. Just act like I'm not there."

Black Fish could not be ignored. Months earlier, the Shawnee and his warriors had gone on the war path. Furious at the treachery of British officials in Detroit, they seized white men at every opportunity. In February 1778 they captured Daniel Boone not far from the Blue Licks at which salt makers regularly camped.

"Your warriors are wearing British paint," Boone charged.

"No," Black Fish responded. "When the Redcoats came to us with guns and money, we would not take it as pay to fight you and the other Long Knives. Our great chief Cornstalk went to a fort of the Long Knives to talk peace. They took him inside. Then they killed him and his son. His spirit calls to us to take revenge. Tomorrow we will kill the men at the salt licks. Then we will take your fort and your women."

Boone managed to convince the war chief that Redcoats at Detroit would pay twenty pounds each for men taken alive, and nothing for those killed. He then led the way to the Licking River and ordered his riflemen to stack their weapons without resistance.

As the frontiersman later told the story, Black Fish immediately took a liking to him. Long before the party reached
Detroit, the Shawnee had decided to make the leader of the
Long Knives his adopted son. So when they reached the
headquarters of Lt. Gov. Henry Hamilton, the Shawnee informed the British official that he had decided to keep Shel-
to-wee, or "Big Turtle," for himself.

At the Shawnee village of Chillicothe, Daniel Boone went
through a ceremony by which he became a member of the
tribe. Soon he was well liked, especially by the young
squaws, he later reported. "But I was always careful not to
beat the other Shawnees in shootin' matches," he said.

The vigilance of the Indians gradually relaxed, giving the
tribesman by adoption an opportunity to escape on June 16.
Somehow he covered the 160 miles to Boonesboro in just
four days, never explaining how he got across the Ohio
River, which was swollen by spring rains.

More than any other spot, Boonesboro was home to the
man who took to the woods at age twelve. Situated on the
south side of the Kentucky River and named for its builder,
it was Virginia's first defensive post and settlement west of
the Allegheny Mountains.

Some colonial leaders interpreted Virginia's charter to
mean that her western boundary extended indefinitely. Others held that the colony's land claims—contested very early
by Indians—ended at the Mississippi River, which few
white men had then seen.

In London, more than three thousand miles away, the
king and members of Parliament became concerned that
"His Majesty's subjects in Virginia" might become rebellious
if given too much freedom of movement. So an edict issued
in 1763 forbade purchase of land from Indians and pro-
hibited settlement west of the mountains.

Lord Dunmore, governor of Virginia, was too far from the
seat of power to fear punishment for disobedience. Hence he
organized expeditions against the Shawnees that brought
military defeat to the tribesmen. Chief Cornstalk signed a
treaty of peace in 1774 and under its terms ceded all claims
to land south and east of the Ohio River. This region, which

the Indians called *Ken-tuck-y,* or the "dark and bloody ground," became the focus of America's first speculative land development.

Richard Henderson and fellow investors formed the Transylvania Company and bought a vast tract north of the Cumberland River from the Cherokees. Henderson employed Daniel Boone to build the Wilderness Road through the Cumberland Gap to open the region to settlers. Pushing his road to the Kentucky River, Boone built Boonesboro. Soon he brought his wife and daughter there, the first white women to live in the extreme western region of Virginia.

Having invested so much of his life in Boonesboro, its builder was willing to die, if necessary, to thwart Black Fish on the day the Shawnee called for him to come out and parley.

At Boonesborough the fort was completed just in time to fend off the first of several Indian attacks.

Observers from one of Boonesboro's two blockhouses saw animated gestures that included much shaking of heads. Finally, to their surprise and relief, they saw Black Fish and Boone smoking the peace pipe. They did not know it, but their leader had persuaded his father by adoption that the settlement lay on land purchased from the Cherokees. Once Black Fish accepted that explanation, he offered to leave peacefully if the settlers would swear loyalty to the Great White Father across the sea and to his deputy, Henry Hamilton.

The whites accepted these terms, prepared a document to which they affixed their signatures, and nervously agreed to go outside the stockade for a ceremony of handshaking with the Shawnees.

Something—no one ever knew precisely what—went wrong during the ritualistic shaking of hands. Initially there was nothing more than a minor scuffle, but it soon mushroomed and shots were fired. Grappling with Boone, Black Fish was knocked to the ground and stunned. A Shawnee lifted his tomahawk to kill his white brother, but Big Turtle ducked and took a glancing blow to his shoulder. Then he and his men raced to the fort.

Once Black Fish recovered his senses, he examined the stockade from all sides and decided he would take heavy losses if he staged an all-out attack. Knowing that drinking water and food were likely to be scarce, he decided to starve out the settlers. That decision launched the longest American Indian siege on record.

After three days, most women and a few of the men under Boone's leadership were ready to surrender and take their chances. "No!" he shouted angrily. "Never! Never give up! We will show those redskins what we are made of before we are through!"

He put men to work splitting a tree trunk and then gouging much of the wood from the center of each half. With the sections bound together with iron stripped from wagon wheels, Boone made a crude cannon. It was fired only once, since it exploded at the instant it spewed rifle balls among the Indians massed together. What the attackers did not know was that the "big gun" was now useless, so they with-

Daniel Boone [JAMES B. LONGACRE ENGRAVING]

drew to what seemed a safe distance.

Starting at the river bank, the Indians dug a tunnel hoping to enter Boonesboro without being exposed to rifle fire. They were within twenty yards of the stockade when heavy rains caused the roof of the tunnel to collapse. Two hundred Shawnees then abandoned their eleven-day siege and slipped into the forest, leaving Boonesboro badly scarred by fire arrows and barely standing.

Although the siege was a dramatic event of the time, it was barely noted in contemporary chronicles. Also, those who knew him best did not bother to preserve a record of Daniel Boone's life and accomplishments. Barely literate himself, he left nothing approaching an autobiography. Hence much that is known about him depends upon hearsay.

Born in Pennsylvania, Boone developed love for Virginia when with his parents he spent some time in the Shenandoah Valley at about age sixteen. Six years later, by then a married man, he fled from North Carolina to Virginia during the French and Indian War. Working as a wagoneer, he and George Washington were among 2,100 Americans who followed Gen. Edward Braddock to fight the French. In a disastrous encounter, Braddock was mortally wounded and

Boone was captured. Soon, though, he cut one of his horses loose from his wagon and made his escape.

Governor Dunmore later hired him to go into "the westernmost regions of the colony" to warn surveyors that Indians were on the war path. That expedition, and an earlier trip into what is now Kentucky, persuaded him that it was the land of opportunity. Once the American Revolution was fully under way, Virginia made Kentucky into a county and organized a formal military force with Boone as its captain.

When Boone's daughter was captured by the Shawnees, he staged a dramatic rescue, which James Fenimore Cooper recounted in his novel *The Last of the Mohicans*. Perhaps because he had accepted adoption by Black Fish, Boone was put on trial by his fellow whites. He refused to admit guilt and won acquittal and promotion to the rank of major.

Land claims of the Transylvania Company having been thrown out, Major Boone collected $20,000 and set out for Williamsburg to seek new titles. On the way he was drugged and robbed, forcing him to work years to repay others for their losses. Captured by the British at Charlottesville in 1781, he managed once more to escape.

When his claims for more than 100,000 acres of land were disallowed, he found himself as poor as he had been in boyhood. But he moved to Point Pleasant in Kanawha County (now West Virginia) to make another fresh start. Hunting in that region proved so poor that he followed the advice of his son and went to the Ozarks, where he once more lost his land as a result of defective titles.

Considering another westward move to make one more fresh start, he returned to his adolescent pursuits. Soon he was making what he called a "better than passable living" by shooting deer, beaver, and other animals to cure and sell their pelts. At age eighty-two, the man who opened Virginia's far west was not about to quit fighting.

It is understandable that when Lord Byron learned about some of Daniel Boone's exploits, he devoted seven stanzas of his poem *Don Juan* to him. Today the man who never gave up is popularly seen as the romantic epitome of America's early frontiersman.

5

George Washington's Longest Battle Was with His Own Countrymen

"My military career started when I fought the French and Indians," George Washington is said to have reminisced to intimates late in life. "At that time I was under the command of a distinguished British officer who did not dream that I would later fight his countrymen on many a field.

"My fortunate success in battle led Americans to insist that I place myself at the head of the new nation. Neither they nor I then conceived that my longest battle would be fought with my own countrymen, over the location of our Territory of Columbia."

Washington's "longest battle" began four years before the adoption of the U.S. Constitution. Mutinous members of militia companies staged a near-riot in Philadelphia, pointing muskets at members of the Continental Congress to emphasize their demand that they be paid long overdue wages. The frightened lawmakers hastily adjourned and moved their session to Princeton, New Jersey, where they considered themselves safe.

A special district with armed protection was essential to the future of the legislative body, its members decided. Hence on October 7, 1783, the Continental Congress adopted a resolution calling for erection of federal buildings "on the banks of the Delaware, near Trenton, or of the Potomac, near Georgetown."

Until then, George Washington had remained silent on the question of establishing a permanent seat for the central government the Founding Fathers hoped soon to create. Once Congress acted, the man who had led the Continentals to victory over the British spoke decisively.

"Our effort to establish a centralized government for the colonies has led Congress to six—no, seven—cities," he pointed out. "First it was Philadelphia, then Baltimore. Another session in Philadelphia was followed by a period at Lancaster and one at York in the same colony. Congress then returned to Philadelphia and has now retreated to Princeton."

Washington had no way of knowing that the site of the conclave would later be moved to Annapolis, Maryland, Trenton, New Jersey, and then to New York City; but he is said quietly to have helped circulate a satire by Francis Hopkinson who suggested building a capital on wheels "so that it may easily be transported from place to place."

Presiding over a 1787 convention called to revise the Articles of Confederation, George Washington helped guide delegates toward a radical decision. Instead of patching up the loosely drawn agreement under which the American Revolution was fought, they adopted an entirely new document, the Constitution of the United States. A clause in its first article stipulates that Congress shall have exclusive jurisdic-

George Washington compared the struggle over the site of a national capital with a long-drawn military campaign.

tion over "such district (not exceeding ten miles square) as may, by cession of particular states and the acceptance of Congress, become the seat of government of the United States. . . ."

Having formulated a clear-cut plan to create a federal district as the site of government, matters might have proceeded swiftly and smoothly had it not been for sectional rivalry and jealousy.

Philadelphia, considered by many Americans to be the only possible city in which to put the new government to work, abounded with Quakers. Since many of them were "notorious abolitionists," southern delegates balked at the prospect of seeing Congress meet always in the City of Brotherly Love. New York City entered a strong argument for being the home of the national lawmakers, but rural congressmen let it be known that they feared Manhattan's "money power."

Soon after the Constitution went into effect through ratification by nine colonies, Maryland offered to cede ten square miles to Congress; Virginia lawmakers followed with a similar offer. At the national level, many top leaders made no secret of their hope that the permanent seat of government would be somewhere within the Susquehanna River Valley.

Seldom making a public statement that might add to sectional antagonism, George Washington never stopped fighting for a location somewhere close to the region he most loved. Annapolis added to the uncertainty and confusion by making a strong but somewhat ambiguous offer. New Jersey heard of the Annapolis bid and promised to provide a free site "anywhere in the colony."

Probably at Washington's instigation, the tobacco planters of Virginia formed a coalition to top all earlier offers. Provided it would become the permanent seat of the new federal government, they said, Virginia would cede to Congress the town of Williamsburg, 300 additional acres, and 100,000 pounds in cash.

Their offer is a revealing clue to how battlefield victories were less difficult than the laborious process of welding thirteen independent colonies into one nation. So far, the English pound and its colonial counterparts dominated U.S. finance.

Two more years passed before the Continental Congress established the dollar as the U.S. monetary unit, stipulating that "the small coin be of copper, of which two hundred shall pass for one dollar." Most fledgling states, burdened by big war debts, were eager to see "assumption." That is, they wanted the emerging federal government to take responsibility for the debts of the former colonies. Anti-Federalists, outnumbered but vocal and powerful, were violently opposed to such action.

George Washington, who had had experience using spies to learn battle plans of the British, discovered that it might be possible to win over some anti-Federalists. As a result, his secretary of state called opposing factions together for a conference.

"Some leading Federalists may be willing to put their influence behind the move to fix the new capital on the banks of the Potomac," Thomas Jefferson suggested. "But they will do so only if some anti-Federalists will support Mr. Alexander Hamilton's proposal for assumption."

After considerable haggling, the first, and perhaps the biggest, political horse trade in American history was consummated in a nameless tavern that was a prototype of later "smoke-filled rooms." George Washington, who masterminded the deal, was quietly happy that the long fight about the location of the nation's capital was finally over, with the South being the clear winner.

On July 16, 1790, President Washington signed an act that called for Congress to remain in Philadelphia for another decade, then move to the Potomac River "at some place between the mouths of the Eastern Branch and the Connogocheague."

Having previously sold all of his holdings in the immediate vicinity, the president negotiated terms under which nineteen landed proprietors ceded their rights on March 30, 1791. Lots for public buildings were to be paid for at $125 per acre, with streets conveyed to the government without charge.

With the building of Washington well under way, a State Department spokesman called it an "ill-arranged, rambling, scrambling village."

By presidential proclamation, Washington established the terms of the sale. One-fourth of the purchase money was to be paid immediately by the treasurer of the United States, with "the residue to be paid in three equal annual payments, with yearly interest of 6 percent on the whole principal unpaid."

Virginia had previously donated a tract of six hundred acres, virtually worthless because it included only a few settlers. Alexandria, included in the original district and retained until 1846, was the largest town involved. On September 9, 1791, the first boundary stone was set in Jones's Point, Hunting Creek, Virginia.

Before construction began, Washington stipulated that "the outer and party-walls of all houses within the said City shall be built of brick or stone." In an additional bid to guarantee a city of pleasing proportions, he informed builders that "the wall of no house is to be higher than forty feet to the roof in any part of the city; nor shall any be lower than thirty-five feet on any of the avenues."

Thomas Jefferson, who later let it be known that he was displeased at not having been consulted, agreed with Washington's dictum that "no vaults shall be permitted under the streets, nor any encroachments on the foot-way above by

A home that stood near the middle of the site that became Washington.

steps, stoops, porches, cellar doors, windows, ditches, or leaning walls; nor shall there be any projection over the street, other than the eaves of the house."

A few southern leaders thanked George Washington for having taken time to select the site, by then usually called the District of Columbia. Many of his contemporaries never learned of the president's behind-the-scenes struggle that ended with satisfaction of his personal wishes.

Northern newspapers immediately dubbed the federal site the "Serbonian Bog." When power was officially transferred from Philadelphia to the city named for the man who picked its location, a Connecticut congressman described Pennsylvania Avenue as "a deep morass covered with elder bushes."

To jubilant political leaders of Virginia, Georgia, and the Carolinas, scathing criticism by the northern press did not matter. Philadelphia, New York, and other rich cities in the North had lost in the battle for the site of the national government. For good or ill, the capital of the United States was where it rightly belonged, within easy traveling distance of George Washington's beloved Mount Vernon.

6

Little Books of William McGuffey Shaped the Mind of Nineteenth-Century America

"I am a teacher of children with little or no competence in the field of philosophy," William H. McGuffey reputedly wrote in reply to an invitation to join the faculty of the University of Virginia.

"Whether you know it or not, you are teaching a philosophy of life to tens of thousands of children," he was informed in reply. "In Charlottesville you will have a free hand to teach moral philosophy in any fashion that you may choose."

Legend says that it was the shadow of Thomas Jefferson, rather than the prestige of membership in a distinguished faculty, that brought McGuffey to Virginia. On arrival he found that the influence of Jefferson, whom he revered, was to be found everywhere. Although he had been restless and constantly on the move early in his life, he spent his last twenty-eight years in Charlottesville, teaching until shortly before his death in 1873.

Born in a Pennsylvania log cabin, at age two William moved with his parents to another log cabin near Youngstown, Ohio. Opening of the "Connecticut Reserve," which offered free land to veterans of the Indian wars, was the magnet that drew the family to the Buckeye State.

McGuffey attended the intermittent sessions of rural schools and showed an astonishing capacity for learning and for memorization. Hence, his father worked extra hours on another man's farm to send the boy to a Latin school operated by the pastor of a Presbyterian church.

Before age eighteen, William was noted for his ability to quote entire books of the Bible and passages from great writers. He studied briefly at the Old Stone Academy in Darlington, Pennsylvania, before moving on to Washington College. Because he took time out to teach in rural Kentucky schools to earn the money for his own studies, graduation did not come until he was twenty-six.

Word of the bright young teacher-student came to the attention of the trustees of Miami University. Therefore, before he had received his diploma, he was invited to teach languages in the school at Oxford, Ohio. During the decade that he spent in the little college town, he was ordained as a Presbyterian minister, which enabled him to develop his own sets of moral principles and rules while preaching weekly in Darrtown, four miles away.

Leaders of Cincinnati College persuaded McGuffey to become its president, hoping that he would be able to solve its financial problems. He was unable to achieve that goal and saw the institution close its doors during the fourth year of his administration. However, while he was in Cincinnati, he organized an association to promote education and, with a few colleagues, established the public school system of Ohio.

With the West expanding rapidly, Cincinnati became a new center of the publishing trade. Winthrop B. Smith, of Truman and Smith, became convinced that the West would purchase and use grade-school textbooks in quantity, provided that they conveyed values associated with farm life, patriotism, and religion.

Catherine Beecher, sister of the future author of *Uncle Tom's Cabin*, seemed to Smith to be eminently qualified to turn out such textbooks. After she listened to his proposal, she turned him down. It seems that she may have suggested that he make contact with an exceptionally able teacher: William H. McGuffey.

"Of course I am interested!" McGuffey responded when approached by the publisher. "I have spent my adult life in the classroom and the pulpit. I have preached more than three thousand sermons without writing out one of them. I rely entirely upon my memory, you see."

Not convinced that a man so overtly religious would be able to write school books, Smith conferred with his partner.

Soon he offered McGuffey a contract for production of six volumes: a primer, a spelling book, and four reading books. If written to the satisfaction of the firm, he said, a royalty of one thousand dollars would be paid for the entire lot.

Drawing upon his prodigious memory and a sheaf of brief sayings he had used to teach the alphabet, McGuffey worked rapidly, always in the same fashion. Thus when he came to lesson #46 of the *Second Eclectic Reader*, he hesitated only a moment before writing:

Seven-year old Ralph Wick went walking with his mother. She loved him very much, in spite of the fact that he cried easily and loudly.

His mother gave him a nice red rose, and he was glad. Then he saw that she had a white rose. When his mother did not give it to him, Ralph screamed and kicked.

That had no effect upon his mother, so Ralph snatched the white rose from her hand. Thorns on the rose tore his hand and made it sore.

After that, when Ralph screamed for something he did not need to have, his mother pointed to his sore hand.

Almost all schools in the West were private, and few had money to spend on anything but essentials. But the reading books, initially not identified by the name of their author, were instantly successful. At the celebration of his fortieth birthday in 1840, McGuffey was proud to tell relatives and guests that his "little books" were selling nearly five hundred thousand copies annually.

Over a period of seventy-five years, the five "McGuffey Readers" made millionaires of Truman and Smith, and eight successor publishers. Yet when a *Rhetorical Guide* was needed in 1843 as an addition to the series, Winthrop Smith offered only five hundred dollars for the manuscript. Neither then nor at any other time was McGuffey greatly interested in money. When invited to join the faculty of the University of Virginia, he did not even inquire about the salary.

In contrast, he was barely settled in the position that would give him something he valued more than money—stability—before he launched a crusade to establish a pub-

William H. McGuffey, professor of moral philosophy, University of Virginia.

lic school system in Virginia. After years of hard work, he saw that dream realized.

During more than a quarter of a century in Charlottesville, McGuffey constantly revised and sometimes enlarged his now-famous readers. Almost without exception, teachers and parents were delighted with them. Short words and simple sentences made for easy reading, and best of all from the standpoint of adults, nearly every page carried a clear-cut lesson that was designed to help boys and girls be very, very good.

A typical selection dealt with two boys who quarreled over a nut. A larger and older boy volunteered to serve as referee. He cracked the nut and gave half of the shell to each small boy. Then he kept the kernel for himself as payment for having settled the quarrel.

In another reading lesson, small Bessie persuaded her Aunt Annie to allow her to hunt wild flowers to plant in a garden. Busy digging violets, dandelions, and other flowers, Bessie forgot about the time.

When she heard a bell calling her home, Bessie did not waste a second. She dropped her flowers and ran home so that dear auntie would not have to wait for her.

Adults who browsed through an *Eclectic Reader* usually gave enthusiastic recommendations to friends and relatives. As a result, by the turn of the century combined sales of volumes making up the set had topped 100,000,000 copies.

Advertised almost entirely by word of mouth, reading books that taught moral values as an extra were firmly entrenched in the nation's private schools when tax-supported institutions began to emerge. In his Charlottesville office, the author smiled triumphantly when he learned that the new public school systems were as enthusiastic about the *Eclectic Readers* as were the private systems. Eventually McGuffey's books were formally adopted in public schools of thirty-seven states.

Small enough to fit comfortably into a child's hand, the

"As soon as Bessie heard the bell, she dropped what she was doing and ran home so auntie wouldn't have to wait."

thin volumes taught a great deal more than reading. Their moral and cultural emphases helped to shape the lives of generations of boys and girls. No other textbooks ever issued have had quite the same influence as did McGuffey's.

About 1920, teachers and parents began to pride themselves upon being more sophisticated than those of the past. Inevitably, they turned away from the *Eclectic Readers* to textbooks considered more up to date and less moralistic in tone.

Later, however, the pendulum swung again. Henry Ford paid for production of a facsimile edition of the 1857 series about the time that he bought William McGuffey's log cabin birthplace and had it moved to his famous Greenfield Village at Dearborn, Michigan.

Criticism of the public school system, especially "Why Johnnie can't read," spawned increasing numbers of private schools. Patrons of these new schools, who often had strong negative feelings about textbooks used in tax-supported institutions, returned to McGuffey's little volumes in droves. New editions of them, handsomely printed but using the language of the University of Virginia faculty member and reproducing their early illustrations, again became best-selling textbooks.

If he could have known that his little books would influence tens of thousands of Space Age boys and girls, the ranking professor at the University of Virginia, widely known as "Old Guff," would have given a quiet smile that signaled, "I told you so!"

After having seen *McGuffey's Readers* through edition after edition, he decided that their style and contents could not be further improved. Always mindful that he came to Charlottesville to teach moral philosophy, Old Guff set to work upon a textbook of philosophy. He spent a decade upon the project, but died before finishing it, quietly conscious, no doubt, that the "moral philosophy" in his little reading books would have far greater impact than the contents of any textbook of philosophy.

7

Booker T. Washington Took His Own Medicine: "Let Your Buckets Down Where You Are"

"Are you the lady that lets boys go to school?"

Miss Mary F. Mackie was startled. Busy reading papers spread on her desk, she had not seen the boy as he stepped timidly into her office. For a moment she made no reply but looked him over critically. *Ragged,* she thought to herself. *And dirty. But eager. Must be about fifteen. Too bad we have no room for him.*

Aloud, she said, "Yes, I let boys go to school . . . when there are places for them. But just now, the institution is full."

Swaying slightly, the young applicant started away. At the door he stopped. Eyes filled with tears but lighted with new hope, he turned back.

"Couldn't I sleep on the floor in the hall?" he begged. "I'm a good hand. Honest, ma'am, I'll work hard. I really will! And I won't eat much. Please let me in! Please!"

Miss Mackie rose. "I believe you mean what you say," she responded as she opened the door of a small classroom next to her office.

"Come here," she directed, pointing to a broom that stood in the corner. "Take this and let me see how well you can clean up this room. While you are working, I will go and talk with General Armstrong about you."

Years later, Booker T. Washington told large audiences about what he termed the most momentous day in his life. "I swept that floor three times," he recalled. "Then I pulled a ragged shirt from my little bundle and dusted every chair in the room four times."

He was standing quietly in a corner when Miss Mackie

Dr. Booker T. Washington, educator, urged both blacks and whites to "Let down your buckets where you are" [TUSKEGEE UNIVERSITY].

returned. Without a word, hardly looking in his direction, she examined the classroom. She moved several chairs and peered into every corner. Then as Washington held his breath, she took a fresh white handkerchief and rubbed it over some of the woodwork.

At last she smiled and said, "I guess we can find a place for you, even if we are already crowded. General Armstrong has consented to let you enter, and you may work as janitor to earn your board and keep. A friend of the general, a gentleman from the North, will pay your tuition."

Born on the plantation of James Burroughs at Hale's Ford in Franklin County, Booker T. Washington is believed to have been the son of a neighboring white man. As a baby, he was listed on plantation records as being worth nothing, but by the time he was about six years old, he was valued at four hundred dollars.

His mother, Jane, gave him the best she had, a few rags for a bed. Just twelve feet wide and sixteen feet long, her shack had no windows. The only floor was the bare earth, and winter rain dripped through the roof.

Slave boys typically received from their owners only one piece of clothing, a tow shirt. Made of flax, such a garment was so coarse and stiff that it tormented its wearer for the first six to eight weeks it was in use. In adult life Booker laughingly told of his brother John, two years his senior, who once did him the great favor of wearing his new shirt for a month to break it in!

Soon after emancipation, Jane and her new husband took their children to Malden, West Virginia, where coal mines and a salt furnace offered hope of jobs. At about age ten, Booker began working fourteen hours a day in the salt mines, earning barely enough to help keep corn bread and sorghum molasses on the family table.

One day he saw a black man reading a newspaper. Never having spent a single day in school, his mind was fired. He, too, would learn to get some sense out of those queer black marks on white paper!

There was not a single piece of printed matter in his mother's cabin, not even a leaf torn from a book; but Booker knew that the barrels with which he worked at the salt mines were marked with names and numbers. By observing them closely, he learned some of the letters of the alphabet. His mother was so impressed that she made great sacrifices to buy a spelling book for him. Studying at night without help, the boy learned to read a few words.

To his joy, a young black opened a school for boys of his own race. Informed of it, Booker's stepfather shook his head. "You gotta work, boy, if you want to eat," he ruled. Weeks later, he relented and agreed to let Booker go to school half-time, provided that he worked in the mines from 4:00 to 9:00 A.M.

On his first day at school, Booker was embarrassed when the teacher asked his full name. Somewhere, he had heard of a great man named Washington, so he responded, "Booker Washington, ma'am." Not until years later did he learn that at birth his mother had named him Booker Taliaferro.

Although Booker did well in school, his stepfather soon brought his studies to an end, making him return to full-time work. Part of the day he toiled in the mines, then worked until night cleaning the house and yard of the owner's wife, Mrs. Lewis Ruffner. Whenever he could, he

*Students and faculty members erected many of Tuskegee's
buildings* [TUSKEGEE UNIVERSITY].

would walk five or six miles to the home of a rural teacher to
study a few hours at night, but his progress was slow.

          One day the fifteen-year-old overheard two miners
talking about a new school for Negro boys at Hampton, Virginia. They said that it was a place where a boy could go
without money.

Excited as he had never been before, Booker determined
to go to Hampton Institute. He told his brother and his
mother about the school. Between them, they got together a
few nickels and dimes; and, with his clothing tied in a rag,
he set out on the 500-mile trip across the mountains.

He reached Richmond at night, without a cent in his
pockets, so he crawled under a plank sidewalk and slept on
the ground. Next day, he found work unloading a vessel of
pig iron and earned enough money to take a train for the
eighty-five remaining miles. When he reached Hampton, he
still had fifty cents in his pocket.

After three years he graduated with honor and returned
home determined to help less fortunate young blacks. A
hastily organized school attracted ninety pupils, yet he

found time to teach a class of older students at night and to organize two Sunday schools.

After two years, he spent a term studying at a school in Washington. Then he was called back to Hampton as a teacher. Given a class of seventy-five Indian boys, he was assigned to teach them to speak English. He did so well that Gen. Samuel C. Armstrong, principal of the school, called him to his office one day.

"I have had a letter from 'way down South," he said. "Mr. George W. Campbell, a banker who formerly was a slaveholder, has secured a charter for a Negro normal school that will receive two thousand dollars a year from the state of Alabama. He has asked me to recommend a principal, and I have selected you. I'll find someone to take your place here at Hampton, so I'd like for you to start to Alabama at once."

Upon arrival, Booker T. Washington found that the new school had no building. He managed to get the use of a small church belonging to black worshipers, and in it opened the Tuskegee Normal and Industrial Institute on July 4, 1881. Later, with about two hundred dollars borrowed from a friend back home, he made a down payment on five hundred acres of worn-out farm land and moved to the new site. The buildings of his institute consisted of a stable, a hen house, and the ruins of a partly burned kitchen.

Some of his students wanted to learn Latin and Greek, but Washington told them that it was more important to learn how to make a living. "We need good buildings," he told them, "and good buildings need bricks. Let's all get busy and put up a brick kiln."

When 25,000 handmade bricks were finished, the kiln was constructed. It failed within days, so they tried again. A second failure was followed by a third attempt and a third failure. Washington pawned his watch for fifteen dollars, then made a fourth attempt that proved successful. Students used the kiln to make bricks for the first permanent buildings. Eventually the campus grew to 250 acres and 150 buildings.

Always, Tuskegee's head was busy raising money. He trav-

A national monument to Washington shows him "lifting his veil of ignorance."

eled widely and made many speeches through which he won respect and honor. The slave boy who had fought for a crust of bread had tea with Queen Victoria at Windsor Castle; he became a friend and adviser of President Theodore Roosevelt; Harvard University awarded an honorary degree to the man who first mastered some of his letters by studying salt barrels; and he wrote books that were so well received that they were translated into eighteen languages.

"Let down your buckets where you are," he advised blacks and whites. "When you do that over and over, you will help to bring a new day to the South."

Now Tuskegee University, the institution long headed by Dr. Washington, is a living memorial to him. Elected to the Hall of Fame of Great Americans in 1946, the ex-slave from Franklin County stands for all time as an example of a man who became great despite seemingly insuperable obstacles.

Not simply to the South but to the entire nation, Dr. Booker T. Washington was the prophet of a new era of better racial understanding and more opportunity for blacks. His greatest joy was not reception of another honor, but the thrill of seeing young blacks learn trades, gain educations, and enter mainstream American life.

8

Puzzled but Obedient, Hill Lamon Left Lincoln Unguarded

"Mr. Secretary, I am deeply worried."

"What troubles you this time, Hill?"

"The president has instructed me to spend several days in Richmond. If I go, I cannot protect him."

John P. Usher, U.S. secretary of the interior, leaned forward and inquired, "Precisely what am I supposed to do about it? Is it not common knowledge that I submitted my resignation more than a month ago?"

"Yes, it is known," admitted Ward Hill Lamon. "But I heard somewhere that it does not take effect until the middle of May."

"Heard somewhere? You got that straight from the president!"

Nodding assent, the marshal of the District of Columbia returned to the purpose of his visit. "You have considerable authority here in the capital. I beg you to use it to guard the president in my absence."

"I'm willing to do what I can, of course. But you and I both know that he is not particularly fond of me. Wouldn't it be better for you to stay by his side?"

"That's what I would like to do. But Mr. Lincoln has made up his mind. He remembers having sent me to Charleston before the firing started but has forgotten that I didn't do any good on that mission. Now he wants me to iron out some of the problems that block the calling of Virginia's reconstruction convention."

"Why doesn't he send someone from the department of state?"

"Since I was born in Frederick County, he believes that

Ward Hill Lamon was big, tough, and determined to protect the president.

leaders of the Old Dominion might listen to me. Besides, it is common knowledge that every black abolitionist in the country despises me."

"These are not persuasive reasons for sending you on such a vital mission," mused the secretary of the interior. "It seems to me that it would be better for you to stay in the capital and let someone else bargain with the rebels. Instead of accepting the burden of guarding Mr. Lincoln's life, I believe I prefer to try to have another agent sent to Richmond."

Far from satisfied, the man who for years had taken personal charge of Abraham Lincoln's safety tried to think of someone else on whom to call. Ward Hill Lamon correctly believed that Usher would do nothing.

Nearly a decade earlier Lamon had become a law partner of Lincoln when the future president was practicing in Danville, Illinois. He joined the new Republican party soon after it was organized and campaigned for Lincoln in 1860. When party leaders learned of assassination threats, Lamon was chosen to guard the president-elect during his journey to Washington.

Big and burly, the handsome Virginian became a familiar figure in the capital. As marshal, he liked to make spectacular arrests and execute orders of the circuit court. At many levees, he introduced visitors to the president.

Political foes derided Lincoln for putting a proslavery Virginian in a responsible position that kept him close to the chief executive, but the president did not waver. When plots were widely suspected in 1864, Lamon supervised the patrolling of White House grounds and himself slept next to the president's bedroom.

In Lamon's judgment, protection of the president became urgent near the end of 1864 when Horace Greeley's *New York Tribune* publicized a notice that had originally appeared in Alabama's *Selma Dispatch*. Apparently inserted by a Col. G. W. Gayle, an open letter offered a reward to killers:

> If the citizens of the Southern Confederacy will furnish me with the cash, or good securities, for the sum of one million dollars, I will cause the lives of Abraham Lincoln, William H. Seward and Andrew Johnson to be taken by the first of March next.

When the letter was brought to the attention of the president, he waved it aside. "Pluck a banjo for me, Hill," he requested, "and sing me a sad little song. What does anybody want to assassinate me for? If anyone wants to do so, he can do it any day or night, if he is ready to give his life for mine."

"Maybe so," admitted the burly Virginian, "but I would like for you to make me a promise."

"What is it?"

"I want you to promise me that you will not go out after nightfall unless I am at your side. And I particularly want you to promise that you will not go to the theater without me."

Abraham Lincoln hesitated, then shook his head. "I cannot promise," he said, "but I tell you what I will do. I'll do the best I can."

*   *   *

On April 5, 1865, the president was aboard the U.S.S. *Malvern*. In the cabin of the warship he received Gen. Edward H. Ripley, who wanted to arrest a former Confederate who had belonged to Rains's torpedo bureau. According to Ripley, men of the secret Confederate organization had been ordered to take action against "the head of the Yankee government."

Informed of this and urged to speak with the one-time rebel who had changed sides, Abraham Lincoln would have nothing to do with the matter. "I must go on the course marked out for me. I cannot believe that any human being lives who would do me any harm," he said.

However, the next week the president told Hill Lamon about a strange dream he had had a few nights earlier. According to the chief executive, "I retired after having waited for dispatches from the front. Once in bed, very late, I began to dream.

"There seemed to be a deathlike stillness about me. Then I heard subdued weeping that led me to climb from my bed and walk downstairs.

"I went from room to room and saw no one but continued to hear sounds of mourning. In the East Room, I met with a sickening surprise.

"A corpse wrapped in funeral vestments lay on a catafalque that was guarded by soldiers. 'Who is dead in the White House?' I demanded of one of them.

"'The president is dead,' he informed me. 'He was killed by an assassin.'

"A loud burst of grief from mourners caused me to awaken, but I slept no more that night. Though it was only a dream, I find myself strangely vexed by it."

"Then, Mr. President, let me do all I can to ease your vexation," Lamon urged. "I will detail additional guards here at the White House and put them on duty when you travel to the Soldiers' Home. I will cast other duties aside and remain with you day and night."

"No, Hill, that would never do. I would feel foolish surrounded by soldiers. And you have other things to do, some of them for me, personally."

*   *   *

Laura Keene, star of Our American Cousin.

Keenly aware of Lincoln's dream and of his refusal to take extra precautions, the native of Frederick County repeated his concern when told to devote several days to the Virginia mission. Reminded that he was being given an order rather than a request, he stood hat in hand as he said goodbye to his friend.

"I don't understand why I must go," he told the president, "but I am accustomed to obedience. Please exercise extreme caution. Go out as little as possible, and never to the theater, while I am gone."

Silent for an instant, Lincoln responded, "I know you have my interests at heart. That is why you must go to Virginia."

Good Friday fell on April 14 in 1865, three days after Lamon was ordered to the former Confederate capital. Since the popular English actress Laura Keene was playing in *Our American Cousin*, the president and Mrs. Lincoln decided to go to Ford's theater that night. They invited Gen. Ulysses Grant and his wife to accompany them, but Julia Grant declined because she disliked Mary Todd Lincoln.

At the theater, no one noticed that a peep hole had been bored through the door of the box normally occupied by the president and his party. Action on the stage caught the attention of a substitute for the regular theater guard, and he deserted his post. After having peered through the hole bored with a gimlet that afternoon, John Wilkes Booth burst into the box wielding a one-shot brass derringer in his right hand and a steel dagger in his left.

Assassin John Wilkes Booth was depicted as inspired by the devil.

At a distance of less than five feet, he raised the derringer and sent a half-inch ball into Abraham Lincoln's head. It passed through his brain and lodged behind his right eye. Soldiers, policemen, the substitute guard, and a surgeon rushed to the side of the president; but from the first it was clear that he had no chance of recovery.

Word of the assassination reached Ward Hill Lamon in Richmond the following day. Cutting off his negotiations with Virginia leaders, he hurried back to the capital asking himself over and over, *Why on earth did he send me away, after so many warnings?*

Lamon's question is as profound today as it was in the aftermath of the assassination. Some historians theorize that the president was a fatalist who believed nothing could interfere with the course of foreordained events. A few have speculated that he harbored a death wish. Others think that with more than eighty threatening letters stored in a special pouch, all talk of danger came to be ignored. But why Abraham Lincoln ordered his long-time bodyguard to Richmond at the approach of Easter 1865 remains an unsolved mystery.

PART TWO:
North Carolina

General Joseph E. Johnston.

General William T. Sherman.

9

Sherman's Plan Would Have Avoided Reconstruction

"The mass of the people south will never trouble us again, Ellen," wrote Gen. William T. Sherman to his wife. "They have suffered terribly, and I now feel disposed to befriend them."

Posted from Raleigh in April 1865, that little-known personal letter reveals the Sherman whom few people in the North or the South know.

Most Americans remember Sherman for his infamous "march to the sea." Nearly forgotten are events that took place near Durham.

Joseph E. Johnston commanded the Confederate Army of Tennessee in 1865. The last major fighting force of the Rebels, it had moved into North Carolina to evade Union armies.

However, the Federals moved too rapidly to give Johnston a breather. Weighing his options, he decided to seek the best terms he could get. At his headquarters he drafted, then revised, a letter.

The Confederate leader's document was hand-delivered to William T. Sherman on April 14. It requested an armistice for the benefit of both armies and ended with a short but vital question, "What are the best terms upon which I may surrender my army?"

Sherman and Johnston met under a flag of truce at noon on April 17 in the yard of the James Bennett place, about two miles from Durham Station. After two hours, they came to a general agreement. Johnston would disband the last effective fighting force of the Confederacy. He also would order Rebels in Alabama, Mississippi, Louisiana, and Texas to lay down their weapons. In return, Sherman drafted terms designed to create an honorable peace and a swift return of seceded states to the Union.

All fighting men of the rank of colonel or below would be pardoned upon taking an oath of allegiance to the United States. Every soldier who would return home, observe his parole, and obey the laws "would be entirely free from disturbance by U. S. authority."

Southern legislatures would remain intact. Elected officials would keep control of weapons held in their own armories. Every Southerner ready to submit to the authority of the U. S. Constitution would "regain his position as a citizen, free and equal in all respects." Incredibly, Sherman even promised that citizens could sue the Federal government for the value of freed slaves.

Sherman had offered far more than Joe Johnston had dared to expect or hope. With spirits soaring to the point of ecstasy, he ordered his men to surrender their weapons. Every available building was soon filled with rifles, sabers, and pistols.

Meanwhile, Secretary of War Edwin M. Stanton, who had already shown himself to be an implacable foe of the South, now demanded that North Carolina native Andrew Johnston, successor to assassinated Abraham Lincoln, convene his cabinet at once. Their session started at 8:00 P.M. on April 21, only hours after Sherman's telegram was received from Raleigh.

Following a marathon cabinet meeting, Sherman was ordered to resume fighting. Each of his top subordinates received a telegram instructing him to disregard any and all promises of peace. Gen. U. S. Grant was ordered to relieve Sherman of command, and Sherman was ordered to report to Washington at once for interrogation.

Opponents of "an easy peace" grilled Sherman minutely, then reprimanded him. To his face some of them called him a lunatic and a traitor.

"To say that I was merely angry would hardly express the state of my feelings," Sherman wrote to Ellen. "I was outraged beyond measure."

Having repudiated the Sherman–Johnston pact, Stanton of Ohio—Sherman's native state—led a group of Congressmen in shaping harsh new terms for the stricken South.

Some of the effects were felt at once.

On learning that the armies had laid down their weapons, Zebulon Vance went to Greensboro to surrender to Gen. John M. Schofield. Schofield refused to make him a prisoner and told him to go home.

Therefore Vance put his saddle horses and two mules in a freight car and went home to Statesville. Once Stanton's terms superseded Sherman's, Vance was arrested at his home and shipped to Old Capitol Prison in Washington. His experience was indicative of the military occupation and repressive Reconstruction era that followed.

Had Sherman's generous terms not been rejected out of hand, the South would have been spared Reconstruction. Because he was a popular commander, his peace plan would have had a fighting chance for success if Stanton and his allies had not prevented its implementation.

Sherman had been in long conferences with Lincoln and was confident that the peace he made with Johnston reflected the president's views. But Abraham Lincoln was mortally wounded on April 14, the same day Sherman received Johnston's overture for peace. In the emotional climate that followed the assassination, Sherman's plan for an honorable peace and healing of the wounds between North and South was doomed.

10

Gunmaker Said He'd Put an End to War

"I witnessed almost daily the departure of troops to the front and the return of the wounded, sick, and dead," said Richard J. Gatling in describing the origin of the gun upon which his name was bestowed.

"It occurred to me that if I could invent a machine—a gun—which by its rapidity of fire could enable one man to do as much battle duty as a hundred, that it would eliminate the necessity for large armies.

"Such a gun would reduce exposure to battle and disease, and would become a great life-saving device."

Writing to Miss Lizzie Jarvis, that's how Richard Jordan Gatling, M.D., explained his invention of a rapid-fire gun.

Born in Hertford County, North Carolina, Gatling began tinkering with machinery as a small boy. As an adolescent, he helped his father perfect a cottonseed sowing machine. His experience on Jordan Gatling's prosperous farm launched him on a lifelong search—frequently successful—for better and faster machinery that could do work formerly performed by hand.

Richard worked with his father on a machine for thinning cotton plants. Then he taught school for a year and at age twenty opened a country store. His business venture lasted only a few months because his fascination with machinery led him to devote most of his time to the invention of a screw propeller.

Next came a rice sowing machine that was so successful he won a patent and attracted the interest of financial backers. Since Carolina had no facilities for mass production of his rice-sower, he went to St. Louis and then to Indianapolis and Philadelphia in search of a manufacturer.

Icebound on a river steamer during the winter of 1845, Gatling came down with smallpox and found that there was no physician on the boat. Ever busy, he enrolled in the Medical College of Ohio in Cincinnati to study medicine so he could take care of himself and members of his family. Though he never practiced medicine, for the remainder of his life he was addressed as Dr. Gatling.

Prior to the Civil War, Gatling invented a hemp braking machine and a steam plow. With the outbreak of war, he turned his mind toward military machines and invented a steam ram for naval use.

On November 4, 1862, Gatling won patent #36,836 for a rapid-fire gun. Six rifled barrels, each equipped with a striker, revolved around a hand-powered central axis. Charges fed from a hopper by gravity.

Two men were required to operate the gun, which was first produced in Indianapolis. Explaining his invention, the man trained to save lives by medicine said, "I made inquiry at the depot, and found that out of eighteen dead, only three or four had been killed by bullets. The rest died in hospitals from disease.

Dr. Richard J. Gatling.
[DICTIONARY OF
AMERICAN PORTRAITS]

"Out of my own experience, I knew that it was possible to sow seeds in a scientific way by machinery. Why not shoot by machinery—and have one man do the work of one hundred, leaving the other ninety-nine at home?"

At maximum efficiency, Gatling's original gun sprayed out about two hundred bullets per minute. Nothing remotely like it had ever been seen on a battlefield; yet top officials in Washington showed little interest.

Gen. Benjamin F. Butler bought twelve guns without authorization from higher authorities. Fighting men used these $1,000-weapons in the James River campaign of May and June 1864.

Gatling's guns performed so well that official Washington sat up and took notice. Leaders decided to adopt his invention; but by the time orders were placed and manufacture was under way, Lee and Grant had met at Appomattox, Virginia, and the war was over.

An improved 1865 model with ten barrels raised firepower to three hundred shots per minute. Gatling still was not satisfied. By 1898 his latest model—already called a gat—had a battery-operated motor. It could shoot at the rate of three thousand rounds per minute.

Heralded as a substitute for troops, the gun devised by the inventor who had started with farm machinery attracted the interest of Napoleon III and other European leaders. Gatling, who seemed to have forgotten his claim to have devised the rapid-fire weapon to put an end to war, demonstrated it in many parts of the world.

The Gatling gun played decisive roles in the Spanish–American, the Franco–Prussian, and the Russo–Japanese wars, as well as dozens of smaller conflicts. For the British Empire at its zenith, it was *the* device for keeping restless colonials at bay throughout the world.

If the machinery-minded son of a Maney's Neck planter ever had misgivings about being a weapons inventor, he said nothing. Ironically he became wealthy from a gun that magnified war's horror instead of reducing it.

11

Wright Brothers Started Over
En Route to Kitty Hawk

"Will, you insisted we had to have the right wind. That has put us on the way to Kitty Hawk," Orville Wright reminded his older brother as they rode the train from Ohio to North Carolina.

As Wilbur nodded in agreement, Orville continued, "We're going to have to scrap every idea anyone else has ever proposed."

Radical as Orville's idea was, the two bicycle mechanics from Dayton, Ohio, implemented it when they arrived at North Carolina's Outer Banks in September 1900. Discarding all they had learned, they took an entirely new direction as they began building a heavier-than-air machine.

Just eighteen months earlier, Wilbur had penned a fervent plea to the Smithsonian Institution. "I believe that simple flight at least is possible to man," he wrote. "I am an enthusiast, but not a crank. I wish to avail myself of all that is already known."

Poring over booklets and pamphlets and diagrams, the operators of the Wright Cycle Shop in Dayton arrived at a radical conclusion. For centuries men had been dreaming of flying like birds, and many had attempted the feat. All had failed, however, *because they tried to imitate the motions of a bird flapping its wings.*

"We can fly, and we will fly," Orville insisted. "But we will fly like a bird that uses the wind to soar with motionless wings."

Wilbur Wright (l) with Orville (r) in 1910. They were almost inseparable until Wilbur's death in 1912. [NATIONAL AIR AND SPACE MUSEUM, SMITHSONIAN INSTITUTION]

Wilbur concurred, but only after insisting that they find the right spot to test their ideas.

Inquiries to the U. S. Weather Service brought a stack of publications. Some prospective sites were eliminated because there were too many hills and trees. Others were eliminated because winds were too variable.

Questioned by letter, Joseph J. Dosher reported in August 1900 that the beach at Kitty Hawk, North Carolina, was one mile wide and clear of trees for sixty miles. "Wind mostly from north and northeast September and October," he reported. "Sorry to say you could not rent a house here, so you will have to bring tents."

Postmaster William Tate, a commissioner of Currituck County, heard from Dosher that "Some fellows from Ohio think this would be a good place to test a flying machine."

Tate immediately sent a detailed report. At Kitty Hawk, he wrote, experimenters would find level sand covering an area one mile wide and five miles long "with a bare hill in center eighty feet high, not a tree or bush anywhere to break the evenness of the wind current. Our winds are always steady, generally from ten to twenty miles velocity per hour."

The brothers' first experiments in North Carolina, using gliders, were not dramatically successful. They were not totally unsuccessful, either. Soon they had expanded their vision to include using a motor to propel their machine.

Each year they returned to Kill Devil Hill, edging closer to flight. Money, however, was scarce. They seldom had net profits of three thousand dollars a year from their bicycle business, so they skimped, substituted, and improvised. A Dayton tinsmith made for them a gasoline tank about three inches in diameter and twelve inches in length. They modified bicycle hubs to fashion wheels and built a "launching track" from scrap lumber at a cost of four dollars.

Scoffers derided them as geese, ridiculing Wilbur and Orville for always wearing stiff white starched collars complete with neckties.

With Orville at the controls, a heavier-than-air machine flies for the first time. [NORTH CAROLINA DEPARTMENT OF ARCHIVES AND HISTORY]

Starched collar, necktie and all, Orville took off against a twenty-seven miles-per-hour wind on the morning of December 17, 1903. Their 605-pound *Kitty Hawk Flyer* was airborne for twelve seconds at a speed of about thirty-one miles per hour before it landed 120 feet from the take-off point.

On the train headed back to Dayton, the jubilant brothers agreed that the *Flyer* was likely to change the world nature of warfare. Later they confessed that had they been offered ten thousand dollars for all rights at the time, it "might have been too tempting to refuse."

*   *   *

Mankind was ushered into the air age at a point that had special meaning for native Americans. For generations coastal Indians had come every Fall to hunt migrating flocks of geese. The site of their "Killy Honk" hunt became the white man's Kitty Hawk.

A strange twist of fate, indeed!

Jocular post card sent to Orville by Will when the younger brother made headlines by setting new records. [WRIGHT STATE UNIVERSITY]

12

They Called Elizabeth Blackwell "Mad or Bad"

"Women and children—most of them, anyway—would welcome you," agreed John Dickinson, the clergyman-physician of Asheville, North Carolina. "Many men—perhaps most of them—will view things in a different light. If you persist in your goal of becoming a doctor, you must be prepared to pay the price."

"I realize that!" interrupted Elizabeth Blackwell, the twenty-five-year-old teacher who had been Dr. Dickinson's pupil. Local tradition declares that she seized Dickinson's black bag and marched up and down the room, bag in hand. "I'll do whatever it takes! I'll pay whatever price is demanded!"

Born near Bristol, England, and brought to the United States by parents at about age ten, Elizabeth had studied under private tutors in early childhood. Then her father's fortunes had waned in their new country, and his death in 1838 left the family in poverty.

Elizabeth and two of her sisters opened a private school in Cincinnati. Later she taught in Henderson, Kentucky, before moving to North Carolina.

It was while teaching in Asheville that she began reading pamphlets and books about medicine. Soon she turned to John Dickinson for help. He guided her reading, and at intervals borrowed books from his brother in Charleston, South Carolina.

At first, he had regarded Elizabeth's interest as a hobby. When she declared her intention to win an M.D. degree,

Dr. Elizabeth Blackwell (far side of carriage), age 91, in a New York City suffrage parade.

he became deeply concerned. No female had ever been granted that degree.

Elizabeth insisted that she wouldn't stop without achieving her goal; so Dickinson sent her from the mountains to the sea, to his brother in Charleston. Dr. Samuel Dickinson, an instructor at Charleston Medical College, tutored her without charge.

When Ms. Blackwell applied to the School of Medicine at Harvard University, officials didn't take the letter seriously. "Clearly, she is either mad or bad," they concluded.

Rejected at Harvard, Elizabeth applied to Yale and then to Bowdoin. Next she tried every medical school in New York City, followed by applications to every school in Philadelphia.

Only when she had been turned down by these medical schools of national prominence did she begin applying to less well-known ones. Her thirtieth application went to the medical college of Geneva, New York.

There, officials sidestepped the issue of her sex. They polled members of the student body—some of whom probably considered the question a joke—and were surprised that a majority said they'd be willing to have a woman among their number.

In 1847, at age 36, Blackwell began her studies at Geneva, a school later incorporated into Syracuse University.

Many students, including some who had voted to admit her, refused to speak to her. Others harrassed her. Townsfolk ridiculed her openly, and professors initially barred "a member of the tender sex" from classroom anatomical demonstrations.

Incredibly, on January 29, 1849, she graduated with the highest academic record in her class. Yet she flatly refused to take part in the commencement procession. "It would be unladylike for me to participate," she said.

No clinic or hospital would give her a place on a staff; so she went to Paris for additional study at a famous maternity hospital. Then she did additional study at St. Bartholomew's in London.

Encouraged by Florence Nightingale and Oliver Wendell Holmes, America's first female M.D. went to New York City. There she found financial backing and launched an infirmary for women and children. Eventually it grew into a teaching institution for women.

First of its kind anywhere, the Women's Medical College of 1868 aroused so much opposition that its founder reacted by becoming a militant suffragette, remaining active in the movement for women's rights until her death.

Until the rise of the modern women's movement, Blackwell's feat had been largely forgotten. Today she is nearly universally revered, not simply for having been the first of her kind, but because she refused to quit when most persons—male or female—would have given up.

Dr. John Romulus ("Goat-gland") Brinkley. [INTERNATIONAL NEWS SERVICE]

13

Jackson County M.D. Pioneered in Organ Transplants

"I've got the mountains and their waterfalls in my blood," listeners to radio station XER were told often and earnestly. John Romulus Brinkley, M.D., had built the station just across the Mexican border from Del Rio, Texas, far from his native Jackson County, North Carolina.

Gesturing gracefully with his diamond-heavy hands, Brinkley used radio to enrich himself. "My dear, dear friends," he often began, "I thank you for your love—and for your letters. I promise to answer each and every letter, soon. But, oh my friends, you must help me. Remember that I must pay office rent, hire stenographers, and buy postage stamps.

"Only when you send my small fee of two dollars along with your questions will it be possible for me to share my medical knowledge with you."

No one knows how many listeners wrote regularly, faithfully enclosing Brinkley's fee. But the wattage of XER was boosted several times, until it became the most powerful radio station in the world. John Brinkley had come a long, long way from his Smoky Mountains boyhood.

Yet that powerful radio station and its hosts of listeners constituted only a sideline—and a small one at that—for the physician. Decades before surgeons made world news by transplanting a baboon's heart into a dying child, Brinkley was specializing in transplanting testicles from goats to men.

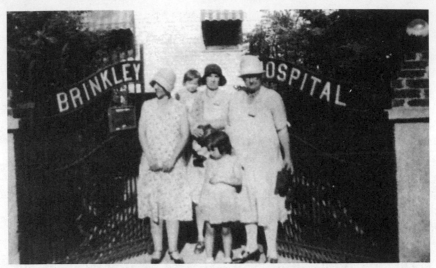

Tourists and visitors liked to pose for photos at hospital entrance.

John Brinkley's career may well have been launched by his unique middle name, Romulus, the same as the founder of ancient Rome who was saved from starvation by being suckled by a she-wolf. "Anyone who bears so great a name is surely destined for greatness," his father and mother assured him over and over.

A rural mail carrier at age 16, Brinkley spent much time dreaming about great things a 20th-century Romulus could do. Having determined that medicine was the coming thing, he decided to study it by mail since he was unable to attend college.

By 1911 Brinkley was an "undergraduate doctor," by permission of the North Carolina Board of Medical Examiners. Later he earned his medical degree by mail from the Eclectic Medical University of Kansas City.

Arkansas was one of the few states willing to honor a diploma from Eclectic as a valid M.D. degree. Once he was recognized in Arkansas, Dr. Brinkley used reciprocal agreements among states to build a pyramid of licenses in Tennessee, Connecticut, and Kansas. That enabled him to open a practice in Milford, Kansas, late in 1917. Milford had no hospital and no nearby doctors to ask embarrassing questions.

For years Brinkley had read about the ancients from whom his name had come. He learned that many cultures considered the goat the most sexually potent of animals. He pondered legends about gods who took on the form of goats and mated with the daughters of men. That led him to what he announced as a medical breakthrough without precedent.

"I learned to transplant goat glands," he said. "A childless patient from Wakefield went home and began chasing all the farm women. Within ten months, his wife, Dora, had a baby!"

Brinkley had found a medical pot of gold.

After he made his announcement, seven other males practically stood in line for the surgery. Each paid two hundred dollars for goat glands. Quickly borrowing money, the transplanted Tar Heel built a fifty-bed hospital. Then he won a Texas license by reciprocity with Arkansas.

Newspapers soon were running feature stories about his work. Since the "great surgeon" refused to reveal details about his astonishing new technique, the stories were rather vague. He told reporters rivals would steal his business if they knew exactly how he functioned.

By 1921 a steady stream of males was pouring into Dr. Brinkley's clinic in Milford, Kansas. The price of goat testicles rose steadily, peaked briefly at $750 a pair, and then doubled. Many Monday mornings found fifty men waiting for their operations.

Publicity soon brought the American Medical Association into action, and "Goat-gland Brinkley," as he was widely called, was charged with misrepresentation, outright fraud, and "gross immorality." When Brinkley lost his Kansas license, he quickly rebounded in Mexico. Eventually State Department pressure forced the closure of station XER, although Dr. Brinkley kept most of his luxury possessions.

A trickle of lawsuits grew into a stream. Eventually the

Twenty thousand people protested closing of Brinkley's radio station. [Texas State Library]

man who had parlayed a myth into a take of at least ten million dollars filed for bankruptcy.

While waiting for the federal court in San Antonio to act, John Romulus Brinkley ran for the U. S. Senate. Opponents called him "the greatest charlatan in the history of medicine," but many of his patients still swore by him.

Brinkley might have made it to Washington, had it not been for a lanky ex-teacher. Although he was world famous, Dr. Brinkley was beaten at the polls by a nearly unknown fellow by the name of Lyndon B. Johnson.

14

"Poorest of the Vanderbilts" Built Largest Mansion

At his father's death in 1885, George Washington Vanderbilt found himself almost impoverished, by family standards. As the youngest son, George received merely five million dollars, plus a trust fund of the same amount from his father's two-hundred-million-dollar estate.

William H. Vanderbilt was following the pattern established by dynasty founder Cornelius, widely known as "Commodore." At his death, just eight years before that of William, the Commodore had left him 90 percent of his $100 million. From generation to generation the first-born son served as head of the family and guardian of its fortune.

George already had inherited about $2.5 million from his grandfather. Yet at age twenty-three, the youngest male Vanderbilt had ideas far bigger than his assets.

Educated by private tutors, he spent much of his youth in Europe and was a master of eight languages. Uninterested in the world of high finance, he decided to make his mark in another arena.

In the year of his father's death young George visited the mountains of western North Carolina. Like most who see them for the first time, he was intoxicated. Unlike the typical visitor from up East, he picked a particularly spectacular site near Asheville and decided to build himself a mountain house there.

George's oldest brother, Cornelius, moved into immediate control of a fortune ten times that of George. Soon he was a director of thirty-four railroad companies. William

Childhood home of George W. Vanderbilt on New York's Fifth Avenue. [NEW YORK PUBLIC LIBRARY]

K., second in seniority among males, inherited nearly one hundred million dollars.

Their serious-minded younger brother who'd fallen in love with the Smokies was eager to become a resident of North Carolina. With seven million dollars cash in hand, he set out to build a house along the lines of those he had enjoyed most in Europe.

The chateau he envisaged as the Biltmore House would require a proper setting. So young Vanderbilt bought up about 125,000 acres nearby, with Mt. Pisgah included in the tract.

Richard Morris Hunt, finest Beaux Arts architect of the era, gladly tackled the assignment of planning the most magnificent country home in North America. He chose Indiana limestone as a building material and did not stop until he had sketched plans for the 254th room.

Frederick Law Olmsted, revered in Atlanta for having drawn up the master plan for Druid Hills and nationally acclaimed for having designed New York's Central Park, said he couldn't possibly prepare an acceptable land-scape plan unless he had at least 250 acres with which to work.

That suited George Washington Vanderbilt. After all, Versailles and Fontainebleau wouldn't be architectural gems without proper settings.

By the time Hunt and Olmsted were reasonably well satisfied with their work, their employer was committed to spending more than seven million dollars.

The Biltmore has a library with a seventy-foot ceiling whose shelves are lined with fine leather-bound volumes. Its tapestry gallery is seventy-five feet in length. A banquet hall that measures seventy-two feet by forty-two feet has such acoustical qualities that persons sitting at opposite ends of the vast table can converse without raising their voices.

The Biltmore house.

Each of the thirty-four main bedrooms has its own bath. An indoor swimming pool has seventeen private dressing rooms.

Landscape artist Olmstead delighted at having created "America's finest British garden." To keep it at its best, gardeners annually plant and dig up 40,000 tulip bulbs.

When completed after five years of work by one thousand men, the Biltmore had just the right atmosphere to make King Louis XIV feel at home, although it was equipped with some of Thomas Edison's earliest filament light bulbs.

In order to experience Europe at its finest a few hours from home, more than 650,000 paying visitors come annually to the house George Washington Vanderbilt erected with almost his entire inheritance. Immense fortunes held by his older brothers have been largely dissipated, but the Biltmore has gained worldwide fame. Listed as the world's largest private home in *Guiuness Book of World Records*, it could not be built today for $50,000,000—even if the skilled craftsmen who worked on it were available.

George Washington Vanderbilt as a student.

15

Dorothea Dix Shook Up the Lawmakers

At age forty-six, Dorothea Dix was "an invalid in the process of recuperation." She had staged many a one-woman fight; more often than not, she had been victorious.

Now she was ready to square off for one of her toughest bouts—against the North Carolina legislature.

Two factors boosted her chances. Of the original thirteen colonies, only Delaware and North Carolina were without institutions for care of the insane. Dorothea's appeal to state pride would be enhanced by her growing national reputation, which would cause at least one major newspaper to back her crusade.

She also had heavy liabilities. In an era when most women avoided public controversy, she was noted for stirring it up. What's more, she hailed from "way Up North" in Maine—in the era when North/South friction was mounting.

To make matters worse, the self-styled woman reformer was known to be determined to ask for an impossible sum: $100,000. That amount of money would double the budget of the state.

Arriving in 1848 without a single aide, Dorothea Dix followed a practice that had worked elsewhere. First she spent weeks traveling through major population centers gathering case histories of brutal treatment meted out to the mentally ill.

Then she enlisted a powerful friend, the editor of the

*Dorothea Dix as portrayed on a
commemorative stamp.* [U.S. POSTAL
SERVICE]

Raleigh Register. By early December, the newspaper was
praising her as "a high-souled, earnest, persevering
woman" who was working wholeheartedly for "a most
noble charity; that of procuring a home for the most
wretched of her fellow beings."

In spite of that tribute, veteran capital watchers didn't
give the upcoming "Memorial by Miss Dix" any hope.
Lawmakers were primarily concerned with fostering the
state's infant railroad system.

Incredibly, though, railroad backer John W. Ellis of
Rowan County sponsored the bill that the woman from
"Up North" wanted. Under its terms, the legislature
would provide funds with which to erect an asylum. Lu-
natics would then be transferred from county poorhouses
and jails to "an institution offering the most modern medical treatment known."

Though the Ellis bill was believed doomed before it
could reach the floor, Dorothea Dix remained in Raleigh

and actively lobbied for its passage. Staying at Raleigh's Mansion House hotel, she spent much of her spare time attending to another guest, Mrs. James C. Dobbin.

In spite of her efforts, Mrs. Dobbin died on December 18. Momentarily giving up her political activity, Ms. Dix traveled to Fayetteville for the funeral. Richard A. Faust, who meticulously investigated the work of Dorothea Dix in North Carolina, pointed out that she knew Mrs. Dobbin was the wife of an influential legislator.

As expected, the "asylum bill" was voted down when it reached the floor of the legislature on December 21. According to Faust's account, "at this point, chance and the result of Dorothea's kindness brought success."

Returning from the funeral of his wife, James Dobbin made a stirring appeal for reconsideration of the bill calling for erection of an asylum. His influence led to development of a compromise.

Quick action by the House, on the heels of the Dobbin appeal of December 22, brought an overwhelmingly positive vote. Dorothea Dix was hailed as having "presented North Carolina with the finest Christmas present on record."

Commissioners of the new insane hospital of North Carolina wanted to name the institution for her. She adamantly refused. Then, yielding a bit, she agreed to let them name the site for her grandfather, Dr. Elijah Dix.

Dix Hill became a byword in Carolina. Then the legislature acted once more. During the centennial celebration of the first patient's admission in 1956, lawmakers renamed the Dix Hill Asylum as Dorothea Dix Hospital.

Dorothea Dix was instrumental in founding institutions for the care of the mentally ill in a dozen states and many cities. Only two in the nation perpetuate her name.

Frail in childhood and an invalid during a period as a young woman, she was drafted to teach a Sunday School class in a Massachusetts jail when a pastor failed to keep an appointment. Finding terrible conditions among the insane confined there, she was so shocked that she forgot her own infirmities and launched a one-woman crusade that lasted for decades.

16

Tsali Gave His Life for Fellow Tribesmen

Eastern Cherokees, who were among the most culturally advanced of all native Americans, established themselves as a nation in order to resist the encroachment of whites.

They adopted a constitution, established a capital, and published a newspaper, *The Cherokee Phoenix.* Instead of placating their enemies, these moves made the whites more determined to take over tribal lands.

A few leaders decided that compromise was the lesser of the evils confronting the Cherokees. Hence they signed the Treaty of New Echota, which called for removal of tribesmen to new lands in the West.

Seven million acres "in the Arkansas River region" were to be assigned to deported Indians. Federal authorities agreed to provide two thousand dollars a year for the education of Cherokee children, plus one thousand dollars for purchase of type and a printing press to replace the one destroyed by whites.

Each family moving west of the Great River was to be provided with "a good rifle, a blanket, a kettle, and five pounds of tobacco."

Stockades were built, and Cherokees were herded into them in preparation for the start of removal in June 1838. An estimated 18,000 men, women, and children were ready to begin the march now famous as "The Trail of Tears."

Some of the tribesmen resisted and fled into the wild mountain country of western North Carolina. General

Winfield Scott, who headed U. S. Army units superintending the removal, decided not to pursue fugitives for the moment. He would escort the large contingent of Cherokees to Oklahoma, then send seasoned troops back to flush out the escapees. Scott, who had won national fame by riding into Mexico City as a victor in the Mexican War, was following the orders of Congress, whose decision was strongly advocated by President Andrew Jackson.

Soon after the march began, it became obvious that it would be a debacle. Children, a few women, and occasionally a weak male were unable to stand the pace. Prodded by uniformed soldiers, they staggered forward until

General Winfield Scott. [LIBRARY OF CONGRESS]

they died. At least one Cherokee woman at the limit of her endurance was prodded by a soldier's bayonet.

Furious at the white man's treatment of his wife, Tsali—or Charlie—that night made whispered plans with his relatives in their native language. Sentries on duty heard them speaking but did not understand what was being said.

At dawn Tsali led a suicide squad of young men willing to die to escape to the hills of their birth. In the melee that followed, a soldier was killed.

Tsali, his sons, and other fugitives, joined a band led by Utsala, or Lichen, who had found refuge on the upper Oconaluftee River.

General Winfield Scott believed that the killing of one of his men gave him an opportunity. Instead of waiting, he immediately determined to come to terms with the refugees. Using veteran trader William H. Thomas as a go-between, he made the fugitives an offer.

In 1762 these Cherokees came to London to reaffirm the pact made by Sir Alexander Cumming.

If Tsali and his band of escapees would turn themselves in, said Scott, he would permit the remainder of Utsala's followers to remain in the mountains. They could negotiate a settlement with the federal government later.

Comfortably and securely established in a remote cave at the head of Deep Creek, Tsali received word of Thomas's mission and Scott's offer. "I will come in," he said. "I will bring my own. But the rest must be allowed to stay in the mountains."

Speaking for Scott, Thomas gave his solemn word in agreement.

Tsali led the culprits who had reacted to a soldier's brutality: his brother, his oldest son, and two younger sons. Together they marched to the white man's command post and surrendered.

Tradition says that a female missionary, alerted to what was happening, interceded with Army leaders. "Look at Tsali's youngest son," she reputedly urged. "Wasituna (better known to whites as Washington) is only a child. Spare him, in the name of humanity and decency!"

Thus was Wasituna's death sentence commuted, and he survived into the twentieth century. His father, his uncle, and his two older brothers were taken out and shot.

"Tsali did right," Wasituna always said. "He gave himself up and led the others along, for the sake of our people."

As a result of Tsali's sacrifice, eastern Cherokees who had escaped to avoid deportation were permitted to remain in the Great Smokies. Their descendants make up most natives of the Qualla Reservation in western North Carolina.

Unto These Hills, widely believed to be America's most popular outdoor drama, gives a vivid portrayal of the Cherokee Indians' story, including the life—and death—of Tsali.

17

Benjamin Hawkins Smoked the Peace Pipe

"Tustenuggee Thlucco will sign," said the Indian chieftain of mixed blood whom whites knew as Big Warrior. As he stepped forward to make his mark giving consent to the treaty framed by Andrew Jackson, Benjamin Hawkins burst into sobs. Later he explained to his son that "Twenty years of my life were wiped out by a single stroke of a pen."

Commissioners had come together with Indian leaders at Fort Jackson. Hastily erected near the confluence of Alabama's Coosa and Tallapoosa rivers, Fort Jackson was in the heart of Red Stick territory.

Big Warrior, the affluent owner of sixty black slaves, was not there by choice. He and other chiefs invited to the council by Andrew Jackson had been warned that "Destruction will attend a failure to comply."

Numerous Creeks had fought under Jackson at Horseshoe Bend; they came expecting to be rewarded. Many others had been on the side of their own people, loosely allied with the British. Soundly defeated, they came expecting to be punished.

Jackson treated all Creeks alike. Former allies and former enemies were told that they had only hours to decide whether they would cede tribal land to whites or be exiled to the region near Pensacola, Florida.

Since military forces under Jackson had already demonstrated their overwhelming superiority, most Indian leaders—of whom a majority were of mixed blood—followed the lead of Big Warrior. That night they signed away more than half of the Creek domain, an estimated twenty-three million acres. This area included most of present-day Alabama and much of Georgia.

Eyes still moist with tears, Benjamin Hawkins that night resigned as Indian Commissioner for the region south of the Ohio River. He had done all he could to help native Americans, and he had seen years of effort wiped out by a treaty widely described as "unequalled for exorbitance."

Born in Warren County, North Carolina, Hawkins was personally selected by George Washington as an aide. After the Revolution, he became North Carolina's first full-term U. S. Senator.

Partly because he had learned French at the College of New Jersey, Hawkins had been asked to help negotiate several early treaties with Indians. He was so successful in dealing with Cherokees, Choctaws, and Chickasaws that George Washington again appealed to him. This time he wanted Hawkins to become permanent agent for the Creeks. He also was to be superintendent of all Indian tribes south of the Ohio River.

Hawkins' first daughter showed his passionate interest in native Americans. He named her Cherokee.

Hawkins left his Roanoke plantation in November 1796 and entered northwestern South Carolina on the way to his new post. Creek territory was then about four hundred

William McIntosh, field commander of Creeks loyal to Hawkins.

miles from east to west and about two hundred miles from north to south. Hawkins established headquarters near Macon, Georgia, and built a fort named for him; later he moved to a permanent post on the Flint River.

Once firmly established in Creek territory, the ex-senator brought his slaves from Roanoke and used them to teach agriculture to the Indians. He developed a model farm, so large that he often put his brand upon five hundred calves in a single season. Milk was churned by machinery activated by water power.

Tools and implements manufactured at his model plantation were distributed to Creeks and other natives. Those willing to do so could spend weeks on the Flint River model farm, learning how to use tools and to select and plant seeds.

Symbolically "smoking the peace pipe" year after year, Hawkins's dream of reconciliation between red men and white men was shattered in 1811 when the noted orator Tecumseh came to the South. His mission was to enlist as many Indians as possible on the side of the British in the War of 1812.

Hoping to counter the influence of Tecumseh, Benjamin Hawkins organized a regiment of loyal tribesmen. At their head, as commander, he placed half-breed William McIntosh, who was closely related to a governor of Georgia.

McIntosh and his followers fought fiercely against other Creeks in the battle of Horseshoe Bend. Like Hawkins, they felt betrayed when they were given the same treatment as the Red Sticks who had murdered whites at Fort Mims and had opposed Jackson's troops.

Following the debacle at Fort Jackson, Benjamin Hawkins returned to North Carolina after an absence of twenty years. Once more assuming the role of a wealthy and well-educated white man who had experienced political power, he grieved over the treatment given to the Indians he had tried to help. Four years after having been forced to leave the Indians he loved, he died. Until his death he grieved at the wicked ways of his own people.

18

Dan Morgan Masterminded "Most Imitated Battle"

"Remember, boys, three shots is all I ask!" Wincing from rheumatism, buckskin-clad Dan Morgan wore no insignia of rank. Members of his militia companies regarded him almost as one of them. Even though he had been a brigadier general for a few months, his attitude hadn't changed at all.

Using his lungs as though he were bellowing at men and horses during his years as a wagon master, Morgan shouted assurances to the militiamen. "You will win! Follow my orders exactly! You'll see the enemy run! Get ready, boys, they're on the way!"

Morgan had taken part in the expedition against Canada and in the bloody Saratoga campaign. Still, he was untried as a commanding officer.

Gen. Nathanael Greene, defeated by the British at Camden, was in trouble; and George Washington sent Morgan to his aid. Badly outnumbered, the patriots split their force. Pursued by Cornwallis—perhaps the finest professional soldier of the Revolution—Greene retreated into North Carolina.

Morgan's small band was being hunted by the elite corps headed by Col. Banastre Tarleton, all seasoned regulars. They knew that most of Morgan's men were hastily summoned militia with no battle experience and little stomach to get it. Men of this sort had been known to turn tail and run when confronted by booming artillery and flashing sabers.

Artist's conception of Morgan in hand-to-hand combat with an Indian ally of the British.

To the bewilderment of his subordinates, Dan Morgan picked a field and deliberately waited for Tarleton and his men to mount an attack. From a boy of nine who'd taken one of his father's old bulls into the British camp and sold it, he learned that enemies were close on his heels. They would catch up soon, no matter what he did. His only chance was to have a meeting ground of his choice, plus unconventional deployment of his forces.

Hannah's Cowpens, named for a man who once grazed a herd of cattle at the site, was a rolling slope topped by two small hills. To the rear was Broad River, which was too turbulent to be crossed and effectively cut off retreat.

"Remember Tarleton's Quarter!" Morgan shouted again and again as he rode along his lines early on January 17, 1781.

His message—actually a warning—required no explanation. It was well known that Colonel Tarleton was so disdainful of patriots that he had more than once refused to take prisoners. Men who had thrown down their weapons and surrendered had been cut down by the sword blades of Tarleton's redcoats.

Although Dan Morgan didn't say it, his message to his inexperienced men was clear: "With the river behind you,

you have two choices. You can fight like veterans and whip the British here, or you can die in these Cowpens."

Ignoring tried and tested strategy by which men facing attack always put their finest troops in the forefront, Morgan deliberately stationed his militia where they'd meet the first wave of assault. Behind them he placed a second line of troops made up of Continental soldiers, plus a small force of mounted dragoons.

Members of his militia company understood that once every man had fired three of the twelve rounds he carried, the entire body was to make an orderly withdrawal. Continentals knew they were expected to hold their positions regardless of what happened.

British scouts described for Tarleton the unusual spot at which the colonists were deployed. Delighted at the ignorance of the American commander who'd placed his forces in such fashion, the redcoat leader sent his little three-pound cannon (commonly called "grasshoppers") forward.

One volley from the grasshoppers should have dispersed the untrained men in Morgan's front ranks. Incredibly, they stood their ground. It was too late for Tarleton to change his tactics; his battleline was already moving forward.

Though they had no combat experience, many of the militia were skilled hunters. They used their weapons so effectively the British advance faltered, then halted. As ordered, the first line of patriots made an orderly retreat to the rear.

The British regrouped. Tarleton threw in the seventy-first Highlanders—his last fresh troops—in a frantic bid to take the hill held by Continentals. Repulsed, they swirled around in confusion.

Precisely at this point, Morgan did what no other commander had done. He sent his militia back into the fray. Having nearly circled the American position, they struck the British left rear. Simultaneously, Morgan's dragoons hit the British right.

Redcoats began surrendering. Jubilant patriots yelled

"Tarleton's quarter!" and prepared to cut them down. Their commander intervened, but not before 39 British officers and 61 enlisted men lay dead on the field. More than 200 of the enemy had been wounded; about 600 were taken prisoner. Patriots had lost 12 men and counted less than 60 wounded.

Military strategists who learned of what had happened in northwestern South Carolina at first refused to believe the news. When fresh reports made it impossible to deny, many dubbed the battle of Cowpens as "the most extraordinary event of the American conflict."

Nathanael Greene received from Morgan a firsthand account of tactics used. Later, at least twice, Greene would employ the same strategy against numerically superior forces. Again in the War of 1812 "Morgan's battle plan" was used so effectively that Cowpens became famous as the most imitated battle of the American Revolution.

One-time wagon master Morgan had done what everyone thought impossible. He had used raw recruits to turn the tide against battle-tested veterans!

General Dan Morgan, dressed much more elegantly than usual.

19

The Battle That Changed Naval Warfare Forever

The most famous naval battle of the Civil War took place on March 16, 1862.

Union forces used the ironclad ship *Monitor*, designed and built with the goal of making wooden warships obsolete, while the Confederates had a converted wooden vessel which they had covered with a partial shield of iron. One-inch sheets of iron made in Atlanta and Richmond were applied in three layers to the partly burned Union gunboat *Merrimac*. Though the name *Merrimac* has stuck in many records, Confederates called their makeshift ironclad the CSS *Virginia*.

In order to fire, the *Virginia* had to turn because she carried just one seven-inch gun. There was no iron at points three or more feet below water. Worst of all, the *Virginia* could not maneuver in less than twenty-two feet of water.

Her rival, designed by famous inventor John Ericsson, had two eleven-inch guns inside a revolving turret. She was completely iron clad and had a draft of just twelve feet.

Most military experts would have said the clumsy *Virginia* didn't have a chance against the *Monitor*. Under the command of John L. Worden, the world's first warship designed and built as an ironclad left New York City.

Its destination was the Carolina coast, where it was to be stationed for blockade duty. But Confederates in the *Virginia* found the mighty ship in Hampton Roads, Virginia, and launched an attack.

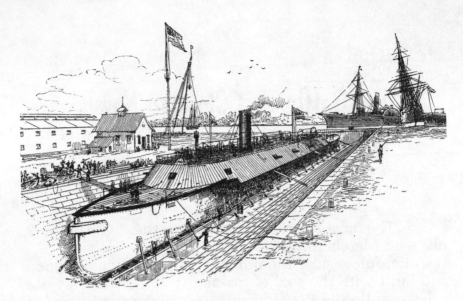

The Merrimac under conversion into the Virginia at Norfolk.

They fired at one another at close range for two hours. Both withdrew with no winner, but their meeting forever changed the navies of the world. Reporting the engagement, the *London Times* said there now were just two first class vessels in the world, both superior to Britain's 149 "first class warships."

Her enemies didn't know it, but the *Virginia* was crippled. Her smokestack was gone, and her steam pipes had been shot away. Railings, stanchions, and even boat davits had received direct hits. A rafter was cracked, and her engine, always creaky, failed frequently. Still, she had survived!

The jubilation of crew members was brief, for a series of Union victories drove Confederates from Norfolk and made capture of the *Virginia* seem inevitable.

Since Commodore Josiah Tattnall, head of the Confederate Navy, refused to allow the *Virginia* to fall into the hands of the enemy, he hastily scuttled the ship before it could be captured. To a court of inquiry, which exonerated him of wrongdoing, the crusty commodore tartly explained, "At least, we didn't lose a single man of our crew."

Union leaders decided to send the *Monitor* to Charleston, but she never reached her destination. On December 30, 1862, the ironclad hit heavy seas off Cape Hatteras and foundered. Four officers and twelve men perished with the vessel.

For more than one hundred years the *Monitor*'s whereabouts were unknown. A 1973 discovery showed her lying off the coast of North Carolina, bottom up, under 220 feet of water. Ambitious salvage schemes have been devised and promoted, but the vessel that inventor John Ericsson hailed as "totally invincible" remains a captive of the sea.

Eleven-inch guns of the Monitor.

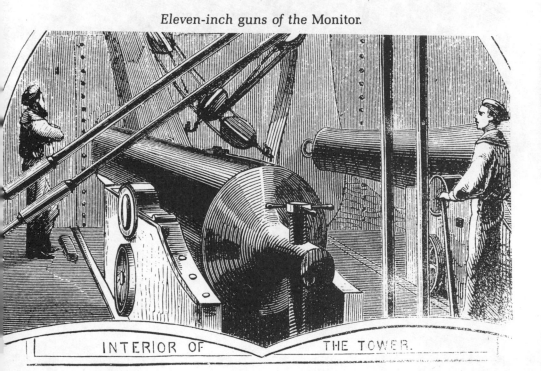

INTERIOR OF THE TOWER.

Neither the *Monitor* nor the *Virginia* (or *Merrimac*) ever won a victory of any consequence. But the four-hour battle of the two ironclads served notice that from that day on wooden warships—the standard for centuries—had become obsolete.

Sinking *of the* Monitor *off the Carolina coast.*

20

"Sherman in Gray" Burned a Wide Swath Around the World

"Put her to the torch, boys, and waste no time doing so!" ordered Capt. James Iredell Waddell. Master of the Confederate warship *Shenandoah*, North Carolina native Waddell had just captured his first prize, the Maine-owned bark *Alina*.

Headed toward Argentina, the unarmed merchant vessel posed no threat to fighting men in gray as her cargo consisted only of railroad iron. However, because she belonged to Yankees, destruction of the vessel would slightly weaken the Union cause.

Encountered in waters off Dakar in the Senegal, Africa, the cargo ship surrendered without a fight. She had no other choice; Waddell's vessel carried enough big guns to blow the *Alina* out of the water.

James D. Bullock of near Savannah had made a secret deal for the ship commanded by Waddell. In England, he bought the *Sea King*, with plans to outfit her as a warship. Soon after sailing from London on October 8, 1864, the ship was renamed the *Shenandoah* and took aboard heavy guns.

A smokestack, clearly visible in engravings of the era, reveals that although the ship was equipped with a full spread of sails, for some unaccountable reason it also had an auxilliary steam engine. Crew members of merchant vessels who noticed it were puzzled. James Waddell gloated. The engine gave him the extra speed he needed to overtake and capture Yankee ships.

Captain James I. Waddell of Pittsboro, Chatham
County, North Carolina.

Having burned an unarmed merchant ship, the Confederate officer and his men had no place to hide. Under international law they had become pirates. Having nothing
more to lose, they embarked on an eight-month voyage of
destruction.

Gen. William Tecumseh Sherman, whom Henry Grady
twitted as having been "a bit careless with fire," is hated
for having burned Atlanta and destroyed Columbia, South
Carolina. However, in terms of systematic, planned destruction, C.S.A. Capt. James Waddell was even more
careless with fire on water than Sherman was on land.

After burning his first prize, Waddell captured and quickly disposed of three more vessels. By then his own ship was crowded with prisoners. Capture of the clipper ship *Kate Prince* offered a solution to overcrowding of the *Shenandoah*.

"I've taken four prizes, and I've burned four," Waddell told the master of the merchant vessel based in New Hampshire. "I'll spare yours if you'll take my prisoners to South America and sign a bond requiring your owners to pay $40,000 to the Confederate States of America."

Compared with the torch, those terms were lenient and generous. A bargain was struck, and the *Kate Prince* was soon on her way to Brazil.

Some of the many vessels burned by "North Carolina's Sherman in Gray" were: the *Lizzie Gray*, carrying barrel staves; the whale ship *Edward*; the whalers *Hector, Edward Carey, Pearl, Harvest, William Thompson,* and *Euphrates*.

Soon the Confederate seaman received troublesome news. One of the ships he had captured carried newspapers reporting the fall of Richmond, and the surrender of Robert E. Lee at Appomatox.

"Never mind," the Pittsboro, North Carolina, native told his crew members. "We're a long way from the action on the ground. We'll use the torch as long as we can."

Before the Confederate seaman was finished, he and his men burned at least thirty-one ships. Many were destroyed weeks after land forces of the Confederacy had ceased to fight.

A professional Navy man who enlisted as a midshipman in 1841, Waddell had studied at Annapolis and briefly taught there. He resigned his commission in January 1862 in order to become a lieutenant in the tiny Confederate navy.

As master of the *Shenandoah*, the Tar Heel was the only Confederate to carry the stars and bars around the world. He gave up the fight only when it became clear that the war had ended long ago on land. Finally he turned himself over to British authorities in November 1865.

When his vessel docked at Liverpool, it ended a voyage of 58,000 miles during which he had put into port only once, in Australia. Since he and his men were classified as pirates, they remained in England until President Andrew Johnson declared universal amnesty for former Confederates.

Waddell's global spree of capturing, pillaging, and burning puts him in a class by himself. No other man, whether wearing blue or gray, made such widespread use of fire as a form of punishment for enemy civilians.

Rare old photograph reveals sleek lines of the CSS Shenandoah.

21

Boy Hero of the Waxhaws Defied the British

Exactly where did pioneers establish a settlement that in time became a tiny village called Waxhaw? Respected authorities disagree on this point. Many insist it was in the area now encompassed by Lancaster County, North Carolina. Not so, say others, believing it lay just below the line dividing North Carolina from South Carolina.

Because Andrew Jackson spent his boyhood in the disputed settlement, the birthplace of our seventh president thus is claimed by both North and South Carolina.

The story of Andrew Jackson—the boy hero of the Waxhaws—is much clearer than the exact location of the village in which he was born.

Settler Andrew Jackson strained himself trying to lift too heavy a load; as a result, Elizabeth Jackson was a widow when her third son was born on March 15, 1767. She named him for his dead father and took refuge with him in the home of her sister, Jane Crawford.

A bright youngster, Andy learned to read at age five. By the time he was eight, he was praised by his schoolmaster as being able to write "a neat, legible hand." One year later, he often served as "public reader," standing on the steps of Captain Crawford's home and reading columns of newspapers aloud to anyone who cared to listen.

The calm and tranquil life of the Waxhaws vanished after July 4, 1776. High excitement prevailed at news that the British had attacked Charles Town. Should they take

Andrew Jackson's birthplace, claimed by both Carolinas.

the city, they'd no doubt move out into the countryside, perhaps as far as the Catawba River.

"We ought to get ready to fight," young Jackson is reputed to have said to friends and relatives.

Words like that from a boy of nine would have been ignored under ordinary circumstances, but Andy was no ordinary boy. Time and again he had demonstrated his willingness to fight fellows twice his weight, usually when taunted about his tendency to drool almost constantly.

In 1776 the boy didn't have to do more than make threatening noises about the British. Repulsed at Charles Town, they did not mount a major offensive in Carolina until 1779.

South Carolina's capital fell on May 12, 1780. Lieutenant Colonel Banastre Tarleton then led his redcoats toward the Back Country. After a long forced march, they clashed with patriots and left the ground covered with the dead. Many wounded were brought to the Waxhaw church, hastily converted into a makeshift hospital.

During weeks of action, the region was sometimes securely held by patriots. At other times it was overrun by the British, who burned crops and houses and destroyed the cattle they did not kill for food.

By 1781 young Andy Jackson was a seasoned member of Crawford's mounted militia. Along with his older brother, the boy was captured in early April, while eating breakfast in the Crawford home.

Redcoats proceeded systematically to smash furniture in the sparsely equipped home. One of their officers, cursing profusely, commanded Andy to clean his boots. The

Upon Andy's refusal, the officer lifted his sword and struck him.

order was instantly refused as being below the dignity of a prisoner of war.

Andrew's brash refusal brought quick reprisal. Lifting his sword, the officer delivered a violent blow aimed directly at the head of his juvenile captive. Throwing up his left arm, Jackson received a cut that left him badly scarred for life, but saved his skull except for a deep gash that reached the bone.

Forced to mount a horse, the bleeding boy was made to guide the British to a nearby home. He, in turn, duped his enemies and managed to warn the man they expected to capture. As punishment, he was forced to march more than forty miles to Camden.

Days later, Elizabeth Jackson rode from the Waxhaws to the prison compound in Camden. Somehow, she persuaded Lord Rowdon to release Andy and his brother Robert, who died two nights after reaching home. Andy became delirious and for hours was at the point of the death.

Gradually recovering, the boy of fourteen made a solemn vow. God being his helper, some day he'd make the British pay for what they had done.

22

Original Siamese Twins Reared Families in Carolina

"Hurry!" Eng Bunker urged his wife in the pre-dawn hours of a January day in 1874. "There's something badly wrong!"

One look was enough to tell her the worst. Chang—Eng's Siamese twin—was dead.

Eyes dilated with terror, Eng cried, "Then my last hour is come! May the Lord have mercy on my soul!" Three hours later, Eng joined his twin brother in death.

A recently discovered autopsy report gave the verdict that modern science accepts. Eng died of fright. Joined to Chang's corpse, Eng's terror triggered his own death.

Connected by a mostly cartilaginous band, Chang and Eng were the original Siamese twins. Generations after their death, they remain far and away the best known.

Abel Coffin, skipper of a Yankee clipper ship, had discovered the pair on a visit to Bangkok. He instantly saw commercial opportunities and arranged with their mother for a "settlement" that nearly amounted to a purchase.

"I have two Chinese Boys seventeen years old," Coffin wrote to his daughter Susan. "They enjoy good health. I hope they will prove valuable as a curiosity."

Brought to Boston, the teenagers created a sensation. Coffin next decided to exhibit them where the real money was, in Europe.

Britain's famed Royal College of Surgeons invited Chang and Eng to tea, then the members eagerly examined them, sure they were a fraud. But the conjoined twins, as they are now called, baffled scholars. Pronounced authentic, Chang and Eng attracted 300,000 paying customers in England alone.

It was the London *Times* that first incorrectly called them "Siamese." A news story of November 1829 told readers that "Paris papers have announced that the Sardinian girl with two heads is dead. The Siamese twins will therefore have a clear field in France."

At that time their combined weight was just 180 pounds, yet they were so agile they could defeat four ordinary men in a rope-pulling contest. Although they could walk only side-by-side, they often took jaunts of six to eight miles. To sleep, they had to lie face-to-face.

Trouble between the curiosities and their manager came to a head on May 11, 1832, on their twenty-first birthday. They agreed to stay with Coffin for the rest of the month, but then they would go into business for themselves.

Nimble-minded and already proficient in English, the conjoined twins toured much of the United States on their

Chang (l) and Eng (r) with their wives and two of their twenty-two children.

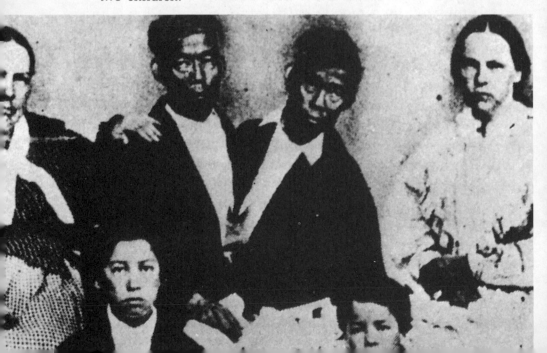

own. They usually charged fifty cents per person for admission to an "exhibition."

Showman P. T. Barnum then signed the brothers to a contract and for five years they drew more customers to his famous American Museum than did any other performers. They lived in frugal style and managed to put aside savings of about fifty thousand dollars.

Applying for U. S. citizenship, they were baffled when a clerk told them they had to have a surname. A stranger who overheard the conversation introduced himself to the twins as Fred Bunker and offered his name to the immigrants. This made it possible for them to win their citizenship.

Only strong-willed men would have considered marriage in such circumstances. Chang and Eng let it be known they'd gladly share their savings with "the right two girls."

They found Sarah and Adelaide Yates, from Wilkes County, North Carolina. Since they had decided to give up show business in favor of normal lives, after their marriage at the Baptist Church, they selected land in Surry County. There they built houses one mile apart.

For the next twenty-five years they lived near Mt. Airy. Except when on tour, they followed a strict schedule: three days at Chang's house with Adelaide, then three days at Eng's house with Sarah.

"Adelaide and I had the first child!" Chang liked to brag. "A fine boy—perfectly normal!"

Their son was followed by two more boys and seven girls. Eng and Sarah had seven boys plus five girls.

According to Dr. Robert Hollingsworth, though Chang contracted severe bronchitis, he insisted upon going to Eng's house at the customary time. It was there that he died of complications from illness—and his brother of fright.

Medical specialists today insist that Chang and Eng's bond was not that complex. Had modern surgical techniques been available then, it would have been a simple job to separate the brothers.

PART THREE:
South Carolina

Submarine Hunley on Charleston dock.

23

Every Voyage of the *Hunley* Was a Suicide Mission

"Until about 8:45 P.M. it was a routine evening," wrote J. R. Crosby, acting master of the warship USS *Housatonic*. His vessel was on blockade duty in the Charleston, South Carolina, harbor on February 17, 1864.

"Suddenly the lookout spotted something. It was about one hundred yards away, and at first looked like a huge log. But it was moving too fast to be drifting with the tide.

"Our chain was slipped, the engine was backed, and all hands were called to quarters. Then the torpedo hit.

"It struck the *Housatonic* forward of the mizzenmast, on the starboard side. With our after pivot gun bearing to port, we were unable to fire.

"Within a minute after the explosion took place, we started down—with our vessel sinking stern first and heeling to port. Five members of our valiant crew died at once."

Crosby's record constitutes the only on-the-scene account of the world's first kill by a submarine. Not until decades later, early in World War I, was another warship sunk by an underwater craft.

Confederates built their submarine at Mobile, Alabama, and named her for designer Horace Hunley of New Orleans. An old steam boiler about twenty-five feet long and four feet wide provided the shell of the CSS *Hunley*.

Cut in two lengthwise, the boiler was strengthened by twelve-inch iron strips. Ballast tanks, equipped with sea cocks and force pumps, were riveted across the stern and bow.

There was only one source of illumination, a big candle. When it began to flicker, crew members were warned that oxygen was running low.

Power for the craft that some derisively called "the fish" came from Confederate muscles. Each of the eight crew members helped turn the shaft to which a small propeller was attached.

From the outset, builders of the *Hunley* knew their goal, to break the Federal blockade of Charleston harbor. So the thirty-five-foot craft was loaded on two flatcars and shipped to the port city early in 1864.

Only volunteers were accepted for duty inside "the fish." A trial run at Mobile had ended in tragedy; someone had failed to turn a sea cock, and every man in the *Hunley* died.

Once in Charleston, Lt. George E. Dixon, who had helped to build the craft, took command. With the man for whom she was named at the helm, "the fish" dived under the receiving ship CSS *Indian Chief*.

The *Hunley* failed to surface on the other side of the ship. It was a week before salvage crews pulled the sub from the bottom and found that, this time, the after valve had not been closed tightly.

In spite of the murderous record of "the fish," there was no scarcity of volunteers for her first mission against an enemy.

Confederate Gen. P. T. G. Beauregard, in command at Charleston, stipulated that for the sake of safety, the *Hunley* would have to resort to use of a spar torpedo. Lashed to a long pole, it projected from the bow of the craft.

When George Dixon scanned the harbor, he saw no shortage of targets; enemy vessels had tightened their grip upon Charleston. He picked a handsome sloop—rigged like a small frigate—and told his volunteers that it would make a fine prize.

A prize it was. Nearly everything ahead of the mainmast of the *Housatonic* was crumpled by the blast of the *Hunley*'s torpedo. Even the rudder post and screw were blown away. From a distance of a few hundred yards, the

USS *Canadaigua* came to the rescue, so that 21 officers and 137 men from the *Housatonic* were saved.

Not until February 27 did Confederates learn that the big blockade ship had gone down. They knew the *Hunley* had not returned, but they didn't know that her torpedo had ripped the converted steam boiler open at the bow.

In trial runs and in her only assault upon an enemy, the *Hunley* claimed thirty-three Confederate lives. But she was one of the most unusual innovations of the Civil War and was the distant ancestor of today's nuclear-powered submarines.

A full-scale replica of the *Hunley* now sits in front of the Charleston Museum. Another replica, said to be somewhat more accurate, is displayed in the South Carolina Museum in Columbia. Differences between the two are not readily apparent to the casual viewer. Both replicas, viewed thoughtfully, bring overwhelming realization that men who manned the submarine placed the cause of their region above their own lives.

Hunley's torpedo hits the Housatonic.

24

Charlestonian Added Twenty-Eight Million Acres to the Nation

"Mr. President, we must ignore critics," said U. S. Secretary of War Jefferson Davis. "History will judge us by what we do about the Mesilla Valley. I urge that we send new instructions to Gadsden."

Already committed to the goal of securing a land grant from Mexico, President Franklin Pierce mused briefly. In his imagination he could see a transcontinental railroad snaking its way through the region south of Arizona's Gila River.

"Send for Marcy," he directed. "Final arrangements belong to him and his department."

U.S. Secretary of State William L. Marcy, weak and indecisive, had abolitionist sentiments. That meant he leaned toward a northern route for the contemplated rail line.

A southern route, considered least expensive of three under consideration, would bring new industry to the entire South. A rush of settlers would help maintain the delicate balance between pro- and antislavery states. Davis was determined to get the coveted land.

As a key actor in the international drama, Jefferson Davis's friend James Gadsden would have to conduct the negotiations. A native of Charleston, Gadsden had piled up an impressive track record by the time Franklin Pierce took office in 1853.

Gadsden had gone into Florida with Andrew Jackson as his adjutant general during the Seminole War and had remained in the conquered region to supervise the removal

James Gadsden. [Gibbs Art Gallery]

of the Seminole Indians to reservations and to build Florida's first roads.

Back home by 1840, he became president of the Louisville, Cincinnati, & Charleston Railroad. If he was not the first man of influence to advocate creation of a strong southern rail network, he was perhaps the most persuasive early spokesman for this cause.

At Memphis in 1845, Gadsden caused delegates to a regional commercial convention to take better notice of tiny Atlanta. Small as it was, he insisted, it was a vital rail center sure to gain rapidly in importance.

It was at this convention that the Charlestonian suggested building a transcontinental railroad "along an easy and economical southern route." To make that possible, the United States would have to acquire thousands of square miles from Mexico.

Stressing Gadsden's "extraordinary vision" and experience as a rail executive, Jefferson Davis helped win him a hearing. Franklin Pierce was so impressed that in 1853 he named the South Carolinian as minister to Mexico.

Gadsden had been in Mexico City only a few weeks before he sent an optimistic report. "Times are very hard here," he wrote. "Money is so scarce that some of the governmental departments seldom meet their payrolls on time. An offer of hard cash, right now, can hardly be refused. Perhaps we can get even more land than we actually need for the railroad."

This intriguing report led Jefferson Davis to push for immediate action. Fearful of Mexican bandits, Davis persuaded the secretary of state to take unprecedented action.

Once Gadsden's new instructions had been prepared, they were delivered to Christopher L. Ward as messenger. In order to foil bandits, Ward was required to memorize long and detailed orders so, if captured, he would have no documents on his person.

There's no certainty that Ward remembered every detail committed to him. What he did recall, he relayed to Gadsden in Mexico City.

This chain of events had the effect of giving the Charlestonian a free hand. Having no written instructions, he could proceed as he wished, then claim that Ward forgot or misunderstood debatable points.

Gadsden immediately went into a series of negotiations, emerging with a treaty he had drafted. For ten million dollars, the United States was to get more than twenty-eight million acres in the vital Mesilla Valley. Ratified in 1854, the treaty established the present boundary between Mexico and the United States.

In 1869 the United States became the first continent to have a rail line from coast to coast, when the Union Pacific and Central Pacific lines met at Promontory, Utah. Gadsden's dream became a reality when the Southern Pacific Railroad was completed in 1882.

Small by comparison with the Louisiana and Alaska purchases, the Gadsden Purchase was immensely profitable; it brought our nation a region estimated to have yielded ten billion dollars in minerals alone. Within one hundred years the annual payroll of the Southern Pacific Railroad topped the purchase price.

One crucial aspect is nearly forgotten now. James Gadsden, Jefferson Davis, and Franklin Pierce knew that money paid by the United States would not go into the sagging Mexican economy.

Money for the Gadsden Purchase went directly into the pockets of dictator Santa Anna, the universally hated military dictator responsible for the massacre of Americans at the Alamo.

25

No One Ever Wielded a Cane
Like Preston Brooks

"Pierce Butler and his kind deserve no voice in this august body!" cried U. S. Senator Charles Sumner of Massachusetts.

Fellow lawmakers who had been dozing, bored by the long-drawn debate over Kansas, were shaken awake by startled colleagues. Every man in the house knew and usually obeyed the unwritten law by which no senator was permitted to criticize another by name.

Having breached the "gentleman's code" that had prevailed for decades, Sumner made no apology. Instead, the violently partisan abolitionist kept the floor. He spoke for what seemed an eternity, heaping abuse upon slave owners in general and Senator Pierce Butler of South Carolina in particular.

Few partisan issues in American politics have been debated so furiously as the Kansas–Nebraska Act of 1854. Stephen A. Douglas, "the little giant" of American politics, saw in it what he considered to be a workable compromise on the slavery issue.

Let new territories be organized, said Douglas, without specifying whether or not slavery would be legal. Once settlers establish themselves, permit them the liberty of deciding the issue for themselves.

It was the notion of "squatter sovereignty" to which Sumner and fellow foes of slavery violently objected. They wanted slavery outlawed in every new territory.

Men from slave states hoped that by permitting popular sovereignty they could hold their own in the U. S. Senate.

If the delicate balance in that body should be destroyed, the nation would disintegrate, or would be plunged into civil war.

Senator Pierce Butler was attacked by Sumner because he was reputed to own more slaves—and bigger plantations—than any other member of the lawmaking body.

On the day of Sumner's personal attack, Butler was not present to speak for himself in defense of his character or his views. But one of his nephews, who also was influential in the nation's capital, was close at hand.

Preston S. Brooks, born at Edgefield, South Carolina, and a veteran of the Mexican War, had been elected to the House of Representatives in 1852 at age thirty-three. Six feet tall and widely considered the handsomest man in the House, he was regarded as gracious and gentle, except when angry.

Charles Sumner's vitriolic attack upon his absent uncle made Preston Brooks fighting mad. According to the South Carolinian's own account, he sent a message to the senator from Massachusetts. In it he demanded an apology. When no apology was forthcoming, Brooks stalked the streets of the capital, but failed to find Sumner.

Two days after Sumner's attack, the congressman made his way to the Senate chamber at adjournment. As law-

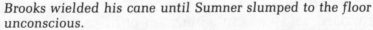

Brooks wielded his cane until Sumner slumped to the floor unconscious.

Senator Charles Sumner.

makers filed out, Brooks worked his way to Sumner's desk.

Having reached his foe, Brooks lifted his gutta percha cane and began clubbing Sumner. By the time the cane snapped, Sumner was slumping to the floor, apparently unconscious.

Senators and aides grabbed Brooks and held his arms, but it was too late. Sumner had received injuries from which he never fully recovered. "Senator Butler's honor has been restored," said Congressman Brooks tersely.

Fellow lawmakers took a different view of his violent actions. A special investigating committee named to consider the incident favored the expulsion of Brooks from the House. Put to the vote, the recommendation failed to get the required two-thirds majority.

Brooks, a noted orator, made an impassioned speech defending his conduct; then he resigned. Constituents promptly re-elected him to the seat he had vacated.

At the University of Georgia, students took up a collection and bought a new gold-headed cane for Brooks. Texas admirers sent him a gold-handled cowhide.

Aaron Burlingame of Massachusetts, a colleague in the House of Representatives, challenged him to a duel on the Canadian side of Niagara Falls. Brooks laughed, taunting his foe, "You might as well have named Boston Common as the place of meeting."

Veteran capital watchers say that nothing in our nation's history quite matches Congressman Brooks's response to Senator Sumner's insult.

26

Joel Poinsett's "Ghost" Is Here Every Christmas

Writing from Philadelphia on December 1, 1835, florist R. Buist bubbled with enthusiasm. "In our collection last winter," he wrote, "the beautiful scarlet bractii on a Mexican imported plant four months from cutting reached fourteen inches in diameter."

Buist had earlier notified Charleston-born Joel R. Poinsett that the exciting new plant would be called the poinsettia in his honor.

The plant had created excitement among botanists at the Royal Botanic Garden in Edinburgh, Scotland, soon after having been brought from Mexico by Poinsett in 1828. Yet no one on either side of the Atlantic then anticipated what would take place. It has become *the* modern Christmas flower.

Nearly forgotten today, Joel Poinsett was in his era the most urbane American to hold high national office.

British redcoats occupied Charles Town at the time of his birth in 1779. Therefore his prosperous father, a Huguenot physician, packed up the family when Joel was three and took them to England for six years. That could have fostered what proved to be a life-long absorption with foreign travel.

After studying medicine for a year, Poinsett set aside his books to spend several months in Scotland and in Portugal. He then spent a year in France, followed by leisurely travel through Switzerland, Germany, and Italy. Then he came home to spend two years touring North

Joel R. Poinsett.
[NINETEENTH CENTURY
ENGRAVING]

America by horseback and boat. Soon he left on an extended trip to Russia and her Asian frontiers.

A few months after returning to the United States in 1810, the world traveler was sent to Chile as the first official North American emissary to Spanish-speaking South America. After playing a key role in Chile's fight for independence, he returned to South Carolina and served two terms in Congress.

Following his inauguration President John Quincy Adams chose Poinsett as the United States' first minister to Mexico. Ironically, Poinsett had spent more years outside our nation than in it.

December 1825, was an exciting time for avid botanist Joel Poinsett. In every marketplace, he found Mexicans offering a colorful flower for sale. They called it "The Flower of the Holy Night" because it was at the height of its brilliance on December 25.

Poinsett examined the plant and discovered that the bright red displays are not blossoms. Instead, he found them to be bracts, or petal-like leaves; the true flower of the plant is the tiny but vivid yellow cluster at its center.

The end of Poinsett's tour of duty in Mexico began with the elections of 1828, which set off a revolt. Having sided with the insurgents, Poinsett found himself in the middle of the action.

"In Mexico City, the house of the American ambassador was the refuge of the persecuted," he later recalled. "It was pointed out to the infuriated military, and they rushed to the attack.

"My only defense was the flag of my country. It was flung out at the instant that hundreds of muskets were leveled at the embassy."

Poinsett's friends and allies prevailed, but so many Mexicans resented his having meddled in their affairs that Andrew Jackson recalled him. Forced to leave Mexico City on Christmas Day 1829, he took with him cuttings of the wildflower that to Mexicans was simply a weed, except at Christmas.

Four years' service as U.S. secretary of war in an era of tension (1837–41) is Poinsett's chief claim to national fame. During this period, he upgraded the U.S. Military Academy at West Point to an unprecedented level of importance in our nation's defense. Yet his most enduring legacy is the "Mexican weed" he introduced to the United States and Europe.

Early fanciers were puzzled. Growing wild in Mexico, plants turned many a hillside red as Christmas approached. But in Philadelphia and London they remained green during December.

Years of experiment showed that the intensity and duration of light governs the growth cycle of the plant. Commercial growers have learned to control exposure to light. Hence, millions of plants bearing the name of Joel Poinsett are now at their peak beauty precisely at Christmas in most major cities of the world.

Colonel William Moultrie, later made a general.

William Moultrie Was First to Fight the British

Major General Charles Lee, immaculate in his elaborate uniform, looked down his nose at ragtag Col. William Moultrie. "You will dismantle this slaughter pen at once," he ordered. "Take your men into Charleston and wait for further orders."

Whistling to his ever-present dogs, the man who despised George Washington, but who was his second in command, climbed on his horse and headed back to Virginia.

Charleston-born Moultrie ignored the orders of his commander. Having personally selected Sullivan's Island, he knew it was the best place at which to place guns to stop the big British ships that were sure to come, sooner or later.

Men of his Second Carolina Regiment had cut palmetto trees, notched their ends, and fastened them together to form a tall rampart. Behind this makeshift barrier, they placed sixteen feet of beach sand.

Any military engineer could have taken one look at Fort Sullivan and known that it was the work of an amateur. General Lee was no amateur. He wanted the place abandoned, but he didn't remain to see his orders carried out. He believed that though the South was important, the real action in the coming American Revolution would be far to the north.

British leaders had other ideas.

They knew that while Charleston wasn't as important as New York, Philadelphia, and Boston, it was the colonies' major import—export center south of Norfolk. Furthermore, its deep, broad harbor was ideal for the British gunboats that sailed up and down the American seacoast.

June 26, 1776, saw Britain's first move toward armed invasion of the emerging United States. Two ships of the line, plus six frigates, mounted 230 guns and carried eight regiments of infantry under the command of Lord Cornwallis. They were sighted on the horizon, headed directly for Charleston.

William Moultrie had thirty-one guns and 400 men, plus palmetto logs and sand. The outcome of the impending battle was clear to everyone except Moultrie and a few subordinates such as Francis Marion. These patriots refused to admit the possibility of defeat.

Under plans developed by Cornwallis and General Sir Henry Clinton, the invaders would make a two-pronged attack. With guns blazing, ships anchored in the harbor would destroy the Americans' fortifications. Simultaneously, regiments of infantry would use small boats to seize positions in the rear and make it impossible for the defeated patriots to retreat.

June 28, 1776, saw the twenty-eight-gun *Actaeon* drop anchor at its preassigned position. Close behind her was the stately *Bristol*, a ship-of-the-line with fifty great naval guns. Next came the *Experiment* with another fifty guns, followed by the twenty-eight-gun frigates *Solebay*, *Sphinx*, *Syren*, and *Friendship*.

When vessels manned by invaders had taken their positions, they let loose a nearly simultaneous blast such as North America had never before heard. Under cover of the noise and smoke, small boats filled with redcoats headed for inlets that would take them behind Fort Sullivan.

Surveying the tiny fortification through a glass, Clinton could not believe what he saw. His expert gunners had hit their mark many times in the first volley, but the soft palmetto logs cushioned by sand appeared to be undamaged.

Moultrie's men began firing their smaller guns, not in volleys but one by one. A lucky shot cut the anchor cable of the *Bristol*, causing the huge vessel suddenly to yaw and shift out of line with the tide. That left the stern of the British ship within easy range of American gunners.

Soon the mainmast of the *Bristol* fell; her mizzenmast followed a few minutes later. Drifting, the stricken vessel diverted frigates from their courses, and three of them became entangled. While sailors tried to free tangled lines, American fire cut the *Actaeon* to pieces. Drifting out of control, the ship ran aground at a spot that later became the site of a U. S. military installation, Fort Sumter.

Pounded by heavy guns from time to time during a ten-hour fight, the palmetto fort that the military expert from the North believed to be "a slaughter pen" stood firm. One by one, the British ships still under sail withdrew. When night fell, sailors and soldiers from the stranded *Actaeon* rowed out to sea, where they were picked up and taken aboard other vessels.

Francis Marion, who had fired the last shot of the battle, directed his gun toward the immense *Bristol*. Two officers and three seamen were cut down, and a cabin was smashed. British observers did not know that their foes had run out of powder, and would be unable to fire again.

After the invading flotilla retreated, Americans boarded the stranded *Actaeon* and seized her bell as a prize before setting her afire. William Moultrie, a mere colonel of a colonial regiment, had turned back the first British attempt at armed invasion of territory destined to become part of the United States.

Grateful South Carolinians renamed Fort Sullivan in his honor. Years later, Fort Moultrie was the prison in which the Indian chief Osceola grieved—or starved—himself to death after being seized under a flag of truce. It was at Fort Moultrie that Edgar Allan Poe conceived and wrote "The Gold Bug."

The finest tribute paid to the first American to defeat the British is symbolic. South Carolina's state seal depicts a sturdy palmetto tree that proudly surmounts an uprooted oak. Warships fashioned from oak logs were turned back by a "hopelessly out-gunned and out-manned regiment of South Carolina amateurs."

28

Penelope Barker Led Nation's First Women's Protest

"It is time for women to act. We must show the men that we are to be reckoned with," Penelope Barker insisted repeatedly in 1774.

Tradition credits her with having gone from house to house in Edenton, the capital of Carolina for forty years. Some friends were easily persuaded to back her scheme. Others held back at first, but yielded under her prodding.

October 25, 1774, saw Penelope and her friends converge upon the home of Mrs. Elizabeth King. There they held the nation's first women's protest meeting. Many had come from outlying counties.

"We cannot be indifferent," began a brief open letter written that day. Stressing the importance of the public good, the document ended with a veiled threat: "we do therefore accordingly subscribe to this paper, as a witness of our fixed intention and solemn determination."

Abigail Charlton was the first to affix her signature, and Penelope Barker added hers halfway down the first of two long columns. By the time the second column was filled, fifty-one women had gone on record as being unwilling to "conform to that pernicious custom of drinking tea."

What's more, they launched what may have been the earliest of all "Buy American" movements. They solemnly vowed not to buy clothing or other merchandise manufactured in England.

Men with hatchets staged the Boston Tea Party in December 1773. Aboard the ship *Dartmouth*, they broke

Unexpurgated version of the "Edenton Tea Party." [NORTH CAROLINA DEPARTMENT OF ARCHIVES AND HISTORY]

open 342 chests of English tea and dumped leaves into the harbor.

Events on that dramatic day are remembered everywhere. Not so familiar is the fact that taxed tea went to three additional ports. Charles Town, South Carolina, southernmost point at which taxed tea entered the British colonies, saw docking of the tea ship *London* on December 22, 1773.

Patriots refused to pay duties imposed by Parliament. Three pence per pound seemed small, until it was realized that the British East India Company planned to pump 600,000 pounds of tea into the colonies in one year.

Most Americans, including the ladies in and around Edenton, knew that even with tax added, tea was a bargain. Untaxed tea was more expensive in Britain than the taxed tea being sent to America by the boatload.

Leaders of the British East India Company were sure

that their American market would grow by leaps and bounds. Edenton ladies showed that bewigged males sitting in a London board room could be woefully mistaken. They pledged themselves not to use tea because they opposed the tax, not the price.

Word of actions by female activists spread rapidly. Along the entire Atlantic Seaboard, tea became the focus of colonial protest.

Britain responded by imposing a large fine upon Boston. It was deliberately made large enough to cover the entire cost of tea dumped into the harbor; so the net effect of the Boston Tea Party upon the colonial balance sheet was negative.

Not so in the South.

Inspired by the ladies of Edenton, Carolinians by the hundreds swore off tea for the duration. So did many in still thinly populated Georgia. With tea not selling, many casks of it remained in the Charleston warehouses for months.

As the Revolution broke out and the patriots eventually gained control of Charleston, they seized the stored tea. Selling it tax free, they quickly sold the entire shipment. Ironically, the same tea upon which the colonists were unwilling to pay a tax to Britain was used to help finance the war!

British artist Philip Dawe is believed to have created the early caricature of "A Society of Patriotic Ladies at Edenton in North Carolina" that circulated in London some time in 1775. In it he included a dog urinating on a chest of British tea. Though he included the dog in order to poke fun at American women, not all viewers were amused. A later artist placed the dog in a sleeping position with its head on the lap of a sitting child.

There is no certainty that Penelope Barker ever saw either version of the sketch that mocked the actions of the women she led. Were she alive today and given her choice, there's little doubt about which artist's conception she would endorse. "That dog is giving British tea exactly what it deserves," she'd surely say.

29

Angelina Grimke Defied
Charleston Tradition

"Stop waving the paper in my face and let me take a look at it," Angelina Grimke said. Her friend, James Bettle of Philadelphia, had rushed into her rooms flourishing a copy of the *Liberator*. Edited and published by William Lloyd Garrison, it was famous—or infamous—as an antislavery journal.

Angelina's pulse began to race. Face flushed, she found reading difficult.

"These are my words," she eventually said, "just as I wrote them. But I was not consulted about publication."

"Why? Oh, why?" stormed Bettle. "You are a woman— a woman from the aristocratic South, a woman from Charleston. Why?"

Wordless, Angelina pointed to the headline: Slavery and the Boston Riot. In May 1835, an antislavery convention had been refused the use of Faneuil Hall. One after another, seven churches then refused to open their facilities to abolitionists. When they persisted and found a meeting place, opponents formed a mob and a riot ensued.

Born and reared in a patrician family of Charleston, Angelina Grimke early formed strong views about slavery. She became convinced that unless slavery was abolished, America would be bathed in blood. Slave uprisings would rock the nation.

Her father, a wealthy, conservative justice of the South Carolina supreme court, owned so many slaves he was never sure of the exact head count. "A tender and reflec-

Masthead of The Liberator, *the abolitionist newspaper that exploited Grimke's letter.*

tive young woman," Angelina refused to accept the gift of a slave in childhood. Later she would not permit her father even to provide a body servant. Slavery was not only dangerous, she decided; it was morally wrong.

Had she remained in the cloistered life of Charleston, one of America's richest and most cosmopolitan cities, Angelina might never have voiced her views except to intimate friends.

However, a stay in Philadelphia at age twenty-seven created new questions. In time, she became a Quaker by choice, turning her back upon her Episcopalian rearing. Though she visited Charleston from time to time, it never again was home to her.

Living in Philadelphia and pondering the evils of slavery and the Boston riot, the shy, courteous, blue-eyed Charlestonian took pen in hand. After several days, she had a letter ready to send to Garrison, but several times she deferred posting it. Years later, she admitted, "I really did fear that he might publish it, but I had no idea he would use my name."

"I was compelled at this time to address thee," she wrote to editor Garrison. "I can hardly express to thee the deep and solemn interest with which I have viewed the violent proceedings of the last few weeks."

News that abolitionist J. Dresser had been publicly flogged may have been the catalyst that changed her from passive to active opposition to "the peculiar institution" of slavery.

"If persecution is the means which God has ordained for the accomplishment of *emancipation;* then, *let it come . . .* for it is my deep, solemn, deliberate conviction that *this is a cause worth dying for.*"

Publication of these sentiments meant cutting most or all existing ties. Her family would repudiate her, and Quakers would turn her out of their meeting because she hadn't shown proper discipline. Sarah, her beloved older sister whom she later converted to the cause of abolition, was initially so horrified at Angelina's actions that she did not communicate with her for weeks.

Her 1836 *Appeal to the Christian Women of the South* was so despised that many postmasters publicly burned copies of it.

In the City of Brotherly Love, she raised the hackles of civic leaders by advocating erection of a special hall for use by abolitionists. What's more, she helped to raise money for it.

Opening night saw the woman from Charleston a featured speaker in Philadelphia's new Pennsylvania Hall. Hecklers were on hand, and a mob gathered. Late that night the hall was burned to the ground.

Charleston had already disowned her most noted—or notorious—daughter. Philadelphia tolerated her but used sticks and stones and firebrands to tell her what she already knew: she was almost alone against a world in which most who didn't foster slavery openly tolerated it.

30

Gibson's General Store Shook and Swayed

Thomas Gibson studied the cards in his hand. The situation called for strategy, not rash action. Across the table from him, John Pipkin waited patiently. Hamp Adams and William Gibson, also sitting around the table, shuffled their feet as a signal calling for action.

Gibson reached for a card

Just as his hand touched the card, at about 9:30 P.M., a low-pitched and wavering moan made each player jerk bolt upright.

Pipkin, at age twenty-nine already a Marlboro County, South Carolina, commissioner, remembered warnings voiced by the preacher a few Sundays earlier. Since then he had doubted the wisdom of accepting the invitation to play cards in the second-floor storage room of Gibson's General Store.

Later, villagers of McColl, South Carolina, remembered that August 31, 1886, was the first day of the cotton ginning season. With pressure in the boiler low, dew probably settled on the whistle cord. That made it just heavy enough to release the steam that produced the eerie moan.

But for wielders of "the devil's calling cards" who'd refused to run, a supernatural sound was just the start. They'd barely stopped discussing the moan, whose nature they still didn't understand, when caskets stacked next to the outside wall began to shake and rattle.

Most general stores of the era kept caskets in stock. Like unopened bolts of cloth and kegs of nails, they were customarily stored on the second floor.

Refuges created a "tent city" in stricken Charleston.

The rattling caskets were simply too much for Pipkin, and he decided it was time to fold up and go home. Clearly, he was receiving a divine warning, or a threat from the devil himself.

Incredibly, the youthful county commissioner and his friends did not panic. They simply put up their cards, doused the light, and calmly walked down the steps and out the front door. Come daylight, they reasoned, they would get to the bottom of that unearthly noise and the rattling and shaking unlike anything they had ever experienced.

News—a bit of it, that is—reached the village before morning. Charleston had been hit by an earthquake—not a mild tremor, but a genuine earthquake. That's about all anyone in McColl knew until the morning train brought a few papers.

At 9:51 P.M., clocks in Charleston all stopped. One newspaper reporter said that "An awful roar bombarded my ears, and the strong-walled building shook as though an immeasurable power intended to tear it asunder."

Soon streets and parks were filled with terror-stricken

men, women, and children. A few tried to flee in small boats. An estimated 50,000 persons were trapped near the center of a major earthquake, later listed as the fifth most lethal in U. S. history.

More than 90 percent of the city's buildings were damaged. Twenty fires were roaring out of control; there was nothing to do except watch buildings burn to the ground. Even if water mains had not burst, firemen would have been helpless; every street was obstructed by rubble.

At Gibson's General Store in McColl the next day, the usual trickle of customers was augmented by a flood of curious people who wanted a firsthand look at "the place where the coffins rattled last night." Most who trudged up the steps to see for themselves shook their heads in wonder. "How on earth did John Pipkin and his buddies manage not to panic?" they asked.

The tale of raw courage on a fearful night has been transmitted orally in South Carolina for a century. Ruthie Pipkin of The Waynesville, North Carolina, *Mountaineer* may have been first to put this tale into print. Amended and amplified by her grandfather, it emerges, not as folk lore or fiction, but as an authentic account of actions in the face of fearful events no one in McColl could explain on the night they took place.

Henry W. Grady won national attention through his coverage of the Charleston earthquake.

31

Showdown in Charleston Harbor

"Carolinians, you have been tested by fire, already. But now the time is at hand to show your mettle more than ever before!

"Let all able-bodied men rush to arms! Come fellow citizens; share with us our dangers, our brilliant success— or our glorious death!"

Published in various forms and distributed throughout the Carolinas, coastal Georgia, and parts of Tennessee, the proclamation issued about Thanksgiving 1862, was calculated to arouse everyone who read or heard it.

"That's Old Bory at his best," said admiring subordinates.

Pierre Gustave Toutant Beauregard was under no delusions. The hero of the assault upon Fort Sumter faced a much tougher fight this time; he would need all the manpower available.

In spite of the Federal blockade, tonnage of goods in and out of major Southern ports was near an all-time high. From Wilmington to Mobile—with Charleston and Savannah between—commerce with Britain and Europe flourished.

Nevertheless, intelligence reports from Confederate spies had assumed an alarming tone. Numerous ironclad ships were under construction by the U.S. Navy, and several were said to be ready to sail. The Confederates feared that the Federals would put everything into closing Southern ports. Beauregard, but not his superiors, believed that Charleston would be the target.

With the flagship at the rear, Du Pont's ironclads formed a line
across Charleston's harbor.

A flotilla of ironclads mounting guns larger than any
included in shore batteries, would mean a showdown.
The outcome of the conflict between sea power and conventional land-based artillery could determine the course
of the war. It definitely would influence military strategy
for years to come.

Beauregard ordered more sandbags. Once Fort Moultrie
was as secure as he could make it, he turned his attention
to Castle Pinckney and Fort Sumter. Then he constructed
a line of signal stations arranged so that he could order
seventy-seven guns to fire simultaneously.

Torpedoes, the most effective mines then available,
were laid in the harbor. Nets made of huge hemp ropes

were arranged to hover just below the surface, ready to entangle propellers of vessels whose captains had out-of-date charts.

Waiting for the enemy to strike, men in Beauregard's command spent days in target practice. When marker buoys were hit, jubilant artillerymen carefully recorded wind conditions and distance.

Meanwhile Washington was as tense as Charleston, with spies under the leadership of Alan Pinkerton bringing back alarming news. At the rate Confederate preparations were being made, the Southern port would soon be invincible. Ironclads must strike soon, or not at all.

Admiral Samuel Du Pont, nephew of the pioneer munitions manufacturer, was selected to lead the assault against Charleston. He knew these waters, as he had scored the first decisive Union victory of the war at Port Royal. Even more important, he had reservations about the ability of ironclads to withstand heavy fire. That made him cautious; he was unwilling to mount an assault unless he was sure of winning.

At the U. S. Department of the Navy, top officials were openly jubilant. They believed once Du Pont had mastered Charleston, their invincible fleet would move south to Savannah. Then it would reduce Mobile before moving north to Wilmington to end Confederate capacity to engage in overseas trade.

To be sure that there would be no regrets, Assistant Secretary of the Navy Gustavus Fox persuaded superiors to give Du Pont the brand-new *Housatonic*. Rated at 1,200 tons, it was believed to be second only to the 3,500-ton flagship *New Ironsides* as the mightiest ship afloat.

Two gunboats, plus seven converted merchantmen, were to accompany the flagship. This was not so much because they would be needed, as the sight of a flotilla with thirty-three huge guns, plus many smaller ones, would throw panic into Confederate lookouts.

While the Federal plan sounded good, it didn't work out very well. Rebel artillerymen found an easy target in the ironclad *Keokuk*, conspicuous for her twin turrets.

When the warship ventured close to Fort Sumter, defenders scored ninety direct hits.

The size of the *New Ironsides* proved to be a liability rather than an asset. Inside the harbor the mighty ship moved clumsily. By darkness on the night of April 7, 1863, every ironclad in the Federal fleet was dented and scarred.

Scanning defensive works with glasses that night, Du Pont found little evidence of damage. "We'll resume the attack at dawn," he told his officers.

Daylight brought a quick revision in plans. Officers and men were hastily taken off the battered *Keokuk*. The only thing preventing it from sinking was that it had run aground on a sandbar. Damage to other ironclads was much worse than it had seemed at dusk; four would be unable to resume the assault under any circumstances.

Keenly aware that he would face censure or worse in Washington, Admiral Du Pont decided to accept defeat as the price of saving his men. Except for the *Keokuk*, the entire flotilla withdrew as rapidly as possible.

Immense naval guns had proved impotent, even when mounted on moving targets, when sent against skilled artillerymen who fired from protected fortifications. Not until World War I did a major power attempt another showdown such as that which took place in Charleston harbor on April 7, 1863.

General P. T. G. ("Ole Bory") Beauregard, Confederate commander.

32

Sharpshooter Who Spared George Washington Lies At Kings Mountain

London's public record office holds the handwritten original of an amazing document. Had it not been preserved, the story of Patrick Ferguson's sighting of George Washington would be dismissed as a myth.

According to researchers, records indicate that the commander-in-chief of still-raw recruits went on reconnaissance on September 7, 1776, to discover whether colonial units at Chad's Ford on Brandywine Creek might be able to stop the British troops that were camped just four miles from the ford.

At the same time, three British soldiers were on patrol far ahead of their own lines. One of them, Major Patrick Ferguson, was a famous sharpshooter and inventor of a light breechloading rifle. Once, while demonstrating his weapon for King George III, he had hit the bull's-eye at one hundred yards, while lying flat on his back.

According to Ferguson's written account, he spotted two American riders. One of them wore "a remarkably large cocked hat."

First he signaled to his men that the foes were to be shot as soon as they came in range. Then suddenly he reversed his orders, stepped out into view, and shouted a demand for surrender. The rider in the big cocked hat wheeled his horse and raced for cover.

"I could have lodged half a dozen of balls in him," Ferguson wrote, "but it was not pleasant to fire at a man's back, so I let him alone."

George Washington, who didn't realize the extent of the danger, rode back to his camp. After fighting in several engagements, Patrick Ferguson was given temporary rank of colonel and sent south at the head of a band of sharp-shooters.

In North Carolina the man who might have altered the course of the American Revolution by one squeeze of his trigger finger decided it was time "to fight Americans with Americans." He issued a call for all Tories, or Loyalists, to get their rifles and join his forces. Three years to the day after his failure to shoot George Washington, he led about 1,100 American Tories in North Carolina against "backwater men, a set of mongrels," known to be getting ready to meet him in battle.

Col. Isaac Shelby had assembled one band in Sullivan County, North Carolina, Col. John Sevier headed others who came from what was then Washington County, North Carolina. About 1,100 patriots were ready to risk their lives in combat with at least 1,700 Tories.

"Nolichucky Jack" Sevier persuaded fellow leaders to pick 900 men with the best horses. Most had Deckhard rifles; all carried bags of parched corn.

These experienced frontiersmen moved slowly up the slope of the long, rugged hill called Kings Mountain. Soon they tethered their horses and proceeded upward, always under cover of bushes and shrubs. During the battle, the Tories had no targets except for brief flashes of gunfire. Trapped at the crest of Kings Mountain, they were so exposed that foes called them "sitting ducks."

The Watauga men and their comrades showed none of the compassion and sportsman-like behavior Patrick Ferguson exhibited three years earlier. They mowed down their Tory foes without mercy.

Patrick Ferguson took at least three balls; when he fell, Col. William Campbell roared to Americans who were killing fellow countrymen almost indiscriminately, "For God's sake, quit! It's murder to shoot now!"

The Tories' defeat was complete; nearly the entire army

was killed, wounded, or captured, while the patriots lost twenty-eight killed, plus sixty-two wounded.

Though the forces involved were small, the impact of Kings Mountain was large. While sending the British reeling in defeat, it boosted the morale of patriots everywhere.

* * *

Partly because it was the site of one of the decisive battles of the Revolution, Kings Mountain was made into one of our largest military parks. Great oaks and pines cover much of its 3,950 acres. Park personnel gladly point out one vast poplar that "maybe was a sapling at the time of the battle." Except for the rock cairn that marks the last resting place of the sharpshooter who spared Washington, there is little to indicate that the fate of America was once in the balance here.

Kings Mountain National Military Park lies in South Carolina, just below the North Carolina line. Only three miles off Interstate 85, it is open every day but Christmas and New Year's.

Osceola. [Engraving after Catlin portrait]

33

Flag of Truce Was Osceola's Undoing

"I speak as a friend," General Hernandez began. "What induced you to come?"

He knew the answer to his question. A huge white banner—an impromptu flag of truce—floated above the spot at which whites and Indians were meeting near Fort Peyton, Florida. Each group was nervous and suspicious of the other with good reason. It was now October 27, 1837, and for twenty-three years the Seminole War had been one of America's longest and most deadly conflicts. General Andrew Jackson had crushed Indian forces in 1818; but their strength had grown under the leadership of Osceola, and they had become a serious threat to whites.

Thus the formal parley on a crisp Fall day was significant to leaders of both sides. A working agreement, however tenuous, would save many lives.

Before white men came in sight, Seminole chieftain Osceola had insisted that Coa Hadjo play the role of tribal spokesman. Coa Hadjo pondered Hernandez's opening words, then replied firmly, "We come for good."

Hernandez nodded gravely. But minutes later, without warning, he announced, "I wish all of you [Seminoles] well. But we have been deceived so often that you must come with me. You will get good treatment. You will be glad that you fell into my hands."

Hernandez gave a pre-arranged signal. Before Coa Hadjo, Osceola, and their comrades could seize their loaded guns, forces of Brevet Major James A. Ashby appeared from ambush. Concealed in a thicket on Moultrie Creek, they were within easy gunshot of the Indians who thought they had come to talk peace.

Surgeon Nathan Jarvis, who was present and reported the conversation, watched Osceola closely. He later said that the famous Indian leader showed no sign of surprise.

Resistance would have meant death. Ashby commanded a force of 250 calvarymen and dragoons. The Indians who had a total of just fifty-two rifles, surrendered without firing a shot.

In addition to Osceola and his spokesmen, soldiers that day captured seventy-one warriors and six women. Cavalrymen formed a hollow phalanx. Prodded inside, Indians walked to St. Augustine, where nearly everyone in the town turned out to gape and to cheer.

Osceola wore the bright blue calico shirt and red leggings for which he was noted. Having dressed in order to talk peace, he had a brightly colored shawl over his shoulders and another wrapped around his head.

Gen. Thomas Sidney Jesup, U.S.A., had arranged the plot. Until his death he defended the seizure of Osceola under a flag of truce as "the easiest way to end a bloody business."

As news of the capture spread, many of Jesup's countrymen denounced him. No other incident in the long-drawn struggle between white men and red men quite matches the perfidy of the man then commanding U. S. forces in Florida.

Today as well as a century and a half ago, little is positively known about the early years of Osceola, the most noted Seminole warrior.

Early writers said he was born about 1804, somewhere on the Chattahoochee River. Others insisted he came from "the Tallapoosa River in what is now the state of Georgia." Tribesmen called him As-se-he-ho-lar, or "Black drink," a famous ritual beverage among the Creeks of Georgia and Alabama.

Some whites said that he was the son or grandson of English trader William Powell. Though undocumented, that tradition is so strong that many reports refer to him as Billy Powell.

Known by whatever name, he remained in obscurity until October 1834. He then repudiated an agreement (widely regarded as a sell-out) under which some Seminole leaders had agreed to removal to the west.

Osceola led the famous Christmas massacre of 1835, reputedly as an act of revenge upon whites who had seized his wife as a runaway slave. He and his men fought at Ouithlacoochee, Micanopy, Fort Drane, and many other battlefields.

Following his capture, Osceola was moved to Ft. Moultrie, South Carolina, where he languished in his cell. There he died at age thirty-four. Today the site of his imprisonment is a tourist shrine.

Osceola's captor, Jesup, is now a footnote to history. No one ever painted his portrait; few reference books include his name.

George Catlin's portrait of Osceola hangs in the Smithsonian Institution in Washington, D.C. A national forest, a state park, three counties, twenty towns, two lakes, and two mountains perpetuate the name of the warrior who grieved himself to death in a Carolina prison.

34

Sergeant Jasper Saved the Flag!

Big naval guns fired from British warships threatened to destroy Fort Sullivan in Charleston harbor. Crowds of civilians watched the action from the city's famous seaside Battery.

"They were looking on with anxious fears and hopes," according to William Moultrie, commander of the patriots.

Some had their fathers, brothers, and husbands in the battle. Their hearts must have been pierced at every broadside.

After some time, our flag was shot away. Their hopes were then gone, and they gave up all for lost! They supposed that we had struck our flag and had given up the fort.

Perceiving that the flag was shot away and had fallen outside the fort, Sergeant Jasper jumped from one of the embrasures. He brought the flag up through a heavy fire, fixed it upon a spunge-staff [used by artillerymen] and planted it upon the ramparts again.

Our flag once more waving in the air revived the drooping spirits of our men. They then resisted so valiantly that the British gave up and retired to deep water.

Nearly forgotten today, except for his impact upon the map, Sergeant Jasper was once the most noted southern hero of the American Revolution. His exploit at Charleston, almost duplicated later at Savannah, made his name a household word: *"Sergeant Jasper rescued the flag!"*

When that message was relayed through the countryside by word of mouth, patriots of 1776 reacted much as Americans did following the raising of the flag on Iwo Jima during World War II.

Southerners named eight counties and at least twenty-two towns and villages in honor of the man who saved the flag. Hundreds of families bestowed the name Jasper upon sons on whom they had high hopes.

Strangely, the record suggests that the man who won fame as a member of a South Carolina regiment was neither an American by birth nor a patriot by choice. Late in October 1767, ninety immigrants took the oath of allegiance to Britain, not to one of her already rebellious colonies, at the Philadelphia office of Thomas Willing, Esq. One who was unable to sign his own name on the register was listed as John William Jasper.

Believed to have been born and reared in Germany and named Johann Wilhelm by his parents, the youthful immigrant didn't find in Philadelphia the opportunities he was seeking. It is believed that Jasper then settled in Georgia. Although land was cheap there, he was unable to send for his sweetheart in Philadelphia for lack of money. Thus at about age twenty-five he enlisted in a South Carolina regiment, not for love of America but because he would be paid in cash.

"Sergeant Jasper saved the flag." [Eighteenth century woodcut]

Small as it was, Jasper's pay enabled him to bring his sweetheart to Charleston. They married there and became parents of twins.

Soon after the twins were born, the British picked Charleston as a major target. It was during the ensuing battle that the German who fought for pay captured the imagination of all who saw him in action and all who heard about it.

South Carolina Governor Rutledge presented Jasper with a sword and offered him a commission. He accepted the weapon but turned down the promotion. A man who could not read and write had no business being an officer, he said.

Universally known simply as Sergeant Jasper, he moved with his unit into the region of Savannah. Legend says that a certain Jones, a handcuffed prisoner of the British, was due to be taken to Savannah to be hanged. With a few comrades Sergeant Jasper got the drop on a band of eight heavily armed British. Forced to surrender their weapons and their prisoner, the redcoats were themselves placed in irons and taken to a nearby American camp.

Days later, on October 9, 1779, when patriots decided they must take Savannah from the British at whatever cost, Jasper was again in the front line of action with the flag in his hands. This time his mission was to plant the colors of the Second South Carolina Infantry upon a redoubt at Spring Hill. He received a direct hit and fell dead, still gripping the pole of the flag.

A redoubt at Fort Moultrie was soon named Jasper Battery in his honor, and Savannah erected a splendid bronze monument to him. Throughout the South political leaders moved to make his name immortal by voting to bestow it upon villages, towns, and counties.

Except for George Washington, Benjamin Franklin, and the Marquis de LaFayette, no Revolutionary leader's name appears on the map of the South more frequently than does that of the illiterate German mercenary who twice offered his life for a flag.

35

Calhoun Sowed Seeds That Led to War

"We hold it as unquestionable that on the separation from the Crown of Great Britain, the people of the several colonies became free and independent states," said John C. Calhoun in an "Address to the People of the United States" in 1832.

Although few Americans, in the North or the South, disagreed with that verdict, the introductory statement hardly prepared readers for what followed: "We hold it equally unquestionable that the Constitution of the United States is a compact between the people of the several states, constituting free, independent, and sovereign communities."

Especially, but not exclusively, in Washington, such an idea bordered upon treason. If the states making up the nation were free and independent, they would do as they pleased about edicts of the national government.

That is precisely what South Carolina had done, at the urging of the state's most persuasive political spokesman. Furious that the tariff of 1828 discriminated against the South, Vice President John C. Calhoun had resigned. He preferred to devote his time to the U.S. Senate, he said, where he could continue to fight the bill.

Even Calhoun was unable to persuade a majority of senators to come to the aid of the South, which he said had been "pillaged, even raped, by Federal legislation."

For at least four years, probably longer, Calhoun had been brooding about the growing tension between federal and state authority. He drafted a long paper entitled

161

"South Carolina Exposition" but did not release it. Even
Calhoun realized that publication could lead to a national
crisis. But when South Carolina passed an Ordinance of
Nullification on November 24, 1832, Calhoun drew upon
this paper when he set out to convince the nation of the
correctness of the action.

Under its terms, Congressional tariff acts were declared
null and void within the Palmetto State. Collection of duties was forbidden, and every officeholder in the state was
required to take an oath supporting the Nullification Act.

Finally—and perhaps most important—Carolinians
pledged themselves, through elected leaders who framed
the ordinance, to denounce any and all efforts of the national government to enforce the tariff. If strong measures
of enforcement were tried, South Carolina warned, the
state would immediately proceed to organize a separate
government.

There had been talk of withdrawal from the Union
much earlier, mostly in the northeast. Proponents pointed
out that the Constitution did not prohibit such action by
individual states.

Decades had passed, however, and the Union had held
firm. Ordinary citizens had come to feel that state authority took second place to federal authority.

While never actually attempted, the notion of secession
was nearly as old as the nation, but nullification was an
entirely different matter. Under Calhoun's doctrine a state
could—and in the case of South Carolina already had—
formally declare acts of Congress to be null and void.

Andrew Jackson, widely claimed as a native son of
South Carolina, was in the White House. He had given his
personal support to the tariff acts. If his own state were to
thumb its nose at Washington, the entire national structure could crumble.

"They can talk and write resolutions and print threats
to their hearts' content," thundered Old Hickory. "If one
drop of blood is shed in defiance of the laws of the United
States, I will hang the first man of them I can get my
hands on, to the first tree I can find."

During the spring of 1833, that threat by Jackson was pondered and debated throughout the nation. In the South many town meetings saw resolutions of defiance greeted by shouts of approval. Old cartoons depicting Jackson as a hangman and as King Andrew I were reprinted and widely distributed, and Jackson responded by setting in motion the machinery needed to send federal troops into South Carolina to enforce federal laws.

Henry Clay, who frankly admitted that Pennsylvania, Massachusetts, New York, and New Jersey were growing rich at the expense of the Carolinas, Georgia, Alabama, and Tennessee, framed what he called "a compromise tariff."

Somewhat mollified by the small concessions gained under the compromise and keenly aware that federal troops were being assembled for invasion, South Carolina retreated. Legislators repealed the ordinance of nullification, and the collection of the hated tariff was resumed in the state.

The union was intact, for the moment. But when the concept of nullification was added to the injustice of economic discrimination and the evils of slavery, civil war became inevitable. It was no longer a question of whether it would come, but when and under what circumstances.

Yet it is doubtful that in 1833 even fiery John C. Calhoun would have predicted that the first shots of the Civil War would be fired in Charleston, where he is buried. Had the old war horse sensed it, he would have been delighted.

Ann Pamela Cunningham. [Mount Vernon Ladies' Association]

36

Charleston Invalid Saved Mount Vernon for the Nation

Editors of the Charleston *Mercury*, widely regarded as the most influential newspaper in the South, did not balk at an open letter signed "A Southern Matron." After all, in 1853 it would have been unbecoming for a South Carolina lady to put her name in print, even at the end of an appeal addressed to "Ladies of the South." Not having the faintest idea of the writer's identity or place of residence, editors considered the letter worthy of use.

George Washington's ancestral home, said the missive, was falling into ruin. Members of the Washington family were unable to maintain it, and they had failed in attempts to have it purchased by the federal government or the state of Virginia.

Because of this melancholy situation, the estate would go to anyone who would pay the asking price, it was reliably reported. There was a good possibility that the site would be used for a resort hotel.

This need not, should not, and must not happen, said the letter writer. Ladies of the South could and surely would, by joint efforts "in village and country square and city" secure "from the mites of thousands of gentle hearts" the money needed to save Mount Vernon.

Years later it was found that "A Southern Matron" was unmarried and was really Ann Pamela Cunningham. Member of a distinguished Laurens County family, she had been crippled in girlhood by a fall from a horse. Yet the semi-invalid who preferred to remain anonymous had the courage also to send a proposal to John A. Washington, Jr. Ladies of the South, she said, would like to purchase Mount Vernon, the sooner the better.

Washington, who had let it be known he'd consider nothing under $200,000 did not bother to acknowledge receipt of the letter from South Carolina.

In Mobile, editors of the *Herald and Tribune* saw and reprinted the plea from the Charleston *Mercury*. Like it or not, the nation was going to be exposed to an idealistic woman's dream.

At a little church near Rosemonte, the Cunningham home, ladies met early in 1854 to form the Mount Vernon Ladies' Association. Ann Pamela's mother, who presided, headed the subscription list, donating one hundred dollars.

Other meetings were held in Laurens, South Carolina, and in Savannah. They yielded several hundred more dollars.

Mrs. Philoclea Eve, of Augusta, Georgia, a "cousin by marriage" of Ann Pamela, published a letter of her own. It deplored America's forgetting Washington and asked for help.

A fellow Augusta resident, Mrs. Tubman, responded with three hundred dollars, one hundred dollars each "for the state where I was born, the state where I was married, and the state where I now live."

Before Augusta ladies stopped voicing pleas, residents gave more than three thousand dollars—twenty-five cents each for every man, woman, and child in the city.

In Mobile and Richmond, ladies joined the effort. Responding to a plaintive plea from Philadelphia, leaders of the still anonymously led movement graciously agreed to permit ladies of the North to join the movement to save the shrine.

Even so, it seemed ludicrous to ordinary folk that a group of women thought they could raise two hundred thousand dollars. However, Edward Everett of Boston did not share that view. Renowned as one of the nation's most sought-after orators, he volunteered to speak on behalf of the ladies and their dream.

Everett prepared a special Washington address, then delivered it 129 times. Traveling always at his own expense, he added fifty-five thousand dollars to the cause. Soon the Mount Vernon Ladies' Association was in a position to buy the property.

Nevertheless, before they could purchase it, they would need to have something no other ladies' group had ever gained, a charter. Once the Virginia legislature acted upon their request, they bought the entire Mount Vernon site of approximately five hundred acres.

To this day the Mount Vernon Ladies' Association operates what has become one of America's most loved shrines. Enlarged and expanded through the years to include outbuildings and gardens designed by Washington, their holdings are now being completely refurbished as a result of another successful financial campaign, this time for ten million dollars.

Open to visitors every day of the year, Mount Vernon sits on a bluff two hundred feet above the Potomac River at a point where it is nearly two miles wide. Few visitors realize that the breathtaking estate would not be there without the work of idealistic, determined Carolina women.

PART FOUR:
Georgia

37

Perilous Voyage to an Unknown Destination

"Come with me," urged James Oglethorpe to an unemployed cloth maker. "Below Carolina, we shall create an ideal colony. No one will go hungry, and everyone will have work. It is the opportunity of your lifetime; if you pass up this chance, you'll never have another like it!"

The former member of Parliament proved as persuasive conversing with the idle poor of London as he had been in debate. While he had never been to the land that was named in honor of King George II of England, he was supremely confident that, under his leadership, Georgia would become a haven for the homeless and oppressed of Europe.

After recruiting male and female followers, Oglethorpe bargained with ships' captains until he finally engaged the tiny *Ann* for the crossing. However, delay followed delay; and on November 16, 1732, departure was postponed yet another day because the pilot was drunk. Since no member of the party had ever crossed the Atlantic, it did not occur to them that delay put the voyage deeper into the fierce winter season.

To the owners and seamen of the vessel, the passengers were only freight, with the trans-Atlantic voyage charged at four pounds per head. An adult was counted as one head, while children were counted in fractions according to age. Rations for the voyage consisted of salt pork, salt beef, salt

Georgia's founder,
James Oglethorpe.

fish, bread, suet, and plums.

Precisely how many persons were aboard, no one knows. A passenger, Peter Gordon, started a detailed journal but gave it up because of seasickness. He recorded that forty-one men, twenty-seven women, and twenty-eight children were housed in the hold. Oglethorpe had a splendid cabin.

Five weeks out of port, with Christmas only a few days away, it seemed an appropriate time to celebrate. A live sheep brought aboard for Oglethorpe's table was slaughtered and roasted over the customary open fire that was the dread of every master of a wooden ship. Along with the mutton, Georgia's founder provided "a quantity of liquor to drink the health of the day."

Even before the Ann's sails were lost, the tiny ship wallowed in heavy seas.

After the evening meal, the passengers who expected to become Georgians "were diverted with cudgell playing," a pair of shoes being the prize awarded to the best player in this form of mock combat. Eventually becoming tired of the contest that used short, thick sticks as weapons, they turned to what Peter Gordon called "skimingtons." In this form of horseplay, someone was ridiculed and thirty-two-year-old Anna Coles was selected as the butt of their humor. A few days earlier, she had loudly berated her husband, a cloth-worker ten years her senior.

When the farce was over, the future colonists went to bed with happy smiles and full stomachs. Christmas Day, they told one another, would be even better.

The holiday dawned with squalls and heavy clouds, and soon the little ship began to pitch and toss wildly. Then a gust swept away the topsail on the mizzen, or third, mast, making it difficult for the seamen to handle the vessel. The *Ann* would not be able to continue its speed, and provisions were running low.

The Reverend Henry Herbert, who had gone along as a volunteer chaplain, didn't have to urge fellow passengers to come to the great cabin for prayers, although earlier they had sometimes balked at gathering for worship and a sermon.

December 26 brought even fiercer winds. Before the day was over, the *Ann* lost her big "main top gallant" sail. Never easy to handle, the crippled ship now moved even slower. Tight-faced and grim, James Oglethorpe ordered that the daily allowance of water and beer be reduced by one pint per head.

The sick and frightened passengers crowded on deck for the funeral of nine-month-old James Clark. A terse log kept by merchant Thomas Christie said simply, "Clark's Child was throwd over board & the Ceremony decently performed."

With seas still running so high that the ship lurched continually, food was reduced to salt fish and moldy bread. Suddenly a sailor spotted a clump of seaweed. "Land ahead!" he shouted joyfully.

His cry brought the entire ship's company running, and the battered, seasick, hungry, and frightened passengers bowed their heads as Dr. Herbert gave thanks for having safely arrived at "the end of a voyage during which each of us despaired many times, but which has brought us to our unknown land of promise."

38

Shotgun Totin' Dentist Was Pivotal at the O K Corral

"It's about time. Sure, I'll go along."

According to an eyewitness, that's all John Henry Holliday said in response to police chief Virgil Earp. Hastily, the officer had outlined a plan of action aimed at putting an end to trouble from the Clanton gang.

Born in Griffin in 1851 and reared in Valdosta, Holliday practiced dentistry briefly after winning a degree from a Pennsylvania college in 1872. However, when his persistent cough was diagnosed as a symptom of tuberculosis, he was advised by a doctor to "Hunt a dry climate, maybe in the West. It could give you an extra year to live."

Doc Holliday stopped at Dallas because the railroad ended there, but it took only a few weeks to learn that dentists were not in great demand in the brawling cow town.

So the Georgian, who was blessed with strong and steady hands, decided to put them to work where they'd pay the best dividends, at faro tables. Soon he had won local renown as a top-drawer professional gambler.

That meant he could handle the cards with the best. It also meant he could hold his own against the assorted deadly weapons present at every card game. Many a hustler carried four, or even as many as ten, assorted weapons; Doc decided that, for him, three were enough.

For his visible weapon Holliday carried a six-gun in his

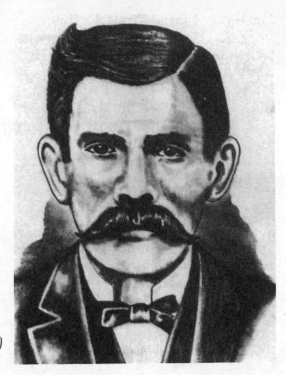

*John Henry ("Doc")
Holliday.*

hip holster. To avoid shooting himself accidentally, he never
put more than five cartridges into the weapon. When not in
use, the hammer always rested against an empty chamber.

A shoulder holster concealed under his left arm put his
second gun within easy reach of his right hand, but the
weapon he used with the greatest zest was a sheath knife in
his breast pocket. Over and over, it found its mark while the
man who had cheated on Doc or had challenged him was
reaching for his gun.

Doc knew all the famous men and infamous places of the
Wild West. He saved the life of Wyatt Earp three times. He
won clemency from the governor of Colorado at the interces-
sion of Bat Masterson. He gambled with Sam Bass and Cole
Younger.

Holliday was in Dallas, Austin, Indian Territory, Chey-
enne, Denver, and Fort Griffin. He coughed his way through

Leadville, Dodge City, Old Town, Las Vegas, Trail City, and Prescott. His traveling companion, Big Nose Kate, sometimes went by the name of Mrs. Holliday. She had saved his life by burning down a hotel where he was held prisoner. Long ago he had severed all Georgia ties, except for exchanging an occasional letter with a cousin in an Atlanta convent.

In 1880 Doc followed Wyatt Earp to Tombstone, where during the last week of October, 1881, law and order collapsed when a long-standing feud between the Earp brothers and a cowboy clan led by Ike Clanton reached the boiling point.

Soon after breakfast on the 25th, Virgil Earp, a law enforcement officer, banged Clanton over the head with his gun barrel because his enemy had resisted arrest when told he'd violated an ordinance.

Within an hour, Wyatt met the unarmed Clanton ally Tom McLowry in the street. Protected by his badge, Earp slugged McLowry until he dropped, bleeding, into the gutter.

By noon, everyone in Tombstone knew that Ike Clanton had sent for help. They'd meet at the O K Corral, an open air livery stable facing the main street.

Virgil Earp decided not to wait for his foes to make the first move. With his two brothers he started for the O K Corral. Doc Holliday stopped them long enough to learn about their plans. Then he grunted approval and said he was ready to join them.

Half a block from the corral, Doc swapped his cane for Virgil's sawed-off shotgun, which he slipped up the sleeve of his long topcoat.

Nineteen-year-old Billy Clanton had two guns in holsters that swung from his belt. Five other members of the Clanton party had a six-gun each. Two rifles were stashed in saddle boots of horses hitched at strategic points.

Since each of the three Earps and Holliday had one pistol, their only ace in the hole was the concealed shotgun carried by Doc.

Lengthy legal hearings never settled the question of who fired the first shot. Witnesses disagreed about nearly every detail of the fight, except its duration and the sequence of events that brought it to an end.

"It was short, awful short," testified Sheriff John Behan, who didn't have jurisdiction over the town of Tombstone but who had watched intently. Some said three men were killed and three were wounded in, maybe, thirty seconds; others said there weren't fifteen seconds between the first shot and the last.

Hit in the belly by a slug from one of the Earps, Frank McLowry bent double with pain. Billy Clanton took one in his chest. All three of the Earps were wounded by now.

Tom McLowry made a jump for a rifle.

Until then, Doc Holliday hadn't had a clear field of fire, but as Tom reached for the Winchester, Doc tore him apart with both barrels of his shotgun.

Holliday dropped the now-empty gun and pulled out his Colt .45, a fine nickle-plated weapon, with the hammer, as usual, on an empty chamber.

By now most action was in slow motion or had ceased altogether, so it was easy for Frank McLowry to know when Doc had fired four shots and had just one left.

Described as "grinning like a stuffed wolf," McLowry bore down upon the gaunt ex-dentist. McLowry and another member of the Clanton gang fired simultaneously. Both shots missed vital spots.

Wounded in hip and back, Doc lifted his piece slowly. Then he squeezed the trigger, put a bullet through Frank's heart, and ended the Gunfight at the O K Corral.

Frank McLowry was Doc Holliday's thirtieth victim, by most counts. Some say the tally would go much higher if the names of men who'd died around faro tables in one-horse towns were included.

In a desperate bid for a few more months of life, the Georgian went to Glenwood Spring, Colorado. There he drank the stinking sulfur water of the health resort, but grew worse rather than better, dying on November 8, 1887. Had he lived two weeks longer, he would have celebrated his thirty-sixth birthday.

39

Beautiful Widow's Problems Led to the Cotton Gin

"Charleston can wait," teased Caty Greene. "There is much more to see and do here."

Irresolute and less than eager to take up a post of tutor, the only job he could find, Eli Whitney hesitated.

"I'll hear no more of your leaving, for now," his hostess said firmly. She gestured to servants and ordered, "Take Mr. Whitney's things back into the guest bedroom; he will be staying a while."

Whitney, age twenty-seven, did not protest because deep inside, he had hoped to be asked to remain at Mulberry Plantation. Never had he met a woman so provocative as the widow of General Nathanael Greene. Since she had already told Whitney that perhaps he could help her with a vexatious problem whose nature she had not described, he had great hopes for his prospects.

"Life is lonely here," thirty-one-year-old Caty told him as soon as he agreed to remain for a few days. "My husband, Nathanael, died six years ago, and I do so miss the balls and levees we once attended so often."

General Nathanael Greene had put himself in financial straights during his campaign to rid South Carolina of the British. Unable to get funds from the Continental Congress, he had fed and clothed his men out of his own pocket.

When the Revolution was over, Green was nine thousand

pounds in debt. He had failed to receive even partial reimbursement, so when Georgia lawmakers offered to make him a gift of Mulberry Plantation near Savannah as a reward for his military service, he accepted it with gratitude.

When the native of Rhode Island died suddenly at age forty-five, his beautiful twenty-five-year-old widow had to care for the plantation, plus five children. She was deeply in debt.

Visits to creditor Jeremiah Wadsworth of New Jersey led to more loans, but Caty could offer him no payment except herself. Their liaison lasted until Mrs. Wadsworth discovered some of their letters.

High-placed friends did their best to help. Alexander Hamilton, secretary of the treasury, became an intimate advisor, as did secretary of war Henry Knox. George Washington, who had once called her the best dancing partner he'd ever had, tried to intervene on her behalf. In France, the Marquis de Lafayette financed the education of one of her sons.

Nevertheless, in 1792 her troubles were worse than ever. Although Congress had voted to pay her more than $40,000—when the money became available—that wouldn't be enough to meet her pressing debts, as every year the plantation was losing more money. The fine upland cotton it produced was unprofitable because of the laborious work of separating the lint from the seeds.

When the handsome young stranger from New England asked for a night's lodging, Caty persuaded him to stay longer than he had planned; he would break the monotony of plantation life.

Days passed, then weeks. After three months at Mulberry Plantation, Eli Whitney gave up all thought of resuming his journey to Charleston.

Fascinated with Caty, Whitney listened with awe as she talked of long evenings spent dancing with famous men. He laughed with her as she recalled times when she openly flirted with her husband's subordinates. Occasionally Whitney managed to brush against Caty or touch her hand.

*Caty Greene gives Eli
Whitney a helping
hand.*
COURTESY OF UNIVERSITY
OF GEORGIA PRESS

Always, his pulse raced at such encounters. Perhaps if he
stayed longer, she might consent to become his wife . . . .

Caty, however, had no intention of marrying him or anyone else because it would be futile to press her claims for
money expended by Greene in any role except that of his
widow. Neither did she expect to accept Whitney as her
lover, as earlier she had turned to Phineas Miller, her over-
seer. The visitor from Massachussetts would provide a
pleasant interlude, no more.

As weeks passed, the young widow Greene discovered
that Eli had an inborn mechanical genius. Confronted by a
broken farm implement or household object, he spontane-
ously moved to repair it, seldom spending more than an
hour or two doing so.

"If you could devise a machine to pull cotton from seeds,
it would make me rich," Whitney's hostess told him one day.
Immediately he plunged into the task. This time he did not
finish in a few hours, and after a week of intensive effort, he
still had gotten nowhere.

Tradition says that as Caty and Eli were strolling one afternoon, she noticed a cat that had been placed in a cage and

called Whitney's attention to the animal. Trying to catch a chicken, the animal reached through the slats to grab at the bird. He did not catch it, but pulled back a paw full of feathers into his cage.

Whitney interrupted his walk with his hostess and raced to his workshop, emerging three days later with a model. "Here is the cotton engine you asked me to produce!" he told Caty.

His simple device consisted of two rollers. One was covered with wire spikes like the cat's claws that could reach forward and grab whatever it touched. A second roller, equipped with bristles, rotated close to the first and brushed off the lint.

Abbreviating the name of the engine to cotton "gin," the inventor formed a partnership with Phineas Miller. They built machines and offered to clean, or "gin," cotton for 50 percent of the lint.

However, fortune did not favor them. Blacksmiths and mechanics who saw the cotton gins could quickly duplicate them. And although Whitney had applied for a patent, he didn't receive one until numerous imitations of his gin were in use. Later he was rewarded with $50,000 by South Carolina, but he spent it—and more—trying to defend his patent rights.

Caty Greene finally received a partial financial settlement from Congress. She invested some of it in Whitney's gin, only to see the money disappear.

Desperate, the still dazzling widow Greene bought heavily when shares of Yazoo, Mississippi, land companies were offered for sale. Georgia legislators, who sold about thirty-five million acres of Yazoo land to speculators for $500,000, did not have clear title to the land, so revocation of the Yazoo sale left Caty Greene "feeling like a plucked chicken." At least $60,000 in debt, she gave up her plantation and took refuge on Cumberland Island. Her death there at age sixty ended a true-life drama in which development of the cotton gin was but one episode.

40

Runaway Thomas Sims Helped Shape the Nation's Destiny

"Sumner Sure to Make His Mark in Washington," read newspaper headlines. Though not identical in language, that prediction appeared on the front page of every Boston daily in July, 1851.

Fiery Charles Sumner, who stood an imposing six-feet, four-inches tall, intended to live up to expectations. In an Independence Day speech, he thanked his supporters. "Most of all," he said, "I am forever grateful to Thomas Sims."

Listeners and newspaper readers applauded that sentiment because no one present during those days of tumult would ever forget the runaway from Georgia.

Despite his potent influence, little is known about Sims's background. No standard history of the state, not even a multivolume set, mentions his name, because Sims was a slave. Not an ordinary, run-of-the-mill slave, he was a cunning, courageous, and altogether defiant seventeen-year-old who chose George Washington's birthday in 1851 as the day for making his getaway.

However, within sixty days, Sims was wearing handcuffs and leg irons in Boston, "the cradle of American liberty." There police had seized him under provisions of the 1850 Fugitive Slave Law. He'd been in the port city for a month, not bothering to hide as he thought he had nothing to fear while within earshot of battlefields where men had died in the name of freedom.

Since Sims was the legal property of Georgia planter James Potter, the law required that he be returned to Georgia and slavery by the first available vessel.

However, abolitionist sympathy was strong in Boston. Richard H. Dana, Jr., and Samuel E. Sewall volunteered their services as attorneys for the defense, as did attorney Charles Sumner, still smarting from his unsuccessful bid for a seat in the U.S. House of Representatives but now being

Boston police, 300 strong, escort Sims to ship.

mentioned as a possible candidate for the U.S. Senate. Although this high-powered defense team was unable to change the law, it could create a public furor. Posters were printed, warning "colored people of Boston" to avoid contact with police officers. Wendell Phillips and William Lloyd Garrison put their tremendous influence behind an organized effort to save Sims from deportation.

Military units were assigned to guard the courthouse where Sims was being held. Boston churches held special prayer meetings; street orators harangued excited crowds.

In an effort to prevent mayhem, authorities ringed the courthouse with a heavy chain. A pack of bloodhounds was held in readiness, and three hundred special policemen were sworn in to guard the prisoner.

Rumors spread like wildfire. Two hundred men from Worcester and another one hundred from Plymouth County were said to be preparing to descend on the port city armed with muskets to effect forcible rescue of Thomas Sims.

Although these armed bands never appeared, Marshal Tukey assembled all three hundred special police officers about 4:00 A.M. on Saturday, April 13, and hustled Sims out of his improvised cell.

Captive and captors marched through Court Square, crossed the spot where the first American freedom fighter had died in the Boston Massacre of 1770, and boarded the *Acorn*. Sims was locked up in a specially built shed and sent to Savannah, where he was publicly whipped upon arrival.

The first person ever returned to slavery from Massachusetts soil, he was heard from no more after his return to the Georgia plantation. However, he was not forgotten, and his *cause célèbre* had far-reaching repercussions.

In Massachusetts, Sumner, Phillips, and Dana repeatedly invoked the slave's name. Although they failed in their immediate goal of repealing the Fugitive Slave Law, they aroused the common people mightily.

*Georgia fugitive
Thomas Sims.*

Members of the state legislature heard the roar of the people and voted to send Charles Sumner to the U.S. Senate.
There the man who owed his seat to publicity about a runaway slave became chief architect of a plan that called for
emancipation, even at the cost of blood. His ardent speeches
in support of that hard-line, no-compromise plan made
Sims's defender a prime mover in bringing about the Civil
War.

41

Vice-President Aaron Burr Hid from the Law on St. Simons

The coattails of history have brushed Georgia's Sea Islands many times. There pirates are said to have buried their loot; John and Charles Wesley, founders of Methodism, preached under their ancient oak trees; and Vice-President Aaron Burr took refuge on St. Simons after his duel with Alexander Hamilton.

Burr is thought to have chosen his hide-out partly because of its seclusion but mainly because it belonged to his long-time wealthy friend, Pierce Butler of South Carolina. A delegate to the Constitutional Convention and then a five-term congressman, Butler retired from public life in 1803. Owning fifteen thousand acres in Georgia, he chose to live at Hampton Point, his "principal residence" on St. Simons Island that was described as being "of feudal magnificence."

From there, the fugitive Burr wrote to his daughter:

I am at the mansion of Major Butler, and am most comfortably settled. My personal establishment consists of a housekeeper, a cook and chambermaid, a seamstress, and two footmen. In addition, I always have two fishermen and four boatmen at my command.

How Burr came to be Butler's "guest" on St. Simons is a sad story in American history.

His background included service on Washington's staff in the Revolution, a term in the U.S. Senate, and then the presidential campaigns of 1796 and 1800. He lost the first election but tied with Thomas Jefferson in the second. Under the Constitution at that time, the winner would be president, while the second vote-gatherer would be vice-president, with the House of Representatives determining the outcome. Alexander Hamilton, brilliant author of the *Federalist* papers and the first secretary of the treasury, used his influence to give victory to Jefferson, thereby incurring Burr's enmity.

Vice-President Burr then ran for governor of New York in 1804 but was defeated. Again Burr felt that Hamilton had been instrumental in his loss.

Just before the election, Dr. Charles D. Cooper had written an open letter published in several newspapers. Hamilton, who had opposed Burr zealously, was mentioned in the letters, although he had not seen the document, and had nothing to do with its circulation.

Nevertheless Burr demanded a public apology from Hamilton, who refused. They exchanged several brief messages through intermediaries, but the notes created an increasingly tense situation. Eventually Burr challenged Hamilton to a duel, and Hamilton accepted immediately, asking only that he be given time to take care of a few personal and legal matters.

Their seconds attended to the details. Burr and Hamilton met at Weehawken, New Jersey, on July 11, 1804.

Both men drew up and signed wills. Burr placed his affairs in the hands of his daughter Theodosia, pointing out that his estate would only cover his debts. Hamilton wrote a long summary of his thoughts and stressed that he bore Burr no ill will.

Wednesday, July 11, dawned hot and muggy as the seconds preceded the principals to a narrow ledge overlooking the Hudson River. There they cleared sticks and stones from the area.

The elaborate ritual began promptly at 7:00 A.M. The seconds counted off ten paces, then cast lots to determine positions and selected the one who would give the commands. Then they loaded the pistols. Hamilton had borrowed his from his brother-in-law, John B. Church.

Upon command, both men fired. Hamilton's shot went wild and snapped a small limb of a tree, but Burr's ball hit Hamilton in the abdomen. He died at 2:00 P.M. on July 12.

Though the duel took place in New Jersey, a New York coroner's jury indicted Burr for murder. When a warrant was issued for his arrest, he fled, taking along his friend, Samuel Swartwout, and his favorite slave.

Hiding briefly in Philadelphia, they then travelled in disguise to Georgia, conveniently close to Spanish Florida. By now also indicted in New Jersey, Burr used the name Mr. R. King, but dropped pretense soon after reaching St. Simons. There he was "serenaded by the island's only band of music."

Burr's Georgia stay was punctuated by a hurricane, but he stayed until time for Congress to convene again. On February 4, 1805, Vice President Aaron Burr—still under indictment for murder—took his seat to preside over the United States Senate until his term ended.

His career did not end there, of course. Politically ruined, he engaged in questionable activities in the West and was tried for treason in 1807 at a trial presided over by Supreme Court Chief Justice John Marshall. Burr was acquitted and went to Europe, returning to practice law in New York City.

However, his sojourn on St. Simons adds another chapter to the exciting tales of Georgia's Sea Islands.

42

Dueling Grounds Saw Blue Blood Flow Like Water

"Our president is a scoundrel and a lying rascal."

Those words, uttered before the Georgia Assembly by General Lachlan McIntosh, were too much for a man of honor to take. Thereupon Council of Safety President Button Gwinnett sent for his friend, George Wells, who agreed to be Gwinnett's second at a duel at dawn and hand delivered a formal note to McIntosh in which Gwinnett demanded "satisfaction accorded a gentleman." He suggested that they meet just before sunrise on the next day, Friday, May 16, 1777.

Although McIntosh grumbled that he wasn't accustomed to rising so early, he agreed to the terms. Honor required that he accept Gwinnett's challenge.

Wells and Major Joseph Habersham, who had consented to serve as McIntosh's second, chose pistols as the weapons that would be used in a meadow near the residence of Royal Governor James Wright.

At the appointed time the antagonists met and "politely saluted one another." As the seconds had not stipulated the distance at which the duelists would stand to fire, Gwinnett indicated that it made no difference to him. McIntosh suggested that eight or ten feet would be sufficient.

Major Habersham, however, insisted upon four full strides, or about twelve feet. Normally, men stood back-to-back as a preface to wheeling and firing, but this time the principals, at the insistence of McIntosh, faced one another with weapons ready to fire at the signal.

Shots rang out almost simultaneously.

Gwinnett dropped to the ground with the cry, "My thigh is broken!" McIntosh, shot through the flesh of his leg, believed his wound to be as serious as that of his opponent and demanded to know if Gwinnett had had enough or was ready for a second shot.

"Yes," indicated Gwinnett, signaling to be raised to take his stand again. Here the seconds stepped between the men and insisted that they exchange perfunctory handshakes.

Button Gwinnett, a signer of the Declaration of Independence and Georgia's chief civil leader, died of his injuries, which led to gangrene.

James Jackson fought twenty-three duels —and lived.

Much of Georgia's bluest blood has been spilled on dueling grounds. During a period of about 120 years after the founding of James Oglethorpe's colony, use of pistols at dawn was the standard way in which a gentleman sought satisfaction for an insult or a wrong.

Just three years after the highly publicized death of Button Gwinnett, a successor in the office he held was challenged by James Jackson. George Wells, who had become interim head of the state government when Richard Howley left the top post in order to attend the Continental Congress, served one of the shortest tenures as Georgia's chief executive, being killed by Jackson in the duel.

Destined to become governor of Georgia and a U.S. Senator, Jackson was the state's most persistent duelist of high rank. He is credited with having fought twenty-three engagements, three of them with a single opponent, attorney Robert Watkins. Tradition says that in one of their encounters Watkins used a dagger as well as a pistol, but he failed to cut down his man.

Another notable duelist was William H. Crawford, a U.S. senator, minister to France, U.S. secretary of war, and U.S. secretary of the treasury. A historical marker on U.S. Highway #78, near Crawfordville, cites his encounters.

Crawford's many duties didn't prevent him from killing P. L. Van Alen in a duel. In another dawn meeting he received a severe wound from Governor John Clark.

Even the president of the United States failed in an attempt to prevent Georgians from fighting. Bad blood between Colonel William Cumming and South Carolina Senator George McDuffie, a native of Georgia, led to taunts and then to a challenge. President James Monroe tried to intervene and make peace between the two prominent men but failed.

Early in the 1820s Cumming and McDuffie met at least four times. Twice they were talked out of firing, but twice they exchanged shots. McDuffie carried Cumming's bullet in his body for the rest of his life.

*William H. Crawford
killed one opponent.*

Finally, to halt the useless waste of life, the legislature enacted a prohibition of dueling, but numerous notables evaded the law by facing their foes in South Carolina. Others simply ignored the statute and met illegally. One of the last such duels was fought near Savannah in August, 1832, when Dr. Philip Minis killed James Jones Stark. The subsequent furor put an end to pistols at dawn.

43

Claiming Innocence, Swiss Doctor Died for War Crimes

"I am innocent," the prisoner said to the soldiers who were busy preparing him for execution.

Calmly, almost dispassionately—in contrast to earlier shouts and pleas—Henri Wirz seemed to be choosing his words carefully. Minutes earlier, as his hands were being tied, he had refused the offer of Catholic priests Boyle and Wiggett to hear his confession. Not being guilty, he told them, he had nothing to confess.

With only General John Winder and a few others present to hear it, the Swiss-born Confederate officer entered his last plea, addressed, not to them, but to the court of final appeal.

"I go before my God, the Almighty God who will judge us all," he said. "I will die like a man. I pray that then I may be found without guilt—simply a soldier who has always obeyed his orders."

Minutes later, at 10:15 A.M. on November 10, 1885, the former commandant of Andersonville prison downed half a bottle of whisky. Wincing from the constant pain of a shoulder wound that had never healed, made worse by surgery in Paris, he made the sign of the cross, then walked calmly across the courtyard of Washington's Old Capitol prison.

Earlier the spot had become famous as the place where the conspirators convicted of President Lincoln's murder had been executed. Now it was about to gain more notoriety, to be remembered as having held the scaffold on which the only "war criminal" of the Civil War was executed.

Since only 250 cards had been distributed for spectators' seats, hundreds more contested for good spots in elm trees surrounding the courtyard. Newspaper correspondents, wearing top hats, were ushered to a reserved section.

As the doomed man mounted the scaffold, onlookers in trees shouted curses. Soldiers, standing at attention, began to chant:

"Wirz! Wirz! Remember Andersonville! Wirz! Wirz! Remember Andersonville!"

"Thank you for the courtesy you have shown me," said the man born Heinrich Hartmann Wirz to his jailers as he left the cell he had occupied during his three-month trial.

With eyes open, he climbed the scaffold, then stood stiffly while a black hood was slipped over his head. A veteran executioner applied the noose and adjusted it.

At the touch of a spring, the trap door opened, and Wirz plunged; but the fall failed to snap his neck. As he slowly strangled, the only sounds came from men in blue still chanting, "Wirz! Wirz! Remember Andersonville!"

Alexander Gardner, a photographer with the studio of Mathew Brady, captured the entire drama in a series of vivid shots.

The chain of events leading to this fatal day caused the presiding judge at Wirz's trial, General Lew Wallace, who later wrote the novel *Ben Hur*, to characterize the accused as "an immigrant who became a rebel almost by accident."

Though he claimed to be a physician, Wirz had no formal medical training. Some time early in the 1850s the man who had come to America seeking opportunity became an assistant to a Kentucky doctor. When efforts to establish his own practice failed, he drifted to Louisiana and took a job on a plantation. Listed as "Dr. Wirz," he may have been employed to care for sick and injured slaves.

When the Civil War started, he enlisted in the Fourth Louisiana Infantry, where he soon rose to the rank of ser-

Execution of Capt. Henri Wirz.

geant. At Seven Pines he took a ball in his shoulder and permanently lost the use of his right hand and arm. Partly to compensate him for his injury, he was promoted to the rank of captain.

Brigadier General John Winder liked the man whom many still called the "Dutch sergeant" even after he rose in rank. As provost marshall in Richmond, Winder was in charge of Confederate prisons in the capital city. Since Wirz was known to be "the epitome of military obedience," Winder made him commandant of a prison.

Wirz performed his duties so well—never asking questions of superiors—that Jefferson Davis sent him on a mission to Paris. While he was there surgeons tried to restore his right arm to usefulness, but they failed.

Back in the Confederate States of America, the self-trained doctor was sent to Georgia's Andersonville prison in March, 1864.

There he found food and water critically low. Prisoners soon began to fight over scraps of bread and the bodies of dead rats. They died by the dozen, then by the score, and finally by the hundred—every day of every week.

The situation became much worse when General Ulysses Grant gave the prison his personal attention. Tens of thousands of men who fought in blue had enlisted for limited terms, and for many who languished in Confederate prisons such as Andersonville, the calendar offered a new life. Their enlistments had expired, or were about to expire. Upon being exchanged, they could put on civilian clothes and turn their backs upon the war.

Therefore, Grant's decision was logical from the standpoint of military strategy, but totally heartless from the perspective of prisoners. He put an abrupt halt to the exchange of prisoners, thereby shrinking the available pool of potential Confederate soldiers that was desperately needed by the hard-pressed South.

More and more captured men were crowed into Confederate prisons with no possibility of relief through exchange. By July, 1864, about 32,000 men were jammed into twenty-six acres of shanties. There were no sanitary facilities, little medicine, and less food. More than 12,900 prisoners died.

Collapse of the Confederate States of America was followed by a national outpouring of indignation about conditions in "the notorious Hell Hole" commanded by Captain Henri Wirz. He was seized and charged with mass murder. After his condemnation, he was offered a reprieve in return for a statement that would make Jefferson Davis guilty of having conspired to murder prisoners.

"No, no," Wirz said. "He did not do it. You cannot make me say that he did." Having turned down a chance to save his own life, the man who had obeyed orders went to the scaffold.

44

Manhunt Netted President Jefferson Davis

"Somebody belonging to the Fourth Michigan Cavalry fired the first shot," insisted Lieutenant Colonel Henry Harnden of the First Wisconsin Cavalry.

"Not on your life!" retorted Lieutenant Colonel B. D. Pritchard. "My men responded when shots were fired at us. We thought we had contacted a rebel unit and had no idea that the First Wisconsin was trying to grab our prize."

These conflicting statements—never fully resolved—came on the heels of the capture of Jefferson Davis, President of the Confederate States of America. For days, he had been the object of a manhunt until pursuers caught up with him in a dense thicket about two miles from Irwinville, Georgia, on May 16, 1865.

Federal authorities, who wanted to bring Davis to trial on a charge of high treason, were frenzied with fear that he might escape. That led to a colossal offer: $100,000 in gold for his capture.

Bounty hunters, plus two military units, followed Davis's trail through parts of the Carolinas and into Georgia. Both the Michigan and the Wisconsin units were close to claiming the reward on the night of May 9. Before dawn, each group moved forward. A fusillade between the two Federal bodies led to at least one death plus several injuries. The ludicrous aspects of the miniature battle were forgotten

Jefferson Davis.

when the fugitive was captured one week later, with official
credit going to the Fourth Michigan Cavalry.

The drama began on a quiet Sunday morning, April 2.
While worshiping in Saint Paul's church in Richmond, Jefferson Davis received a hand-delivered telegram.

General Robert E. Lee, who had sent the message, warned
that Richmond would soon fall and urged immediate evacuation of the Confederate capital. Many people fled during
the next twenty-four hours. Three groups are vividly remembered.

Mrs. Jefferson Davis, with her four children and a small
band of escorts, made up the first such party, heading south
with only vague plans about their final destination.

On the evening of April 2, a larger group left the city with
an armed escort guarding a wagon train carrying what was

left of the Confederate treasury, plus assets of several Virginia banks.

A third refugee party was headed by Confederate President Jefferson Davis. Not yet aware of the price put on his head, the Confederate chief executive hoped to make his way across the Mississippi to Louisiana. If he could reach the Trans-Mississippi Department of the Confederate army, he thought he could rally the remaining soldiers and perhaps bargain for re-admission of the southern states to the union on favorable terms.

Members of Davis's cabinet were told to meet in Washington, Georgia, although no arrival date was set.

Dotted line shows route of Davis's flight.

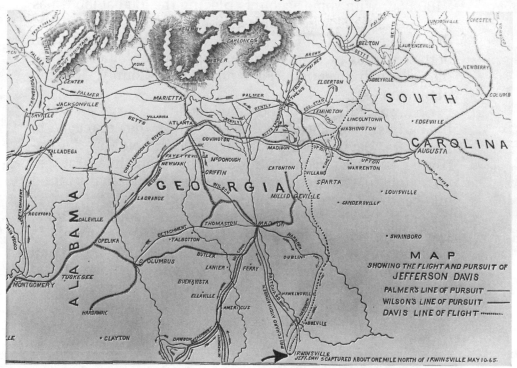

Traveling mostly at night, the fleeing president and his party reached Washington on May 4. The town had been selected as the rendezvous spot partly because it was the home of Confederate General Robert Toombs and partly because it was thought to be safely within Confederate territory.

On the night he reached Washington, Davis signed his last official order, naming M. H. Clark as acting treasurer of the Confederate States of America and giving him a free hand to exercise his office. Clark immediately took charge of the five heavily loaded wagons and headed in the direction of Abbeville, South Carolina.

No one knows how much gold and silver the wagons held, but estimates range from about $250,000 to more than $400,000, with some accounts placing the total at ten times that estimate. However, unidentified raiders surprised the driver and guards on the night of May 5. They seized some of the precious metal and are said to have sunk more of it in the Savannah River or buried it on a Wilkes County, Georgia, plantation.

Unaware of the loss of the Confederate treasury, Davis and his party slowly moved southward, where they managed to meet Mrs. Davis and her party near Dublin on May 7. Continuing to move forward cautiously, they sometimes traveled only eight to ten miles a day until Federal units finally found and captured them.

Sent to Virginia's Fortress Monroe and clapped in irons, Davis stayed in confinement for two years. Never brought to trial, he was released on May 13, 1867, on a $100,000 bail bond whose co-signers included Cornelius Vanderbilt and professional South-hater Horace Greeley. Charges against him were dropped in 1868.

45

First Land Pirate Was an Indian Princess

"It was Coosaponakessa's land, and her labor that produced the first crop of wheat for the colony you call Savannah," read one clause of a lengthy legal document.

"Coosaponakessa is not greedy. Fifty pounds will be enough for this," the itemized list of claims continued.

Using her native name, the woman whom James Oglethorpe knew as Mary Musgrove enumerated the services for which she had not been paid.

While Europeans had failed in attempts to grow peas and potatoes, she pointed out, she had succeeded grandly. Still she'd settle for just 150 pounds. Another claim was much larger. She had been promised 100 pounds per year for service as interpreter to James Oglethorpe and his aides and had filled the post for many years.

Half Indian and half English, Mary was listed in numerous early Georgia documents as "Empress and Queen of the Upper and Lower Creeks." Her title derived from the fact that Old Brim, a noted chieftain, was her uncle. After her marriage to a Carolina-born trader John Musgrove, she helped him operate a trading post at Yamacraw village, not far from the site selected for Savannah. She claimed to have been handling 1,200 deerskins a year when Oglethorpe and his followers arrived from England and immediately hired her as his interpreter. The pay was unusually large for the time.

Another Englishman also thought highly of her. Missionary John Wesley was delighted to learn that the wife of trader John Musgrove was a Christian.

After visiting Mary at her plantation about six miles up the Savannah river from her trading post, Wesley wrote in his diary that she was the most capable "native Georgian ever encountered while in the colony."

When Oglethorpe needed undercover agents, he turned to the Musgroves who went into "the debatable land" that was claimed by Britain, Spain, and France. There they established Mount Venture, a trading post about 150 miles above the mouth of the Altamaha River. Close to the Spanish territory of Florida, it was an ideal site from which to spy upon the vital overland trail that linked Charles Town with Saint Augustine.

When John Musgrove died, Mary married Jacob Matthews, who had come to the colony as an indentured servant. As husband of an Indian princess "he grew vain, dressing gaily and behaving insolently." However, he played

Oglethorpe addresses native Georgians through female interpreter.

The Rev. John Wesley seeks converts at Musgrove's trading post.

the role of prince only a few months before he died in 1742.

Soon afterwards Oglethorpe prepared to return to England. One of his last acts was to take a diamond ring from his own finger and to place it upon the finger of his interpreter. At the same time he is said to have given her 200 pounds of his own money and the promise to send 2,000 more pounds when he arrived home.

Mary then married the Reverend Thomas Bosomworth. As the first native American to become the wife of an Anglican priest, she took no part in his official duties as chaplain to the infant colony and trading post enterprise. She was busy selling illicit rum at high prices. She also busily amassed land grants from various Indian chieftains, both Creek and Yamacraw. However, authorities in London refused to honor the claims based on land transactions among the Indians. To get firm title to her holdings, plus payment in cash for services rendered in the past, Coosaponakessa had to persuade

British authorities to rule in her favor. Her initial request stipulated that she would withdraw from legal action in return for cash payment of 5,714 pounds, 17 shillings, and 11 pence, plus deeds to the islands of Hussoope (Ossabaw), Cowlegee (Saint Catherine's), and Sapelo.

The trustees of the Georgia colony in London stalled her, then eventually decided they didn't have authority to act. So the matter went to the Board of Trade. Month after month passed with no action there.

Angry and determined, Coosaponakessa and her husband sailed to England to present her claims in person. Official bodies shunted them from one to another, pointing out that no native American had ever presented such demands to the home government.

Thwarted but determined not to be defeated, the Bosomworths returned to Savannah and adroitly timed the next move.

Succeeding John Reynolds, first royal governor of Georgia, was Henry Ellis, a man with little administrative experience. Coosaponakessa thereupon recruited a band of Indian followers and invaded Savannah, threatening to launch all-out war against the white settlers unless her claims were settled.

Bewildered and frightened, Ellis convened the colonial council, which decided "to bargain for the sake of peace" and offered their challenger 2,100 pounds, sterling, plus Saint Catherine's Island.

Without consulting her husband other than by brief gestures, the Indian princess accepted their offer and formally released Great Britain from all other claims. Then she took possession of her island, built a splendid mansion and developed a fine plantation.

No other native American ever turned the tables so completely on colonial officialdom, wresting land *from* the British, as did Coosaponakessa. This "Queen of the Creeks" lived happily ever after as a true New World queen.

46

Heisman Guided Yellow Jackets to All-Time Record

Georgia Tech's Golden Tornadoes fared badly during the 1903–04 football season, so college leaders decided to take a bold step and hire a full-time coach.

Ohio-born John Heisman hadn't stayed anywhere very long. He began coaching football at Oberlin where in 1892 he turned out a team with a perfect seven-game record for the season. From Oberlin he went to Akron, then to Auburn, and to Clemson in 1900.

Heisman's salary at Clemson was so low that he became a Shakespearean actor during off-season, and Tech got him by offering him a salary boost of fifty dollars a month.

Critics called him eccentric, but admirers insisted that he was a lopsided genius who might have been right in forbidding his players to use hot water and soap during the week. "The stuff is debilitating," said Heisman in the exaggerated stage voice he nearly always used, a carryover from his moonlighting as an actor.

Although his Golden Tornadoes didn't win a game in 1912, by 1914 Heisman had transformed them into the Yellow Jackets, whom he led to the Southern championship. For three successive years they remained on top. In one period they played a string of thirty games without a single loss.

Concerned for the safety of his players, the coach led a

successful crusade against use of the flying wedge. "The human frame just isn't equal to the wedge," he said. "Use your brain instead of your body whenever you can."

That principle led him to an innovation. Studying rule books, he concluded they didn't prohibit concealment of the ball. So he developed and used the hidden-ball play.

His "Heisman shift," brought out very early, involved having the entire team, except the center, drop behind the scrimmage line. Backs lined up at right angles to the rush line. Awed sports writer George Trevor described the maneuver for the *New York Sun* newspaper: "At the shift signal, the phalanx deployed with the suddenness of a Jeb Stuart cavalry raid, catching the defense off balance."

Along with the famous Heisman shift, the Tech coach decided to put everything he had into a 1916 game. He'd been challenged by assistant coach Bill Alexander, who said that "If we don't beat Cumberland by fifty points, we ought to lose."

*Yellow Jacket Coach
John Heisman.*

Halfback Everett ("Strup") Strupper broke into the conversation between coaches. "If we score 100 will you set 'em up for the gang, Alex?"

"Nope," Alexander responded. "But if you make 200 points, I'll set up the varsity, the scrub, and the frosh."

That was all Heisman and his fire-eating squad needed. Drawn from a student body of 843, the Yellow Jackets didn't have a significant numerical edge. Cumberland, with more than 500 students, had won the All-Southern championship in 1907, and remained a powerful opponent.

Preparing for the big game, Tech's coach cut the water allowance for his players. In typical Heisman style, he demanded that members of the squad eat their meat nearly raw.

Playing before a crowd of less than one thousand spectators who stood because there were no bleachers, Tech made twenty first downs to Cumberland's none. Tech gained 501 net yards rushing to Cumberland's –42. Not counting kick-off returns, the Yellow Jackets moved the ball 959 yards. Cumberland had a net loss of 28 yards for the game.

It was strictly ground action—pure old-fashioned bone-crushing football. Not a pass was thrown.

Six plays into the third quarter, a conversion made the score Tech 154, Cumberland 0. That broke the 1912 world record of 153 points, scored by Michigan.

"Our crew of eleven worked like a mowing machine eating its way through a field of ripe grain," said the jubilant coach. Yet even the man whose name later became attached to the most coveted of all college football trophies consented to stop the carnage

As recalled by Tech's Dean Griffin, "Officials decided to call the game after 7½ minutes into the fourth quarter. If they hadn't done that, the score would have gone past 300." As it was, the final whistle blew when it stood 222–0. Today, Heisman's masterpiece game rates a full paragraph in many editions of the *Guinness Book of World Records*.

Rule changes make chances of a repeat performance of the 1916 debacle just about nil, so the record score is apt to remain tops in college football for a long time.

When Heisman and his wife separated soon after the big win, they tossed coins to decide who'd stay in Atlanta. She won. That sent the coach to New York City near the tail end of his career, where he worked as athletic director for the wealthy, but not-so-athletic, Downtown Athletic Club.

In 1935 well-heeled members of the club put up the money to create a trophy in the form of a two-foot bronze runner who is stiff-arming a tackle. Naturally, they called it the Downtown Athletic Club Trophy.

Before the trophy was awarded for the first time, John W. Heisman died and admirers managed to get his name attached to the award. That is how a Tech coach who wasn't altogether certain he shouldn't have been a Shakespearean actor won a kind of immortality that is afforded to very few.

222-0 game was played on field where spectators stood on sidelines to watch.

47

"Blind Tom" Bethune Awed Crowned Heads of Europe

Who was Thomas Gage Bethune? Precisely *what* was he?

Contemporaries thought they knew the answer to both questions. In the United States, Britain, and France they flocked to hear the musical prodigy perform. After having applauded wildly, they called him "idiot" and "a little nigger boy who's a freak of nature."

Bethune's life story is better known now than it was a century ago. Born and reared in slavery, before he died he was credited with having attracted "more people to see and hear him than any other living wonder."

Idiot, he clearly was not. Given a different set of circumstances, he might have become a great composer.

Born on May 25, 1849, in Muscogee County, Tom belonged to James N. Bethune, a plantation owner and ardent secessionist who was usually called Colonel or General. To him the infant slave was a liability because he was blind.

Today, he'd be called "legally blind," since his vision was limited to light perception plus recognition of familiar persons and objects at close range. When he took to the concert stage, he was labeled "completely blind." His manager realized very early that a blind performer would stir up much more interest than an equally versatile one with vision, however limited.

IRVING HALL!

Irving Place, betw. 14th and 15th Sts., opposite Academy of Music.

Wednesday Afternoon and Evening, May 13th, 1868

BLIND TOM'S CONCERTS

The management would respectfully announce that, in consequence of the greatly increasing interest manifested by the public, and in compliance with the expressed desire of many citizens who have, as yet, been unable to witness the Marvelous Performances of TOM, have decided to remain in New York for

A FEW NIGHTS MORE,

But must Positively Close with the Present Week.

BLIND TOM MATINEES

Will be given during the week, as usual, at half-past 2 o'clock, on the Afternoons of

WEDNESDAY AND SATURDAY.

TOM!

The Blind Negro Boy—of Musical Inspiration!

Sightless and Untutored from Birth—his very soul overflowing with Musical Genius. This Youth is a Remarkable Phenomenon in one direction only, and that is his Wonderful Aptness for the

PIANO FORTE!

There is no Art about him. God has given him a guide, but it is a silent one, that of Nature herself. The manipulations of the GREAT MASTERS of the day are the sole efforts of deep and unwearied study. His instruction comes from a Higher Power, and this, Philosophers are pleased to term, GENIUS.

The Richest and Most Difficult

MUSICAL GEMS

Are to this Wonderful Prodigy but a mere

SONG OF FACILITY!

Which he Plays with all the Correctness, Grace of Manner, Purity of Expression & Brilliancy of Execution, That will PERFECTLY ASTONISH HIS HEARERS.

He is a Perfect

PRODIGY

And Thousands before whom he has had the honor of appearing have expressed the most

Unbounded Satisfaction

And Delight at his

WONDERFUL POWERS AS A PIANIST

THIS BLIND NEGRO BOY—THE

SON OF ORDINARY SOUTHERN FIELD HANDS!

Following the custom of using surnames of owners, the boy was called Thomas Gage Bethune. His fascination with sounds of all kinds was noticed very early. Still, he created a stir one night. Creeping into his master's mansion, he began to play on the newly acquired piano a melody he had heard for the first time only a few hours earlier.

No one in the big house knew what to make of Tom's unplanned demonstration. Totally without schooling, he couldn't even repeat the alphabet. No one had given him any instruction in music, yet his deft touch and sure sense of rhythm announced him as a master musician.

The astonished Colonel Bethune took his slave to a German music teacher in Columbus, the county seat. "No, sir, I can't teach him anything," the musician said after having heard the boy perform. "Just let him hear fine playing. He'll work it out by himself after a while, regardless, but he'll do it sooner by hearing fine music."

Music stores in Columbus ordered a wide range of popular and classical compositions and local pianists played these for the growing boy. As predicted, he drank in melodies eagerly. Soon he demonstrated that he could memorize every note while hearing a composition once.

By now, Colonel Bethune knew he had a money maker on his hands. He turned other interests over to relatives and began exhibiting the prodigy whom he billed as Blind Tom.

The emancipation of slaves had no significant effect on the relationship between the black prodigy and Colonel Bethune, who was his legal guardian. No one knows how much Colonel Bethune made from that relationship. Estimates of the musician's earnings range as high as $100,000 a year, at a time when Abraham Lincoln's salary as president was $25,000 a year.

Blind Tom gave triumphant performances in London, Paris, and most major cities of Western Europe, playing from a repertoire of more than 2,000 compositions. He often demonstrated his ability to reproduce perfectly a new composition, one twenty minutes in length, after one hearing.

As an adolescent he delighted and amazed audiences by playing two tunes simultaneously while singing a third. In Albany, New York, he once played "Yankee Doodle" in B flat with his right hand. With his left hand he played "Fisher's Hornpipe" in C. At the same time, he sang "Tramp, Tramp, Tramp" flawlessly, in still another key.

His career spanned a period of more than thirty years of sell-out performances, yet today, many scholars admit bewilderment that no one during his life gave him serious attention as a composer. He wrote "The Rain Storm" at age five, composed "The Battle of Manassas" as an interpretation of Civil War agonies, and at least seventy other original compositions have been catalogued. How many were lost without mention is unknown.

Georgia's first black to become an international celebrity is a bigger enigma today than during Civil War years. Had he been given the best of musical training rather than being exploited, what would Thomas Gage Bethune have accomplished?

Thomas Gage Bethune.

48

Oglethorpe's "Indian Ways" Stopped Spain Cold

"As Georgia goes, so will all of British North America. May God be with us in these crucial times."

These sentiments echoed over and over in letters of James Oglethorpe, about 250 years ago. Georgia, youngest and weakest of Britain's North American colonies, was just nine years old. There was no certainty that she would endure.

Early in his stay in Georgia, Oglethorpe decided that the Spanish—not the French, as most Europeans said—threatened the future of the colony. Therefore at every opportunity he detailed an early version of a "domino theory." If Georgia should fall to the Spanish, he argued, invaders would move up the coast. South Carolina would be seized, then North Carolina. Before the Spanish tide ceased to flow, the flag of King Philip would fly all the way from Saint Augustine to Cape Cod.

Seeming to prove Oglethorpe correct, a fleet of Spanish ships carrying veteran soldiers left Cuba on May 26, 1742. After a halt at Saint Augustine, the invaders reached Georgia waters on July 1. James Oglethorpe, a veteran of European wars, withdrew from most outposts. Saint Simons Island, he decided, was the place to make a stand.

Florida's Governor Montiano, commanding the vastly superior attacking force, signalled for his fleet to launch an assault about 7:00 A.M. on July 5. They entered Saint Simons sound without resistance and effected an orderly landing.

Then Montiano, who was in no hurry, waited until July 7 to begin moving toward the island's only strong position, Fort Frederica. He expected the forthcoming battle to proceed according to the established European system of combat with troops deployed in well-ordered ranks.

However, Georgia's founder had spent much time with his Indian friends and allies, learning from them the basic concepts of guerilla warfare. Hence, he ignored continental military manuals.

About five miles from Frederica, the attackers would have to cross a marsh on a narrow trail, so there, not at the little fort, Oglethorpe chose to make a stand. He stationed his ragged sharpshooters in dense woods that bordered the marsh.

Released after being captured at Bloody Marsh, a Spanish prisoner took false news fed to him by Oglethorpe.

The Spanish troops knew Frederica to be small and weak, easily mastered they thought. Headed toward the fort, they moved forward in orderly ranks until they reached the marsh and had to form a thin column to negotiate the trail.

There the members of the tiny Georgia militia, their Indian allies, and a handful of British regulars fired from ambush. A few invaders fell, the rest panicked and fled.

Though no English blood and little Spanish was spilled that day, the engagement became noted as the Battle of Bloody Marsh.

In its aftermath, one of Oglethorpe's French-born soldiers deserted to the enemy. Georgia's founder—a perennial gambler—decided upon a risky ploy. He forged a note addressed to the deserter. Supposedly confidential, it indicated that a vast English fleet would reach Georgia within hours.

Oglethorpe gave the bogus message to a Spanish prisoner, whom he released upon his oath that he'd deliver it to the Frenchman and no one else. Montiano's aides, reasoned Oglethorpe, would be sure to search the man.

They did.

Fearful of attack by British warships that didn't exist, the Spanish kept a sharp lookout to sea. When masts were glimpsed at a distance, their worst fears seemed to be confirmed. In a state of near-panic, the Spanish commander evacuated Saint Simons Island and ordered his ships and men to return to home bases in Florida and Cuba.

No list of great battles of the Western world includes Bloody Marsh. Yet the skirmish and its aftermath proved to be decisive. Spain never again attempted a military invasion of North America.

49

Slave Girl Triggered First Big North/South Split

"I don't want to go to that country in a ship," Kitty insisted. "I don't know nobody there. This is my home."

With George W. Lane accompanying him as a witness, Emory College President A. B. Longstreet had made a carefully worded offer. If the young slave belonging to Bishop James O. Andrew of Oxford would only say the word, she could go free.

Conditions were attached, of course. She could not stay in Georgia, state law would not permit that. She could go North to a "free state," where she would find herself alone and helpless. Or she could rejoin her compatriots in Africa.

Common sense seemed to dictate that if she chose freedom she should make "a long trip by water" to Liberia.

Frightened at the prospect of leaving behind everyone she knew and loved, Kitty shook her head firmly as the offer was repeated three times. "No," she said, "I sure don't want to go across the ocean and be free."

Like other slaves she had no surname, but everyone in Newton County knew that an old lady of Augusta had willed her to Bishop Andrew who had become one of five bishops of the Methodist Episcopal Church in 1832.

Kitty was left to him because her owner was confident that he would care for her like a member of the family. What's more, he had solemnly promised to offer her freedom when she became nineteen.

That decisive point in her life was reached in 1842, but by then Georgia lawmakers had enacted new statutes forbidding the practice of permitting freed slaves to remain in the state. Until then the number of free blacks had grown by the natural children of plantation owners gaining their freedom at the death of their masters who were also their fathers, or by freed men moving from other states, or by slaves purchasing their own freedom. Growing fear of insurrection led political leaders to mandate that manumission, or freedom, meant exile.

Keenly aware of the alternatives, Kitty never wavered during discussions about her future. Oxford was home, and she preferred to remain in the Andrew household as a slave.

Neither she nor other villagers had the slightest idea that her decision would trigger the first major North/South split, sixteen years before the outbreak of civil war.

Methodists who converged upon New York's Greene Street Church on May 1, 1844, to discuss slavery knew that sectional differences would be hotly debated. Although only members of the clergy came as voting delegates, they represented 985,598 whites, 145,409 blacks, and 4,129 American Indians, making their church the largest religious body in the United States. Decisions made by Methodists would have implications for the whole nation.

Parliamentary jockeying lasted for several days. Southern delegates, sensing that a showdown was at hand, wished to avoid it, while anti-slavery forces were confident that they had a slight, but decisive, advantage.

As the Methodists debated, delegates to the Anti-Slavery Society's annual meeting convened a few blocks away. In the chair was William Lloyd Garrison, whose name was hated in the South. His fiery *Emancipator* newspaper, launched in 1831, had evoked an unparalleled reaction, even causing Georgia lawmakers to offer a reward of $1,000 for his capture.

With the fiery abolitionist presiding, his followers took

action aimed at persuading undecided Methodists. By a three-to-one vote, the society urged "immediate dissolution of the existing union between Northern Freedom (such as it is) and Southern Slavery."

Methodists established a special committee "to investigate a report that one of our bishops has become connected with slavery." While delegates debated, Andrew tried to resign, but his colleagues wouldn't let him do so.

However, a formal report finding him guilty of slaveholding and recommending his suspension from office evoked a minority protest from thirteen states. Soon the protest coalesced into a Plan of Separation.

Formal North/South division came within a year.

At its organization on May 1, 1845, the Methodist Episcopal Church, South, claimed 332,067 white members along with 124,961 blacks and 2,972 Indians. A precedent and a pattern had been established. Soon the nation would see a similar division that would mean war.

After refusing to go to Liberia, Kitty was given a simple cottage in which she lived with her husband, Nathan. It was moved to Salem Campground, near Covington, in 1938, where it stands today as a mute witness to forces larger than the persons who set them in motion.

Fiery abolitionists from New England made no effort to find for Kitty a home where she could be free with dignity. Bishop Andrew and his supporters did not attempt to provide funds that would enable her to go somewhere other than Africa.

Forced by law to choose among the North, far away Liberia, and a comfortably familiar life with her master and his family, a girl of nineteen chose slavery, setting the stage for the War That Should Not Have Been.

PART FIVE:
Florida

Juan Ponce de León [Sixteenth-century Engraving]

50

Juan Ponce de León Was One of Spain's Most Splendid Failures

10 February 1521
Sire:

Among my services, I have discovered, at my own expense, the Island of Florida and others in its district. I intend to explore the coast of the said island further, and see whether it connects with Cuba or any other; and I shall endeavor to learn all I can. I shall set out to pursue my voyage in five or six days.

Your faithful servant
De León

Writing to King Charles V of Spain, Juan Ponce de León did not anticipate that hostile Indians would attack his band of 250 men when they landed near today's Tampa Bay. However, they did. Seriously wounded, their leader retired to Cuba, where he died a few days later, regarding himself as a conspicuous failure.

Eight years earlier, at age 53, he had set out to find a marvelous fountain, or spring, whose potent waters would restore youth to those who drank them or bathed in them. Natives of Puerto Rico had told him of this great wonder, which he called *Fons Juventutis* or "fountain of youth."

The Spanish adventurer was determined to find the fountain and, for the glory of his king, to conquer the island of Bimini on which it was located. Convinced that trees around the fountain bore "fruit of gold" that beautiful maidens plucked and presented to strangers, with

225

three caravels he set out to master Bimini and its wonders.

On March 27, 1513, Ponce de León sighted land, which
he called in Spanish *Florida*, meaning "feast of flowers,"
a term linked with Easter. In a brief but formal ceremony
on what he believed to be a big island, he took possession
of it in the name of Spain.

Nowhere in Florida did he come close to reaching his
goal, the miraculous fountain. Neither did he succeed in
his secondary, but still vital, purpose of discovering gold
in abundance. Early European drawings depicted Indians
of the country north of present-day Jacksonville retrieving
gold from a river. Although he probably passed through
that region, Ponce de León found no yellow metal.

Thus eight years and many adventures after having
found, named, and claimed Florida for his sovereign,
de León regarded himself as a failure.

He was sure there were wonders aplenty in the region.
He had been told that native rulers were giants because as
children their bones had been treated with herbs that
made them stretch. He looked for, but never saw, such giants.

His search for "men with tails, which they could lash
fearsomely about," was equally futile. Even lions and
kangaroos, which natives told him were abundant, eluded
the Spanish adventurer.

In a region where his men killed 170 tortoises in a single day, he did manage to map a cluster of tiny islands
that he called the Tortugas, or Turtles. And he recorded in
his diary with wonder a notation about the location of an
immense river that flowed through the ocean day and
night without ceasing. That, plus his huge island—minus
gold and a marvelous fountain—was all he had to show
for his years of hardship and danger.

De León's followers thought more highly of him than he
did of himself. When he was formally buried, on his tomb
was inscribed, "In this Sepulchre rest the Bones of a Man
who was Leon (lion) by Name, and still more by Nature."

It was decades before anyone in Europe realized that

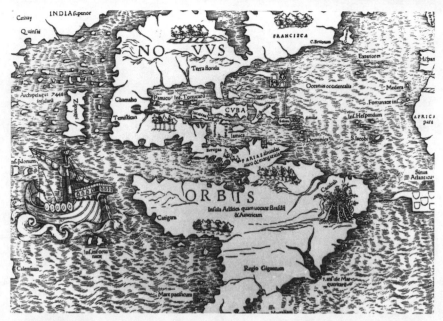

"Terra Florida," Cuba, and South America as depicted in 1540 (land areas are white). [PTOLEMY'S GEOGRAPHY]

Ponce de León's "immense island" was actually a peninsula 400 miles long. Once the true nature of Florida was realized, Spain claimed all North America as her own. For more than a century, Florida was used to name the region from the Gulf of Mexico to the Appalachian Mountains, as well as unknown and unexplored Indian country beyond the mountains.

Long afterward, the thirty-mile-per-hour "great river in the ocean" that Ponce de León found was named the Gulf Stream, one of the globe's most important features. Coupled with what he died believing to be a big island, the Gulf Stream places the man who found neither fountain nor gold among the front rank of all-time great discoverers.

51

A Fair Swap: All Florida for Havana and West Cuba

"England will wrest North America from France and Spain," an impassioned William Pitt promised members of Parliament. He did not mention James Oglethorpe's aborted invasion of Florida a generation earlier. Although Florida—and all of North America—was involved, the decisive military engagements would take place in Europe.

During the Seven Years' War of 1756-63, the struggle between the European powers became global. Germany was the crucial spot, but French soldiers battled English soldiers in India as well as in Canada. Drawn into the struggle between the great powers, natives of Senegal were forced to take sides in the conflict that in America was called the French and Indian War.

Warships of His Majesty's Navy converged upon Havana, the richest Spanish prize north of the equator in the Americas, and forced quick surrender. Gen. James Wolfe led British and Colonial troops against Quebec, where he defeated the great French strategist, the Marquis de Montcalm. In Germany, England furnished much of the money needed by Frederick the Great, whose victories influenced the future of Europe.

Under the terms of the 1763 Treaty of Paris, there were no significant changes in European borders. However, France had to abandon India, relinquish to Britain all its territory on the North American mainland east of the Mississippi, and cede to Spain all her American holdings west of the Mississippi and at its mouth. France thereby

William Pitt promised that England would take Florida from France and Spain.

abandoned the North American continent. Clearly, England was marked as the emerging super-power of the era.

Although the British had taken Havana in 1762, she returned it to Spain in exchange for Spain's Florida possessions, thereby consolidating British American holdings down the eastern seaboard and to the Mississippi.

They then divided Florida into East Florida, with St. Augustine as capital, and West Florida, with Pensacola as capital.

Soon Florida's new owners pushed the northern boundary of West Florida northward to include much of present-day Louisiana, Mississippi, and Alabama. Both Floridas were formally converted into royal colonies, for which London provided generous financial support.

At this time, St. Augustine had almost four thousand inhabitants, including 315 black slaves, 95 free blacks, and 89 Indians who had adopted the Catholic faith. Pensacola, the new capital in the west, was only one-fourth as large.

When news of the transfer reached the New World, Spanish citizens packed up their possessions and left in a hurry. Their departure made England's new American possessions virtually uninhabited, except for roving bands of Indians.

James Grant and George Johnstone were named royal

governors of East Florida and West Florida, respectively. Johnstone could do little more than try to strengthen the already formidable military installations in Pensacola.

But it was a different story in East Florida. It was a prize that some considered to be worth plucking. Dr. Andrew Turnbull procured a grant of land in 1767, and immediately started to recruit settlers in a more methodical fashion than that employed earlier by John White.

Turnbull focused his attention upon poverty-stricken peasants of the Mediterranean basin. During a period of two years, he induced at least two thousand Italians, Minorcans, and Greeks to come to Florida. He provided land and tried to teach them to raise rice, sugar, indigo, and maize, the versatile cereal that Americans today call corn.

Matters seemed to be progressing well in East Florida until truculent colonists to the north launched what they termed "a revolution against British tyranny." Spain pretended to take a neutral stance, but in actuality it did everything possible to aid rebellious colonies, hoping to weaken England.

In Britain's original thirteen North American colonies, patriots stripped Loyalists of their possessions. Many of those refugees flocked to East Florida, causing the prewar population of 5,000 to grow by 5,000 white Loyalists and 8,300 slaves in a single year, 1783.

George Washington and his patriots stunned the world by their victories, which set the stage for new rounds of diplomacy in preparation for another peace treaty. Benjamin Franklin, John Adams, and John Jay represented the new nation at the Paris parleys that brought the American Revolution to a formal end.

Under terms of the 1783 Treaty of Versailles, independence of the United States of America was recognized. Americans promised, in turn, to cease their persecution of Loyalists. To indemnify Spain for her war expenditures, the British returned Florida to the empire ruled by King Charles III.

Britain had held Florida for twenty years, and the American Loyalists who had gone there were dismayed

In Paris, Benjamin Franklin assented to Spain's proposal that England give her Havana in exchange for Florida.

when they learned the terms of the treaty. Unwilling to remain as subjects of Catholic Spain, at least 13,000 persons, including many of the colonists brought over by Dr. Turnbull, fled to the Caribbean islands or Nova Scotia, considered to be firmly in British hands.

Living in retirement on his Irish estates in County Down, the Earl of Hillsborough bemoaned the loss of the region he had long called his "favorite colony." He had spent just enough time in Florida to realize that it was distinctly different from the colonies to the north, but no one in a position of authority listened when the aging nobleman pleaded for England to "recover her crown jewel, Florida, from Spain before it is too late."

Spanish leaders showed no signs of regret at the hasty exodus that followed the change of ownership. Neither did they take seriously the small but rapidly increasing stream of American emigrants who had begun to move into Florida from the north. With France out of mainland America and England now confined to Canada, what possible danger could stem from a fledgling United States of America that had little interest in East and West Florida, except a common border?

52

Governor Bloxham Negotiated America's Biggest Land Deal

Outwardly calm to the extent of appearing jovial, William D. Bloxham was up-tight inside. Steadily drumming upon the table of a Philadelphia restaurant, he suddenly turned to an aide seated beside him and blurted, "Let's forget about sailfish, and go for tarpon!"

With his verdict barely out of his mouth, the governor of Florida jumped to his feet and pumped the hand of the guest he had been expecting.

They ate leisurely, talking only about hunting and fishing. Bloxham waited for just the right opportunity, then he complimented his guest for having learned to distinguish the feather of a hen from the feather of a cock on his first turkey hunt.

Hamilton Disston, who had inherited a fortune as a result of his father's success in manufacturing saws, modestly admitted that, for a novice, he had been exceptionally lucky when hunting wild turkeys. On a first-name basis with the governor as a result of several visits, he repeated what he had often said before: "Bill, you have the best hunting and fishing in the country—maybe the whole world!"

Acting upon that cue, Florida's chief executive talked with enthusiasm about "the greatest sport any man ever indulged in, bar none—salt-water fishing for tarpon." As his enthralled guest listened, Bloxham offered him the use of a state-owned vessel on his next trip south.

Only when the wealthy investor had accepted the invitation to fish for tarpon did the governor turn to a second

233

topic. "Somebody's going to pick up a fortune from the Everglades one of these days," he commented.

Disston asked for more details, although he knew a little about the large land grant to the state from the federal government. Back in 1850 Congress had conveyed nearly seventy million acres of "swamp and overflowed land" to states in which such tracts were located. Florida received by far the biggest part of it, about twenty million acres.

That action on the part of national lawmakers came during a period when they were making a concerted effort to solve the slavery problem. Abolitionists wanted slavery outlawed in newly settled regions while advocates of slavery saw the creation of additional slave states as their only hope for maintaining the delicate balance in Congress.

As chief executive for sixteen months, feisty ex-soldier Zachary Taylor had blocked all proposals for territorial expansion of the United States or relinquishment of federally owned tracts within existing states. He wanted nothing to do with any enterprise that might foster the spread of slavery.

Millard Fillmore, his successor, was a self-taught ex-farmer and mill apprentice. When Henry Clay hammered out what he labeled as a lasting solution to the slavery problem, Fillmore gave his blessing to the Compromise of 1850.

Under its terms, to satisfy the South, Texas received ten million dollars to abandon its claims to the New Mexican territory, and a stricter federal law for the return of runaway slaves was enacted. To please the North, the slave trade was abolished in the District of Columbia, and California entered the Union without slavery. The territories of New Mexico and Utah were organized, each to determine its own stance on slavery.

In the climate of optimism created by passage of the compromise, Congress approved the Swamp Land Act on September 28, 1850. It was the fulfillment of a dream held by Floridians since their region was admitted to the Union.

However, legal and financial problems and the Civil

War had prevented Florida from doing anything with her bonanza. A special Internal Improvement Fund, created to oversee development and sale of state land, became hopelessly in debt.

Trustees of the state fund entered in their minutes such items as: newspaper ad, $5; telegrams, $3.88; monthly expenses of timber agent, $11.50.

Land offices had been opened in principal eastern cities, but even at fifty cents an acre there were few buyers. By 1880 the future of the state hung in the balance; only a really big land deal offered hope of a bail-out for debt-plagued Florida state agencies.

When energetic and personable William D. Bloxham became governor on January 4, 1881, he took it upon himself to clean up the state's financial mess. That is why he made his trip to Philadelphia to see Hamilton Disston, with whom he had become acquainted during the years in which the industrialist came to Florida to hunt and fish.

On the day of their momentous meeting, the president of the Keystone Saw, Tool, Steel, and File Works nodded interest when his friend mentioned the Everglades. Although considered worthless then, the immense region could be rich farming and cattle-raising country if someone with imagination and money drained it.

A general agreement was reached in a matter of hours and a detailed contract was signed on February 26. Under its terms, Disston and associates agreed "to drain and reclaim at their own expense and charge, all the overflowed lands south of specified boundaries."

Technically, it was a reclamation project rather than a conventional land purchase, but the deal required Florida to transfer to Disston four million acres of state-owned land. Thus, at age thirty-seven, Disston became the largest individual land owner in the United States. By December 31, 1881, the state was to be paid one million dollars in no more than four installments.

That contract meant that a nearly bankrupt state could avert disaster. And for Disston and associates, the biggest private land deal on record meant that they gained a tract almost twice as large as Connecticut, for twenty-five cents an acre.

A first payment of five hundred thousand dollars was made in May. Both the Tampa *Tribune* and the Fernandina *Mirror* criticized the sale, but the Apalachicola *Tribune* demanded to know who among the "growlers" would have paid two cents an acre for the vast tract.

The legal transfer of title, often involving two hundred thousand or more acres in a single deed, proceeded during the summer. Before cool weather reached Jacksonville, Disston sold two million acres to Sir Edward Reed of England.

The Philadelphia entrepreneur already had made plans to drain, clear, and develop the remaining two million acres. His engineers actually completed about ten miles of drainage canals. Disston City, not far from present-day

President Millard Fillmore assented to the Compromise of 1850 and the Swamp Land Act. [LIBRARY OF CONGRESS]

Gulfport, was platted into five- and ten-acre tracts, and an extensive advertising campaign was launched in northern cities.

Disston pumped money into projects aimed at fostering the production of sugar cane, rice, fruit, vegetables, and cattle. Kissimmee grew from a bedraggled cow town into what Disston's sale agents—not dimly dreaming of what lay in the faraway future—labeled "a magic city." A few English settlers took up tracts in the region bought by Reed and talked enthusiastically of "restoring this great region to its British heritage."

Side effects were dramatic.

Not only was the state and its agencies suddenly solvent, but Disston money spurred a burst of railroad construction. During 1881–82 more miles of track were completed than during the entire previous history of the peninsula. Florida's tax base doubled by 1885, and Bloxham rejoiced that the state had "no floating debt, and cash in the treasury."

But development plans of Disston and of Sir Edward Reed quickly soured. Colonists came in dribbles, not in droves; and few stayed for any length of time. Homesteaders and squatters caused constant legal problems. The cost of producing sugar proved greater than the market price, and drainage turned out to be far more complex and costly than promoters had imagined.

Then came the Panic of 1893. When Hamilton Disston died suddenly, his heavily mortgaged holdings were soon liquidated. Reed lost out, too. Measured by the standards of the time, both men suffered colossal losses.

Florida, however, proved to be the big winner. Boosted into solvency, the state won the favorable attention of Henry B. Plant, Henry M. Flagler, and other promoters from the north. In spite of boom-and-bust cycles, Florida was never again halted in her progress. The sale of swamp land in a colossal deal that today would be bitterly contested by environmentalists bailed out the state when many observers had gone on record as believing it would "go under, and stay under."

53

Florida's "Founder" Started with Nine Cents

"Now I can die happy; my dream is fulfilled!"

Eighty-two-year-old Henry Morrison Flagler acknowledged the applause of well-wishers gathered at the Key West railroad station. Then he spoke briefly of the fulfillment of his dream: a railroad stretching the entire length of Florida from the Georgia line to the Gulf of Mexico.

Flagler did not tell his listeners on January 22, 1912, that in an era when steak was selling for fifteen cents a pound, he had poured at least twenty million dollars into the last 156 miles of the Florida East Coast Railroad. More than three thousand men worked seven years to link Key West with Miami, with viaducts and bridges accounting for half the total mileage.

More than any other individual, Flagler deserves to be revered as "Florida's founder," modern Florida, that is. He first saw the Sunshine State at age fifty-three, when he spent a belated honeymoon in St. Augustine. It had taken ninety hours of travel to arrive in Jacksonville from New York City and another full day to reach his destination.

The charming oldest city in America, with a population of just about two thousand people, captivated Henry M. Flagler and his bride.

"This really would be a great place for winter visitors," he reputedly mused one day early in 1884, "if only there were decent facilities. One good hotel would make a world of difference."

Back in Florida two years later, the man who was a

The Ponce de Leon Hotel, St. Augustine, later served to house Flagler College. [THE HENRY MORRISON FLAGLER MUSEUM]

native of a village near Canandaigua, New York, found that New England businessmen had erected the San Marco hotel in St. Augustine. Traveling in their private railroad car, "The Rambler," the Flaglers made the trip to Jacksonville, this time—in just two days.

"Got to have hotels to accommodate winter visitors," Flagler concluded. Almost as an afterthought he confided to his wife, "Hotels won't do much, without railroads."

Meditating upon the hotel/railroad combination, the New Yorker took part in St. Augustine's celebration of the landing of Ponce de León 373 years earlier. "That would make a great name for a really splendid hotel," he confided to his wife.

Already many times a millionaire as a result of an early partnership with John D. Rockefeller and a major role in founding the Standard Oil Company, Flagler poured 2.5 million dollars into the Ponce de León Hotel in St. Augustine. When it opened on January 10, 1888, oldtimers in Florida admitted, "This state has never seen anything like the Ponce."

A string of other luxury hotels followed: the Alcazar in St. Augustine, the Ormond in Ormond, and, much later, the Royal Poinciana and the Breakers at Palm Beach, and the Royal Palm at Miami.

Flagler expected to make money, but to intimates he confessed that he already had more than he would ever spend. He was more interested in seeing "this vast sun-drenched wilderness made into a vacation mecca" than in amassing additional millions.

Early in the expansion of his chain of hotels, the New Yorker came back to an earlier conclusion: no matter how delightful hotels in Florida might be, they would be nearly empty unless served by good railroads.

That started his acquisition and combining of short rail lines, later extending new tracks deeper into the Florida peninsula. Because it meant that people from all of the North could travel comfortably to any point in Florida, completion of the line from Miami to Key West really was the culmination of a grand goal conceived nearly thirty years earlier.

At least one modern biographer has called Henry M. Flagler a "visionary robber baron." There is little doubt that the estimated sixty million dollars he poured into Florida enterprises made more millions for him. He clearly was a visionary, but he was not a robber baron, at least not in Florida.

Flagler gave free seed and cuttings to orange growers. The son of a Presbyterian minister, he built Presbyterian, Methodist, and Baptist churches and paid for the renovation of St. Augustine's Catholic cathedral. Throughout his adopted state, "the Flagler impact" from generous gifts, often anonymous, can be seen in public buildings and municipal facilities.

In no other state has a single person had an influence comparable to that of Henry M. Flagler upon Florida. That impact is dramatized by a tour guide's comment: "Mr. Flagler was a high school dropout who left home at age fourteen with nine cents in his pocket."

54

No More Fear of Spain!

*"The city of Miami is helpless to defend herself. Refugees
arriving daily from Cuba talk freely of a coming invasion.
We must have help immediately."*

Dispatched to President William McKinley in secret, that telegram was sent by the mayor of Miami early
in March 1898. It did not bring engineers to build fortifications as citizens had hoped. Instead, McKinley gave
instructions that Miami would become a garrison for
troops.

Oldtimers relaxed when they learned that the fast-growing town would become a staging area for the expected
invasion of Cuba. A few units from the thirty thousand-
man U.S. Army, plus three or four companies of volunteers, began erecting a camp in April.

Late that month, however, panic gripped Miami and all
of Florida. Rumor had it that Spanish Admiral Pascual
Cervera was leading his fleet from the Cape Verde Islands
toward an unknown target on the east coast of the United
States. Once the report was pronouncd genuine, many
newcomers to the land of Julia Tuttle and Henry Flagler
hastened to return north.

During nineteen days of tension, some Miami residents
tried to rig makeshift barriers that they hoped might protect their homes from Spanish bullets. Then it was
learned that the enemy fleet had reached a Cuban seaport.
For the first time since the destruction of the battleship
Maine, Floridians began to feel secure.

The hull of the U.S.S. Maine *was launched at Brooklyn in 1890.*
[HARPER'S WEEKLY]

Strained relations between the United States and Spain in the late 1890s were made worse by a clamor for independence on the part of many Cubans. Tens of thousands of Americans felt it their patriotic duty to go to the aid of revolutionary forces on the island and, simultaneously, to give Spain a licking she would never forget.

President McKinley authorized the mission that took the U.S.S. *Maine* to Havana—into Spanish waters. The battleship was sent there, said the president, to protect American lives and property during the revolution that was sure to break out very soon.

Twenty-one days after her anchor was dropped, the *Maine* was ripped apart by a tremendous explosion that took the lives of approximately 264 crew members. Before an investigation could be launched, the newspaper empire of William Randolph Hearst began clamoring for war with Spain as retaliation for events on the night of February 15, 1898.

"Remember the *Maine!*" became a national battlecry. Congress authorized a three hundred percent increase in the size of the regular army and the creation of a volunteer force of two hundred thousand men. President McKinley asked lawmakers for a formal resolution to permit him to take steps to restore peace to Cuba.

In a joint resolution of April 20, Congress recognized the independence of Cuba, demanded the withdrawal of Spanish armed forces, and authorized the president to use any means necessary to implement congressional wishes.

America's navy, far stronger than the Spanish navy and a great deal better prepared for war than the U.S. Army, threw up a blockade around Cuba. Goaded into action, Spain declared war on April 24. One day later, the United States declared war upon Spain.

Even before the formal declaration of war, Americans knew that Florida would be the jumping-off place for the struggle in Cuba. On the peninsula few failed to realize that the coming military action would pump immense amounts of money into the local economy.

U.S. Army headquarters were established in Tampa, with Gen. William R. Shafter in command. Before reaching his post, he issued orders that led to expansion of the camps around Miami. Soon more than seven thousand men were spending their paychecks in the city that a few months earlier had been described as economically depressed.

So many volunteers flocked to Florida camps that it was difficult to house and to feed them. Everywhere, Americans of almost every persuasion were eager for the war. Assistant Secretary of the Navy Theodore Roosevelt resigned his post to become a lieutenant colonel in a cavalry unit headed for Cuba.

Key West became the headquarters of the American naval operation. Special excitement was created on May 26, when the battleship *Oregon* reached the Florida port after having steamed 14,760 miles from San Francisco. Her tremendous journey around Cape Horn added to growing American interest in building a canal across the Isthmus of Panama to cut weeks off voyages from one coast of the United States to the other.

A naval court of inquiry, established to investigate the

One-time Rough Rider
Theodore   Roosevelt,
president of the United
States.

explosion that sent the *Maine* to the bottom, reported, "A
submarine mine" no doubt planted by Spaniards was
clearly the culprit, said the court.

That hasty conclusion became highly suspect in later
decades. The cause of the explosion has never been definitely proved. Today it is believed that Spain had nothing
to do with it and that careless handling of ammunition,
gun-cotton, or detonators—even coal dust in fuel
bunkers—could have ignited to launch a chain reaction
within the ship. But in 1898 no one wished to examine
alternatives that might relieve Spain of culpability.

Military movement proceeded with such speed there
was much confusion at Florida bases. When the time set
for invasion by land forces was reached, it proved impossible to get horses aboard ships hardly big enough for the
troops consigned to them. As a result, the animals remained in Florida, causing Teddy Roosevelt and his famous Rough Riders to charge up San Juan Hill on foot.

In spite of gaffs such as this, "the splendid little war"
was a howling success for the United States—and for
Florida. So much money poured into Miami that the city

was able to open a telephone exchange before the end of 1898. Throughout the state, buildings erected for military purposes were converted into civilian uses. A few camps and installations were made permanent, notably the naval base at Key West.

Even more important than the big financial gains from the war was the assurance that—at last—Floridians need have no more fear of Spain. The war that lasted for only 105 days of combat resulted in Spain's loss of much of her centuries-old empire. Simultaneously, the United States became established—for the first time—as a world power. It gained new territories: Guam, the Philippines, and Puerto Rico. Accepting its "destiny" of imperialism, it annexed the Hawaiian Republic, previously a virtual protectorate. The U.S. Navy was now dominant in the Caribbean Sea, and long-dormant plans for building a trans-Isthmian canal were revived.

As for the victims of the *Maine* disaster, Spanish authorities initially offered to bury them in Cuba. That idea was indignantly rejected; these heroes would be buried only on American soil—at Arlington National Cemetery.

55

Julia Tuttle Sent Orange Blossoms to Flagler

At St. Augustine on the night before Christmas 1894, it was apparent that Henry M. Flagler's dreams for Florida might well prove to be empty. The thermometer had dropped to about eighteen degrees, and long before word began trickling to his headquarters, the hotel and railroad builder knew that most of the state's citrus and vegetable crops were destroyed.

Flagler acted with characteristic speed. Aides were assigned to stricken areas, told to get there by the fastest possible means, and immediately to begin giving assistance to farmers, ranchers, and citrus growers. Tradition has it that Flagler was at the bank before it opened on December 26 to withdraw one hundred thousand dollars in cash and distribute it among his messengers.

Although the winter vegetable market was strong and growing rapidly, the citrus industry remained the dominant money producer of Florida. While the loss of an entire crop was bad enough, even worse, Flagler insisted, was the probability that many in the north would lose confidence in the ability of his adopted state to produce without interruption.

As Henry M. Flagler paced the floor, firing off telegrams and waiting for firm assessments of damage, a messenger appeared. "This is for Mr. Flagler, personally," he told the aide who stepped forward.

There was momentary uncertainty, during which the messenger remained unyielding. He would not deliver his package to anyone other than the man to whom it was

consigned. When Flagler finally came into the room, to his astonishment he was handed a bundle of orange blossoms.

"They come from Mrs. Julia Tuttle at Biscayne," said the messenger. "She again invites you to visit her at Fort Dallas and to inspect fields and groves without frost damage."

Half a dozen stories circulate about the events that followed Julia Tuttle's gift. One of them, perhaps the most believable, has the railroad magnate and chief aide James Ingraham boarding a launch and heading south without waiting to pack their belongings. After transferring to a mule-drawn wagon at New River, they reached Fort Dallas muddy and bedraggled where Julia Tuttle greeted them at the gate.

"We have corresponded often, but now I am here in person," said John D. Rockefeller's business partner. "I am Henry Flagler, and these must be the shores of paradise itself!"

According to that account, Flagler and Mrs. Tuttle talked for less than an hour, then drew up a tentative agreement for development of the area surrounding Fort Dallas.

Born in Ohio to a mother who had taught in the Indian

school at Tallahassee, Julia Tuttle's ties with Florida were strong. After her marriage, her parents moved to the peninsula, where she often visited them. When Frederick Tuttle died of tuberculosis in 1886, his widow decided to take her two children where they would be unlikely to die of their father's illness.

A quick look at California was enough; after her second day in the state, she decided she preferred south Florida. Long-abandoned Fort Dallas looked as though it could be repaired and used as a residence, so she bought the post once used by soldiers, with 644 surrounding acres.

Soon after having become a permanent resident of Florida in November 1891, Julia Tuttle began badgering Henry M. Flagler. Time after time, she tried to persuade him to visit her region. If he would only come, she insisted, he would decide to extend his railroad to Biscayne Bay.

Usually polite Flagler became impatient at the widow's continued pleas. His replies to her letters became increasingly terse, even abrupt. Yes, he was well aware she was willing to deed half of her land to him. No, he did not intend to extend his rail line below Lake Worth. Yes, he really was planning to dig a great canal, by means of

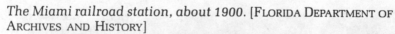

The Miami railroad station, about 1900. [FLORIDA DEPARTMENT OF ARCHIVES AND HISTORY]

which Lake Worth would be linked with Biscayne by water. No, he would not use barges on the canal; it would become an important route for steamers.

Rebuffed many times, Julia Tuttle persevered. And her orange blossoms, delivered during the panic of the great freeze of 1894–95, produced results. No other persuasion was needed. Flagler could see that the great tract of land between the southern tip of the Everglades and the Atlantic Ocean was perhaps the most protected place in all Florida. At least forty miles long, it offered shelter from even the severest winter weather.

The developer and the widow entered into a formal contract in February 1895. She retained Fort Dallas and thirteen surrounding acres. One hundred acres of her land was designated as the site for a railroad terminal, sidings, and a hotel.

More than five hundred acres of undeveloped land remained. Julia Tuttle refused to cede her land in one big block, even though she had earlier promised to give Flagler half of it in return for bringing a railroad to the region. Instead, she divided the acreage into strips, then deeded alternate ones to Flagler, keeping the rest for herself.

Henry Morrison Flagler [THE HENRY MORRISON FLAGLER MUSEUM]

Once the deal was completed, Flagler swung into action. Soon the sleepy fishing village of Miami was incorporated. Gangs of laborers recruited throughout the state worked to build a water tower, lay out streets, and cut a channel deep enough to permit ocean-going steamers to make Miami a port of call. Flagler made plans to build what would be his finest hotel and pushed the promised extension of his railroad.

By the time the first locomotive reached the site of modern Miami in February 1896, Julia Tuttle was busy with her own enterprises. From a small herd of cows, she expanded to form the Fort Dallas dairy, which won the contract to supply milk to all of Flagler's hotels. She bought stock in the Bank of Bay Biscayne, Miami's first bank, and became a director of it. With land values going up, she refused to part with any of the strips she retained in the arrangement with Flagler. Instead of selling, she bought land as rapidly as possible, even when she had to borrow to do so. Many guests from the north who attended the gala opening of Flagler's lemon-yellow Royal Palm Hotel were awed to learn that a nondescript looking woman held title to much of the region.

To finance her dairy and other enterprises, at age forty-seven the widow needed forty thousand dollars. Her bank did not have that much cash to lend, so she persuaded Flagler to endorse her note issued by a New York bank. Then, in the backwash of the Panic of 1893, the directors of the New York bank sounded as though they might demand immediate payment in cash.

Desperate, Julia Tuttle reputedly turned to Flagler once more. This time she offered him her entire Miami holdings for eighty thousand dollars. Flagler is said to have responded that he already owned half of Miami and did not need the other half. Therefore, at her death in September 1898, half of Miami was inherited by her heirs.

At the time the will was probated, a keen observer noted that "The decedent, Mrs. Julia DeForest Sturdevant Tuttle, was a Biscayne resident for only seven years."

56

Key West Was Home to Hemingway

Back in the "good old days" before television, the big entertainment in the sleepy little town of Key West was the weekly prize fight held in the old arena once used for cockfights when the town had been a cigar-making center. Spectators sat on bare pine board bleachers and only bet among themselves.

Suddenly, in 1929, it began to be suspected that dirty dealings had started, that some fighters (they were all nonprofessionals) were throwing fights, for a price.

One Saturday night the big favorite suddenly fell to his knees. A spectator, a self-appointed vigilante, jumped into the ring, grabbed the fighter who had struck a foul blow unseen by most of the audience, and grimly spoke to him. Immediately the boy raced to the center of the ring and shouted the confession, "I did it! I fouled him!"

A wave of huzzahs erupted from the stands in honor of the alert citizen who had settled the problem. His name was Ernest Hemingway.

The writer's "Key West period" began in 1928 when he and his pregnant second wife, Pauline, returned from Europe wanting to find a relaxing, inexpensive place to live, work, and raise children—and to fish. An old book he had read on fishing in Florida had suggested Key West to Hemingway.

In their yellow Model-A Ford convertible coupe, the Hemingways drove and ferried to the southernmost town in the United States, a sleepy, almost-forgotten little spot peopled mainly by small-time commercial fishermen and their families. The last big excitement there had been the

Tennessee Williams in Key West, about 1960 [UNIVERSITY OF TEXAS AT AUSTIN]

Spanish-American War thirty years earlier when Key West was the place for coaling steamers and dispatching news.

A century earlier when the artist John James Audubon had arrived looking for pink flamingos, the now-quiet village had been a booming seaport.

After living in several rental places, in 1931 the Hemingways bought an old Spanish house built in 1851 opposite the lighthouse. They modernized it, adding a pool house with showers and dressing rooms and an upstairs workroom for Hemingway. The author contributed personal touches that revealed his lifelong preoccupation with struggle: a Spanish birthing chair, a silent reminder of the pain with which life begins; a statue of a bullfighter, symbolizing the ever-present life-or-death drama of living; a mounted head of a wildebeest shot on his first African safari, showing that even the fleetest of foot cannot always escape the hunter; and a model of the Civil War ironclad *Monitor*, proclaiming, "Here is the home of a man fascinated by war."

Then there were the cats, six-toed ones, that soon became multigenerational. More than forty of their descendants still live at the same address, 907 Whitehead Street.

Son Patrick was born to the Hemingways in 1928 and Gregory in 1931.

Meanwhile *A Farewell to Arms* was finished, first handwritten because Hemingway refused to use a type-writer, then copied by a secretary.

While Key West was a good place to work, it was also a very good place to enjoy life. For the Hemingways that meant fishing. One of Ernest's fishing cronies was Josey Russell, owner of the bar off Duval Street and a regular rum runner between Cuba and the Keys. He introduced the author to marlin fishing in the Gulf Stream out of Havana, possibly one source of inspiration for *The Old Man and the Sea* that was published years later. It is known that Josey was translated into the character of Harry Morgan in *To Have and Have Not*, which was writ-ten and set in Key West.

As Leicester Hemingway recalled in *My Brother, Ernest Hemingway*, the fishing parties would be well-stocked with gin, key limes, sugar, and ice water. "Papa" Heming-way's preferred costume always was a blue-striped Basque fishing shirt and beltless khaki pants. "One hor-rified local lady declared," Leicester remembered, "that he always looked like he'd just pulled his pants on and planned to pull them off again any second."

The Hemingways did not remain in Florida constantly. They traveled out West, to Cuba, to Europe and Africa. When the Spanish Civil War broke out in 1936, he went to Spain.

The next summer, 1937, as he was preparing to return to cover the war for the North American Newspaper Al-liance, a visitor came to Key West. Leicester Hemingway recorded that magazine writer Martha Gellhorn walked into Sloppy Joe's bar, saw Ernest's name on one of the bar stools, and asked when the author might be expected. "It's almost three o'clock. If he's in town, he'll be coming in," the bartender replied.

Ms. Gellhorn, a statuesque blonde, waited and got her interview. She also got her man, as she became the third Mrs. Ernest Hemingway in 1940. Hemingway did not re-

Hemingway's upright Royal typewriter [HEMINGWAY HOUSE AND MUSEUM]

turn to live in Florida. Pauline, the second Mrs. Hemingway, received the Key West house in the divorce settlement.

Other writers had ties to Key West. In 1926 the poet Hart Crane, while staying on Cuba's Isle of Pines, wrote many of his poems later collected as *Key West: An Island Sheaf* and published posthumously.

In the early 1940s, playwright Tennessee Williams drifted around the country working at odd jobs and picking up impressions of people and places that became the raw materials of his plays, such as *The Glass Menagerie, A Streetcar Named Desire, Cat on a Hot Tin Roof, Camino Real,* and *The Rose Tattoo.* For a while he lived in Key West where he said he had a "love affair with a fishing village barely out of sight of Havana."

57

FDR Was Saved by the Wife of a Miami Physician

"Mr. Roosevelt talked only about two minutes—extending his greetings to the people of the Florida East Coast.

"Then he got back into his open automobile, about fifteen feet away. He had hardly settled in the back seat when I got up from the bench where I was sitting, in order to get a better look.

"That's when this fellow—dark, with curly hair—stood up on the same bench. Since the bench was made to fold in the middle, I thought I might fall. So I turned around and said, 'Please stand still; you're about to knock me off the bench!'

"That's when I first saw he had a pistol in his hand. I think I must have cried out, 'O my God, he's going to kill Mr. Roosevelt!' At the same time, I switched my handbag to my left arm and used my right hand to grab him and twist his arm upward."

Pausing in her story to respond to a question from a Miami reporter, Mrs. Lillian Cross pondered and then slowly shook her head. "I'm sorry," she said, "I really don't know how many shots were fired or who they hit. But I do know that his gun was pointed right at Mr. Roosevelt, over my shoulder. After I grabbed him, I don't know exactly what did happen."

When met by physician-surgeon Dr. W. F. Cross, his hundred-pound wife was visibly shaken, but smiling. Almost instantly, he noticed that her right cheek was grimy, marked by gunpowder from the pistol of the man who

*Voter dissatisfaction with economic ills contributed largely to
F.D.R.'s smashing victory in 1932.*

nearly succeeded in killing the president-elect, Franklin
D. Roosevelt, on February 15, 1933.

Sent to the White House by popular mandate in the
election of 1932, Roosevelt planned to relax during the
weeks before his March inauguration. With the Great Depression gripping the nation, he would have little time for
relaxation once he took the oath of office.

Thus he accepted the invitation of wealthy Vincent Astor for an extended fishing trip in southern waters. Eleven
days after having boarded the yacht *Nourmahal*, Roosevelt docked at Pier 1 in Miami Harbor. Plans called for
him to make a brief personal appearance in Bayfront Park,
accompanied by political allies headed by Chicago's
Mayor Anton Cermak.

Riding in an open car, the president-elect was delighted
to see an estimated fifteen thousand people waiting for
him, with the Dade County Courthouse in the background. Sixty Miami policemen were stationed in the
park, and one hundred more were posted along streets
through which a motorcycle escort of twenty uniformed
men led the motorcade. Six Secret Service operatives

headed by Capt. J. H. Reidy made Roosevelt's personal bodyguard feel "pushed aside." Yet Reidy remained as close to the president-elect as circumstances permitted.

Soon after Roosevelt's election to the nation's highest office, Vice President-elect John Garner, had warned him that he could expect attempts upon his life. Smiling, FDR repeated a Theodore Roosevelt quotation that Garner had heard before: "The only real danger from an assassin is from one who does not care whether he loses his own life in the act or not. Most of the crazy ones can be spotted first."

Because that mood of confidence extended to aides who traveled with Roosevelt, when shots were fired in the bright Florida sunshine, one of them thought he had heard a car backfire. Roosevelt later admitted that he heard the sound, but attributed it to a firecracker. By the time the sound was repeated four more times, almost everyone in Bayfront Park knew that a pistol was being fired.

Chicago's Mayor Cermak, said spectators, was knocked from the running board of the open automobile by the first shot. He dropped to the ground, where he twisted in agony while the gunman emptied his weapon.

In addition to mortally wounded Cermak, four other people were hit by one or more of the five bullets that were fired. William Sinnott, once a New York City policeman, was shot in the head. So was twenty-two-year-old Russell Caldwell of Miami. Mrs. Joe H. Gill, wife of the president of the Florida Power and Light Company, was shot through the abdomen and was listed as in critical condition. Margaret Kruis, visiting from New Jersey, escaped with a minor injury to her hand.

Aware only that she had saved the life of the president-elect, Lillian Cross was bowled over by spectators who rushed to seize the gunman. "Kill him! Kill him!" they yelled as they converged upon Giuseppe Zangara, the would-be assassin.

From his seat in the automobile, Roosevelt shouted at the top of his lungs that he was not hurt. "Leave the poor fellow to the police," he ordered. The men who had seized Zangara obeyed, wordless.

Ready to talk—even eager—the gunman was sufficiently lucid to say he was glad he had hit Cermak. He hated all persons of power and wealth, he told Miami detectives. In Italy, which he had left only a few years earlier, he had seen the rich and powerful send their children to school, while children of poor men like his father went to work mending shoes and baking bread.

Drifting about Miami, the unemployed bricklayer chanced upon a pawn shop where he bought a .32 caliber pistol for eight dollars. A newspaper story about the upcoming visit of the president-elect to Miami had prompted him to spend his last cash to purchase the weapon.

"I tried to get to the park early," he told police. "I thought that it would be easy to get close to him, but lots of people were there ahead of me.

President Franklin Delano Roosevelt

"I sat on a bench, waiting, and my stomach—where I had a big operation that left this scar—kept aching worse than ever. I planned to hit Roosevelt while he was talking, but he sat down very soon and I couldn't get a good shot through the people in front of me."

Zangara, who was only five feet, one inch tall, waited until spectators in front of him tired and sat down. "That gave me my big chance," he said. "I stood up on my bench and took good aim at Mr. Roosevelt. When the bench started to wobble, a little lady grabbed me. I think she must have tried to choke me. Anyway, I got off five shots, but I knew that I had missed my man."

On the twenty-first floor of the Dade County Courthouse where the jail was located, Zangara was questioned by psychiatrists. They agreed that he was very strange, but they were not sure he could not be tried.

Meanwhile, Mrs. Eleanor Roosevelt received the news in New York City from a butler who stammered with excitement. Learning that her husband was not injured, she told reporters, "These things are to be expected." Later she placed a telephone call and managed to reach her husband at the bedside of Anton Cermak.

They talked briefly, then Mrs. Roosevelt told reporters and friends, "He's all right; he isn't even excited." Shortly afterward, accompanied only by her maid, the first lady-to-be boarded a train bound for Ithaca, New York, to fill a speaking engagement.

Security was beefed up immediately. In Miami, Roosevelt's guard detail was doubled. In Washington, Richard Jarvis sent Secret Service agents to augment the two-man force then guarding the White House "in spite of the fact that President Hoover had retired for the night." In New York, where Roosevelt soon reported to keep a speaking engagement at the Hotel Astor, 550 police were detailed to prevent another assassination attempt.

Without exception, professional lawmen who studied the bizarre events in Miami agreed that had it not been for diminutive Lillian Cross, the nation might never have had what came to be called the New Deal. Robert P. Gore of

Philadelphia, a longtime friend of the president-elect, was standing by the automobile when Zangara began shooting. He told reporters for the Philadelphia *Record*, "It happened so suddenly that practically everyone was stunned into inaction." But, he added, while bewildered professionals tried to see what was taking place, "a woman threw her arms around the assailant's neck and tried to strangle him while he was still shooting."

That vivid description may have been somewhat embellished, but there was never any doubt about the significance of the actions of the Florida housewife. From New York, Roosevelt sent Lillian Cross a two hundred-word telegram of thanks for her "prompt and courageous action." Congressman Green of Florida proposed in the House of Representatives that she be awarded the Congressional Medal of Honor for heroism in a moment of crisis.

When Anton Cermak died, the charge against Zangara was changed to murder, followed by a swift trial. He was executed on March 20, barely five weeks after the attempted assassination.

Four months after Zangara went to the electric chair, headlines of the nation were dominated by FDR's proposals to aid millions of Americans made penniless by the Great Depression. Concurrently, Representative Allgood of Alabama was pleased when his colleagues approved a resolution he had introduced. It solemnly expressed "thanks and grateful appreciation to Mrs. W. F. Cross of Miami" for her role in making it possible for a stricken America to benefit from the New Deal.

58

Colin Kelly Became the First Hero of World War II

"No doubt about it; Colin made a suicide run," General Henry H. ("Hap") Arnold confided to aides. "He makes me proud to be a West Pointer—and makes every American hold his head higher."

Before he issued a formal statement, the chief of the newly established Army Air Force summarized the drama-filled last flight of Madison native Colin P. Kelly, Jr.

"Captain Kelly sighted the Japanese battleship *Haruna*, and recognized her to be heavily armed," he said. "Captain Kelly was at the helm of one of our handful of undamaged B-17s and knew that he would come in range of antiaircraft guns long before he could release his bomb load.

"Yet he flew directly into enemy fire to plant three bombs on his target. My greatest regret is that the brave Florida flier may have gone to his death without knowing that he had accomplished his mission."

When news of Kelly's exploit reached the mainland from Manila, on December 12, 1941, Americans took to the streets. Impromptu parades were staged in honor of the man labeled by headlines as "The Nation's First War Hero."

Part of the jubilation stemmed from a national mood of anger and sorrow after Pearl Harbor. Never before had the United States suffered a blow such as that struck by the Japanese at 7:00 A.M. on Sunday, December 7, 1941.

Tension between the United States and Japan had been increasing for months, yet the attack on Pearl Harbor

Colin P. Kelly, Jr., United States Military Academy class of 1937.
[USMA Archives]

came as a surprise, crippling the Pacific Fleet. Five battleships were sunk, nine other naval vessels were badly damaged, 200 planes were destroyed, and 2,344 men died on what President Franklin D. Roosevelt labeled as "a day that will live in infamy."

Meanwhile, the Japanese onslaught continued. Nearly simultaneous attacks were made against Malaya, Hong Kong, and the Philippines. Just ten hours after Pearl Harbor, enemy planes hit Clark Field in the Philippines. This time they lost only seven of their planes but left the American Far East Air Corps in shambles. Half of the thirty-five B-17s stationed there were destroyed, along with fifty-six fighter planes and twenty-five other aircraft.

Wartime censorship prevented reporters from getting timely interviews with comrades of Colin P. Kelly, but later some of them confided that the twenty-six-year-old Floridian took a solemn vow within hours after hearing of the attack on Pearl Harbor.

"My crew and I are going to get the attention of Tokyo," he reportedly promised. "It will take only one Flying Fortress to show Hirohito that Americans can't be given a blow below the belly without hitting back—hard."

Piloting a Flying Fortress bomber out of Manila just forty-eight hours after Pearl Harbor, Captain Kelly spotted the Japanese naval task force in Philippine waters. It included the *Haruna*, a 29,330-ton warship. Enemy fire made it impossible to attempt a practice run over the target, so he had to head directly toward her for a single pass, with antiaircraft fire growing heavier as he approached.

Later, General Douglas MacArthur, commander of the U.S. Army Far Eastern Force, issued a one-sentence communiqué: "With great sorrow, I must announce the death of Captain Colin P. Kelly, Jr., who so distinguished himself by scoring three direct hits on the Japanese capital battleship *Haruna*, leaving her in flames and in distress."

Censorship prevented release of details other than a subsequent communiqué that reported the sinking of the *Haruna* on December 9 somewhere north of Luzon.

A Flying Fortress, hit on the ground at Hickam Field in the attack on Pearl Harbor. [NATIONAL ARCHIVES]

In Brooklyn, where she had gone to be with her parents, Kelly's widow met reporters with her arms around her eighteen-month-old son. "My husband was a marvelous officer," she said, "the first West Point graduate to pilot a Flying Fortress. I am very proud of him, and when Colin III gets a little older, he will be very proud, too."

Colin Kelly had been appointed to the U.S. Military Academy in 1933, when he was eighteen. He played football, sang in the cadet choir, and became a crack shot with the pistol. When he graduated, he was commissioned a second lieutenant of infantry. But at a time when the Air Corps was not generally regarded as very important, he requested and got an assignment to that branch.

Less than a week after his death, Florida congressmen began seeking a posthumous Congressional Medal of Honor for Colin Kelly. Five days later, an army air unit in Detroit was named for him. Planes were sent to Madison for a memorial service on December 20, and on December 24 the British American Ambulance Corps began forming a unit to commemorate America's first hero of World War II.

Colin P. Kelly III,
United States Military
Academy Class of 1963.
[USMA Archives].

On December 17 President Franklin D. Roosevelt wrote a directive that began, "To the President of the United States in 1956." Ironically, that chief executive would be the World War II general Dwight D. Eisenhower. Roosevelt's letter requested special consideration of the future president on behalf of Colin P. Kelly III, should he in 1956 wish to become a cadet at the U.S. Military Academy.

"I make this appeal in behalf of this youth as a token of the Nation's appreciation of the heroic services of his father who met death in line of duty at the very outset of the struggle which was thrust upon us by the perfidy of a professed friend," Roosevelt wrote.

Years later, Colin Purdie Kelly III accepted the help offered by President Eisenhower. Kelly graduated from West Point in 1963 and after twenty years in uniform retired as a lieutenant colonel.

The annals of West Point are rich with human interest. But they include no other saga quite like that of the father-son graduates from Florida.

59

America Probes the Universe from Cape Canaveral

Kennedy, Cape: Point of land extending into the Atlantic Ocean about 14 miles northeast of Cocoa and 51 miles east-southeast of Orlando; named for John Fitzgerald Kennedy (1917–1963), the thirty-fifth President of the United States; Brevard County; 28 degrees 27' 30" N., 80 degrees 32' 00" W. Nautical: Cabo de Canareal, Cape Canaveral.
—U.S. Board on Geographic Names, April 2, 1964

The publication of this brief notice completed the legal procedure to change an American place name. For practical purposes, official Washington and the nation at large assumed that the change took place four months earlier, on November 28, 1963.

That evening, President Lyndon B. Johnson broadcast a Thanksgiving message from the White House. Near the end of it, he announced, "Cape Canaveral, site of the United States space facility on the Florida east coast, will henceforth be known as Cape Kennedy."

Jacqueline Kennedy, widely believed to have urged that the change be made, expressed her gratitude to the president and to the nation. "There has been talk of a permanent memorial to my late husband," she said, "but until now, it has only been talk. Cape Kennedy will commemorate his memory during all future generations."

At the same time that he announced the presidential decision to alter the terminology of Florida's map, Johnson said that installations housed there would become the Kennedy Space Center.

Geographer Amerigo Vespucci gave Cape Canaveral its enduring name.

Most—but not all—Americans took the surprise announcement in stride. It was widely known that a proposed national culture center in Washington, D.C., might be named in honor of the assassinated chief executive. Since that project was still in the idea stage, it was generally agreed that renaming the cape was fitting, timely, and permanent.

That point of view did not prevail in Brevard County.

Public reaction was swift, surprisingly strong, and almost entirely negative. Within days, organizers began planning public rallies to protest the presidential mandate. At such gatherings, many people not generally regarded as activists turned up to register their opposition to the change.

"Cabo de Canareal," as the Spanish called it, is the oldest place name in the United States, listeners learned. It is known that it was given that name by the Spanish who came after Ponce De León.

Many authorities agree that it won a permanent place on the map through the influence of Amerigo Vespucci, for whom America is named. He is believed to have modified it to the form that had prevailed for nearly 450 years—Cape Canaveral.

Almost every public rally held in response to President Johnson's surprise announcement ended with a formal resolution. Most such statements praised John F. Kennedy, noted that he was "almost a Floridian through years spent at his father's West Palm Beach home," lamented his untimely death, and demanded a quick reversal of the change in name. "We must not let sentiment of the moment deter us from working to preserve the oldest symbol of European influence in the nation," one set of resolutions ended.

Editors of reference books, either not aware of events in Brevard County or indifferent to them, proceeded to follow the White House mandate. An edition of a popular encyclopedia includes this paragraph:

> In 1513 the explorer Ponce de León claimed the Florida region for Spain. In 1958, *Explorer I*, America's first earth satellite, soared into space from Florida's Cape Canaveral (now Cape Kennedy). The years between these two famous explorers are rich in Florida history.

Accurate when it was printed, that summary failed to take into account the fervor and tenacity of Floridians who were determined to preserve their heritage. Local leaders won friends in high places and exerted mounting pressure. As a result, Cape Kennedy is no longer on the map. Instead, Cape Canaveral is the site of the Kennedy Space Center.

America's annals include no comparable reversal of a decision to commemorate the memory of a chief executive.

It was another occupant of the White House—Harry S Truman—who gave the go-ahead that made Cape Canaveral the jumping-off place for exploring the universe. In October 1949 he established what was then called the Joint Long Range Proving Ground. Few members of the general public realized that devices to be "proved" or tested there were long-range rockets.

Canaveral projects into the Atlantic in such fashion that it provides a starting point for a five-thousand-mile test range over water. Although that was a decisive matter in 1949, the isolation of Brevard County was also a major consideration. For miles around, the area was practically uninhabited by humans.

Military experts cheered on July 24, 1950, when the first launch was made from Cape Canaveral. A modified German V-2 rocket with an attached upper stage achieved an altitude of about ten miles. America entered the space age on that day.

Col. John H. Glenn blasted off from Canaveral on February 20, 1962. The first American to orbit the earth, he made a five-hour trip that prompted Rep. Victor L. Anfuso of Brooklyn to make an enthusiastic proposal. He introduced a resolution in the House of Representatives whose terms required an official change from Cape Canaveral to Cape Glenn. Unlike the later proclamation of Lyndon B. Johnson, Anfuso's resolution was never taken seriously.

Sir Winston Churchill (right) *helped to persuade President Harry S Truman that the United States should build and test long-range rockets.*

Space Shuttle 41–D seemed ready for liftoff in June 1984, but the launch was aborted when the No. 3 engine failed to achieve ignition. [NATIONAL AERONAUTICS AND SPACE ADMINISTRATION]

Fierce loyalty to the time-honored geographical name has made a relatively tiny piece of Florida real estate familiar throughout the world. A listing of famous first achievements made at Cape Canaveral runs to column after column of fine print.

Germans who landed on the Florida beach in 1942 came to cripple the U.S. industrial and military complex. They were foiled by Floridians much like those who balked at the mandate of Lyndon B. Johnson and succeeded in having it rescinded. Ironically, it was other Germans, Wernher von Braun and Kurt Debus, who played key roles in converting the space center at Canaveral from the theoretical to reality.

Thirty years after *Explorer I* put the United States into the space race, Gov. Bob Martinez announced a long-range plan for a state-funded Spaceport at Canaveral. Envisioned as "a port authority for the universe," it promises an economic boom for Titusville and Cocoa Beach.

It is reasonably certain that federal, state, and commercial interests will focus upon this area for decades to come. At the cape first seen by Europeans from the decks of Ponce de León's little vessels, mighty space ships will roar upward toward the limits of the solar system.

60

Brownie Wise Taught the World How to Give a Party

"This is Brownie Wise, calling from Florida. I'd like to speak to the company president, please."

"Hello. This is Earl Tupper. What can I do for you?"

"Mr. Tupper, I hope you can do a lot for me. I'm Brownie Wise, calling from Florida. I'm distributing a lot of Tupperware® brand products, and my shipment is late—for the second time. Can you do something to see that I get deliveries on schedule?"

"Of course I'll do something to correct this situation. But I don't want to stop there. Can you come to Worcester? I'd like to sit down and have a long talk with you."

"Sorry," responded Brownie Wise. "I'd like to meet you, but I can't come. I have twenty dealers who are looking to me to keep their orders filled. If you want to see me, you'll have to come to Miami."

Late in 1949 the inventor of Tupperware products persuaded the Florida divorcee to come to Massachusetts for a conference. He won her over by promising to bring to the company headquarters the half dozen or so other persons who were already distributing and selling Tupperware products on the home party plan.

In Worcester, Earl Tupper soon learned that Brownie Wise had been a distributor of Stanley Home Products, in Dearborn, Michigan, where she had worked as a secretary. For her, the home sale of Stanley products was a sideline, but an important one. A few pieces of houseware made of an unusual new kind of plastic led her to decide to add Tupperware products to her business. Soon she dropped

Stanley Home Products in favor of the faster-moving household bowls and containers of which few people had ever heard.

Much the same thing happened to Stanley distributor Tommy Damigella. He heard of Tupperware products, began buying them from a Boston distributor, and found them to have so much appeal that he gave up all other lines.

At the 1949 conference in Worcester, Massachusetts, Tommy and Brownie exchanged experiences. Four years on the market, Tupperware products had made no significant impact.

Hardware stores and big department stores handling kitchenware were moving only small quantities. Anyone who tried a product made of the new plastic agreed that it had unique qualities, but the public demand was not great enough to induce store owners to push it.

Before the 1949 gathering ended, Earl Tupper was a convert. He decided to give much less attention to wholesale and retail distributors through conventional channels. In fact, he would go for broke by putting the persuasive woman from Miami in charge of sales.

Tupper, who knew little or nothing about organizing a sales program, was a genius of another sort. Trained in chemistry, he visited an oil refinery one day and noticed that waste produced in the refinement of petroleum was made into blocks about the size of a book. No one had the slightest idea of what to do with these black chunks, and they were thrown away.

Questioned by Tupper, a friend explained that the stuff was called polyethylene. "Sure you can have some of it," he said. "Take all you want and see if you can find some use for it."

Major corporations had already experimented with plastics, but the products produced by their research departments had no sales potential. Items made from these plastics had no eye appeal and seemed to break at the slightest contact.

Experimenting in a home laboratory, Earl Tupper

turned polyethylene into a plastic that could be molded by machinery. His initial test pieces did not look as good as the cheapest glass and china, but they did not break when dropped. Encouraged, but a long way from being certain that he had a successful product, Tupper organized a small South Grafton, Massachusetts, company.

That was in 1942, and Tupper was thirty-five years old. It took months to persuade a few retail stores to begin handling the new plastic pieces and, after having been on the market for a decade, the product line was going nowhere until Brownie Wise was put in charge of sales.

She and the dealers she recruited sold only on the home party plan. At her insistence, dealers met annually to share ideas and brainstorm. "You can't beat people over the head and tell them to buy," she insisted from the first. "Plan a party that will give everyone a good time and will permit participants to make a new friend or two. Demonstrate your products, but only after you know them inside and out. Use the soft-sell approach. Show the merits of Tupperware: their range of colors, the unique seal, and their general eye appeal and utility. When you do a good job with this, you won't have to twist any arms. Party participants will buy without any urging."

By 1951 not a store in the nation was permitted to sell Tupperware products. Brownie Wise made the home party plan the sole sales channel. She traveled Florida for hundreds of miles, above and below Miami, looking for a site at which to erect a headquarters building for what she already envisioned as a global enterprise.

"I've found the perfect place," she exulted in a special report to Earl Tupper. "We can build at low cost between Orlando and Kissimmee and be within easy access of good transportation."

Completed in 1954, the new headquarters building was the site of a "Homecoming Jubilee" that was also a national sales meeting—the company's first. Participants flocked to a newly created lake to help dedicate it to Earl Tupper. They swapped party ideas and applauded with

*Party planner Brownie Wise with inventor Earl
Tupper, dressed for a Jubilee.* [TUPPERWARE
HOME PARTIES]

enthusiasm when they were told that Tupperware was one
of only two major industries in all of central Florida.

In 1951 Brownie Wise agreed to head the newly
organized Tupperware Home Parties Division for only one
year; she did not want to be out of selling for long. Her
first Jubilee in 1954 was so successful that *Life* magazine

ran a special story about it, and she agreed to continue helping others to plan parties instead of holding her own.

Earl Tupper's inventive genius produced a line of products with nearly universal appeal. Brownie Wise developed party ideas so imaginative that approximately eighty million people attend them, worldwide, each year.

In 1970 a three-pavilion headquarters building, with a museum, garden, convention center, and park, began to take shape. Tupperware did for Florida's industry what theme parks did for tourism. Today the brand name is familiar throughout the world, simultaneously American and global in much the same sense as McDonald's® and Coca-Cola®.

From the Florida headquarters, perhaps ninety thousand independent direct sellers in the United States receive guidance, along with at least two hundred thousand more who give Tupperware parties in forty-two countries.

Brownie Wise had no idea of the chain reaction she was about to trigger when she placed her first telephone call to Massachusetts. She would be inordinately proud if she were still at Tupperware, but the Florida woman has not sat back and taken it easy while toting up her triumphs. She now consults with clients throughout the United States.

Men have always sold Tupperware, and the changing nature of the work force has made them increasingly important purchasers. Many purchasers—male or female—are not fully aware of what every independent direct seller knows: Tupperware brand products launched the revolution that has brought plastics into every area of life.

61

"Somebody's Grabbing Up an Awful Lot of Land"

"What's new these days?" inquired California entrepreneur William J. Canole. Owner of a chain of businesses with investor backing, Canole had stepped into a Stuckey's pecan shop. He had a few minutes to kill while he waited for his private plane to take on fuel.

"Not much," responded a native of Orange County. "Looks like we might get a little shower this afternoon." He paused reflectively, eyed the stranger up and down, and commented, "Only real news around here is that somebody's grabbing up an awful lot of land. Everybody I know is selling. One fellow just gave an option for a thousand acres."

Canole thanked the Floridian, canceled his planned departure, and returned to his Orlando hotel room. For at least two weeks, maybe three, he had pored over maps and explored the countryside. From California sources, he knew that central Florida was being considered as the possible site of a vast new Disney theme park. If he could pinpoint the site, he and his clients stood to make fortunes.

Central Florida lore insists that Canole and other scouts for big business studied at least half a dozen other sites east of the Rocky Mountains. Dallas was once believed to have been picked by the Disney people, although many signs pointed toward a St. Louis location.

Trying to appear casual while he followed up on the tip dropped at Stuckey's, Bill Canole went back to the courthouse. His informant was right. Unknown purchasers were acquiring thousands of acres of land.

While tourists flock to Disney World by the millions, excellent fishing is available for tourists and Floridians on nearby Lake Tohepakilaga. [KISSIMMEE/ST. CLOUD VISITORS' BUREAU]

Oldtimers in the region, glad to get two hundred dollars an acre for land that was all but worthless even for grazing cattle, joked about the big buy. With the Ford Motor Company's Mustang surging to popularity, many quipped that "Ford is buying up grazing land to fatten Mustangs before putting them up for sale."

At Disneyland in Anaheim, California, executives were tightlipped. They admitted to having plans for a new enterprise that might entail an initial investment of $400 million or more, but they refused to comment where that money might be spent. First they wanted to acquire all the land they needed at rock bottom prices.

At Walt Disney World today, information is still tightly controlled. Telephone calls and letters inquiring about factors that led to the choice of Osceola and Orange counties as the location for the world's biggest theme park brought no reply. Though eager to have photographs in newspapers and magazines, executives refuse permission to use them in books. But it is a different story at the Kissimmee–St. Cloud Convention and Visitors Bureau.

Staff members are not only willing to answer questions and talk freely; they cheerfully volunteer information.

"Lots of folks called both of these places 'cow towns' until very recently," an executive confided. "They were more than half right. Ranchers drove their herds right through the middle of town, down to the depot where animals were loaded for shipment."

Most people who lived in central Florida before the explosion that took place October 1, 1971, concede that the Disney Enterprise scouts knew their business. "They studied tourist flow, climate, population trends, and transportation systems," say natives. "But most of all, they looked for a place where they could get lots and lots of land."

Irlo Bronson, who once owned large acreage now part of Disney World, points out that until it became the site of an entertainment mecca, it really was not worth much. There were orange groves and some good cattle ranches, but, says Bronson, "Lots of that land was consistently too wet or too dry—no good, really, even for use as cattle ranges or game preserves."

Craig Linton, Sr., of Orlando, operated a real estate firm called Florida Ranchlands. By the time he and other realtors finished closing land deals, the Disney people held title to 27,443 acres, a forty-three square mile undeveloped tract in central Florida, more than twice the size of Manhattan Island.

Much earlier Walt Disney had confided that he had a vision of a completely new kind of family entertainment. He wanted lots of room on which to build, and extra holdings for future expansion. A bit wistfully, he more than once confessed, "Here at Disneyland [in California], we have been cramped from the first; it would be wonderful to have the blessing of unlimited size."

Disney agents chose the Osceola–Orange County region in 1964, but kept their plans hidden for more than a year while they acquired the immense acreage they wanted. When they made their announcement, everyone in Osceola County knew that life would never be the same again.

The population of the county was 19,020 in 1960; in three decades it increased nearly five hundred percent. The number of jobs increased tenfold from 4,606. The average annual income moved from $3,368 to just under $20,000.

These local changes are just the side effects from the colossal impact of visitors. A few tourists visited Osceola County as early as the 1940s, but when the Disney location was revealed to an expectant world, the county had just 482 hotel rooms, a figure that has jumped nearly forty-fold.

The addition of EPCOT Center—an Experimental Prototype Community of Tomorrow—brought another huge increase in the number of visitors. Described by many as "a permanent World's Fair," EPCOT has created a ripple effect. So many people go there that traditional World's Fairs such as those in Knoxville and New Orleans no longer have enough drawing power to be financially successful.

Shingle Creek, only minutes away from Disney World, retains much of the tranquility that marked the "pre-Disney era." [Kissimmee/St. Cloud Visitors' Bureau]

In 1971 Economic Research Associates forecast that during the first ten years of Walt Disney World, the theme park would add $6.6 billion to Florida's economy. Tax revenues were estimated to jump by $343 million during that period, and newcomers to the state were expected to spend $70 million on about thirty-seven thousand new residential units.

If that early projection erred, it was on the side of caution. No one has devised a method to measure the impact made by Walt Disney World and EPCOT. With the Disney/MGM Studios theme park added, growing numbers of international visitors make the complex a world center of tourism.

At the same time, other forces have been at work. Satellite facilities and other amusement parks have sprung up throughout the state to reap tourist dollars. Many vacationers find the climate so alluring that they choose to become Floridians.

At the turn of the century, Florida ranked thirty-second among the states in population. During the next fifty years it climbed slowly, to twentieth place. During the twenty years that followed 1950, populaton jumped nearly three hundred percent—from 2,771,305 to 6,789,443. All of this growth took place before the Disney theme park really got started. This "progress" occasionally disgruntles some oldtimers. While they like the new prosperity, they have been heard to complain that the state is becoming overcrowded. And the boom shows no signs of diminishing.

The Kissimmee–St. Cloud region is truly a world-class center for family-oriented entertainment. Visitors can drive to either the Atlantic or Gulf coasts in about one hour. They can also include in their itineraries these attractions: Sea World, Busch Gardens, the Kennedy Space Center, Wet 'n Wild, Gatorland Zoo, Tupperware Exhibit and Museum, Alligatorland Safari Zoo, Arabian Nights, Medieval Times Dinner Tournament, Xanadu, Water Mania, and other fun activities.

*   *   *

Juan Ponce de León was pleased to sight what he called the "land of flowers." But neither the Spanish who followed him, the French and English who fought over it, the Seminoles and runaways who took refuge in it, nor the Americans who built winter homes by the seashore in the early twentieth century, could envision what war, space, and Mickey Mouse would do to the more desolate region of central Florida.

PART SIX:
Alabama

Tomochichi and Toonahowi. [VERELIST PAINTING]

62

Tomochichi: Early Exile

Native Americans living just west of the lower Chattahoochee River had been there for centuries when Hernando de Soto launched his explorations. Possibly from a term with the general meaning of "swampland," they called themselves Muscogees. When the English settlers made early contacts with these people, they noticed that running streams were especially numerous in the region they inhabited. As a result, they called these "dwellers along the waterways" Creeks.

Since the Creeks had no written language, precise knowledge about them in the seventeenth century is scarce. Tradition says that all male infants were called *ticbanes* at birth and were given names only when they reached manhood at age fifteen or sixteen.

One of the ticbanes who made his appearance just before or after 1650 was called Tomochichi when he went through the rites of passage to manhood. Highly intelligent and inquisitive, he lived relatively uneventfully for more than sixty years. Then, already quite old by tribal standards, he seems suddenly to have become a nuisance or a problem to his tribe.

Precisely what took place within his village, no one knows. This much is certain, however. At about age seventy the Alabamian became an exile. Crossing the Chattahoochee River, he put as much distance as possible between him and the Creeks with whom he had spent so many years.

Tomochichi didn't stop moving toward the east until he was close to the Atlantic Ocean. At a spot on the Savannah River about twenty miles from the sea, he gathered a small band of followers from a subtribal group calling themselves Yamacraws, and they erected a camp that white-skinned trappers and hunters named Yamacraw Village.

Soon the aging Creek, who was homesick for Alabama, learned that two sets of Europeans were struggling for control of the Atlantic Coast. From their base in Florida, the Spanish threatened to overcome the English colonists whose chief settlement was Charleston.

Half a dozen years before Tomochichi selected a site for his new home, a series of Indian attacks had produced what the English settlers called the Yemassee War. Led by the Emperor Brim, the Native Americans claimed to have killed four hundred South Carolinians in a single battle. There were numerous smaller encounters before the tribesmen were defeated and took refuge among the Spanish of Florida.

Tomochichi wanted nothing to do with quarrels among the white factions; perhaps it was defeat in some intertribal struggle that drove him to walk so many miles to the east. Therefore he lived in quiet obscurity until February 12, 1733, when a tiny English ship sailed up the Savannah River.

At a point about four miles downstream from Yamacraw Village, Gen. James Oglethorpe and a small band of followers established a colony they called Savannah. Instead of attacking the newcomers, Tomochichi instructed his warriors to insert white feathers into their hair as signs of friendship. Soon they entered the camp of the Englishmen, dancing to the beat of coconut shells filled with tiny pebbles and shaken rhythmically.

At a spot on present-day Bull Street in Savannah, the Indians reached the tent of Oglethorpe. Communicating through gestures, they offered venison and fruit as tokens of hospitality. Surprised and delighted, the founder of

James Ogle-thorpe, founder of Georgia.

the colony of Georgia wrote to England that he had landed by chance at one of the few spots where the natives seemed to be friendly rather than hostile.

Soon red men and white men found an interpreter. Mary Musgrove, wife of a mixed-breed trader, was distantly related to Emperor Brim and in childhood had learned to speak English as well as her native tongue. Initially relying heavily upon her, Oglethorpe managed to tell Tomochichi that he was ready to draw up a treaty of friendship. On March 21, 1733, just six weeks after the Englishmen had landed, tribesmen and newcomers made a pact.

Eager to display his ally, Oglethorpe took Tomochichi and his nephew Toonahowi, whom he treated as an adopted son, to Charleston for a brief visit. There he learned details of the devastating Yemassee War and realized how fortunate he was to have found an Indian leader who wasn't eager to fight.

When he returned to his encampment less than an hour's walk from Oglethorpe's, Tomochichi arranged for a conclave of Indian chieftains. They gathered in Savannah barely two months after the Englishmen had landed there, and the influence of Oglethorpe's new friend was greatly strengthened. As a result, a new treaty framed in 1735 included dozens of tribal groups that lived along the coast and the interior of what is now Georgia.

Before the treaty became the guarantee that the English colony would survive, Oglethorpe decided to dramatize its importance. Tomochichi was chosen to head a delegation of Yamacraws who would accompany Georgia's founder to London. Others in the party who were treated as dignitaries were Senauki, wife of the aged leader from Alabama, and Toonahowi.

Accompanied by a group of tribesmen, they went with Oglethorpe to Charleston and soon boarded the ship *Algonquin*. Far bigger than any canoe ever seen on the rivers of Alabama, the sailing vessel slowly plowed its way across the Atlantic.

Knowing that the religious leaders of England were eager to claim Indian converts, Oglethorpe had seen to it that someone—perhaps upholsterer Peter Gordon—had taught young Toonahowi well. In a letter written soon after reaching England, Georgia's founder congratulated himself by writing: "A door has been opened for the conversion of the Indians, because one of their chiefs is desirous of having his young people instructed in the science and wisdom of the English, and consequently in the Christian religion."

Described as "a man of advanced age and excellent mind," Tomochichi was considered to be the key to the future success of missionaries. "Toonahowi," reported the English leader, "has already learned the Lord's Prayer in the Indian and English languages."

During a four-month visit to England, the warrior from Alabama and his followers were treated as celebrities. They were taken on tours, showered with gifts, and presented to King George II and Queen Caroline. Tomochichi expressed special delight at "seeing his spirit away from his body." That experience came when William Verelist painted his portrait, his hand resting on the shoulder of Toonahowi.

Recrossing "the great blue water" on "a very large canoe" called *The Prince of Wales,* Tomochichi learned from Oglethorpe that their visit had made many new friends for Georgia. Having been founded as a haven for the destitute and dispossessed of London—not for debtors as often reported—Georgia seemed likely to prosper now.

One major danger for the colony, however, loomed in the distance. Spain hoped to master the entire Atlantic Coast of North America. To do so meant attacking the new, weak colony of Georgia.

Oglethorpe again turned to Tomochichi, and the Native American advised him to make new treaties with large and powerful tribes. Following suggestions made by the warrior who had grown up just west of the Chattahoochee River, the Englishman journeyed into what is now northwestern Georgia. At Coweta Town he persuaded a Creek confederation to confirm earlier grants of land and to pledge loyalty to King George II. After the new treaty was signed on August 21, 1739, it took Georgia's founder nearly a month to return to Savannah.

Upon arrival at his little colony, Oglethorpe was distressed to learn that Tomochichi was lying on his deathbed. Earlier he had been frequently visited by both John Wesley and George Whitefield, two clergymen destined to influence the course of Christianity in the colonies.

Although he respected both men, Tomochichi refused to adopt their religion. "That would go against everything I learned in Alabama," he pointed out. Facing death, however, he made it clear that he wanted to be buried among his white friends rather than among his own people.

This boulder marks the site of Tomochichi's grave.

His only explanation for his departure from Alabama had been to call himself "one who has been driven out" in some of his formal speeches delivered in England. When he died on October 5, 1739, the wish of the first Alabamian to be presented at the court of an English sovereign was honored. Tomochichi was buried in Savannah, far from the Chattahoochee. After a service marked by military honors, the body of the aged Creek-Yamacraw was lowered into a pit in Percival Square, later Savannah's courthouse square.

63

Josiah Gorgas: Quick-change Artist

"It is three years to the day since I took charge of the [Confederate] Ordnance Department. I have succeeded beyond my wildest dreams. From being the worst supplied of the Bureaus of the War Department [in Richmond], it is now the best. Once we could not make a gun, a pistol, a sabre, a pound of powder or a shell for a cannon. Now we make all these in quantities to meet the demands of our large armies."

Clearly proud of his accomplishments when he made that diary entry on April 8, 1864, the writer was a man born in a crossroads hamlet named Running Pumps, which once existed in Pennsylvania.

Josiah Gorgas had received an appointment to West Point in 1837, during the period when cadets spent only four years at the institution. At his graduation in 1841 he was ranked number six in a class of fifty-six men. That meant he didn't have to become a second lieutenant of infantry; he could choose the branch of service he wished to enter.

When the twenty-seven year old picked the Ordnance Corps, he was posted to the Watervliet Arsenal in Troy, New York. During the Mexican War he directed the placement of American guns at Vera Cruz, then he suffered a severe case of yellow fever. (Many years later this dreaded disease was mastered by his son.)

The black-haired and hot-tempered Gorgas became embroiled with Secretary of State James Buchanan and the secretary of war, struggles that cost him an honorary promotion for his Mexican War service.

Possibly because he had come to despise most northerners during his altercations with officials, he asked for and received duty in the Deep South. While stationed at Alabama's then-flourishing Mount Vernon arsenal, he was smitten with Amelia Gayle the moment he laid eyes on her.

Amelia's father, John Gayle, was a district judge who had been governor of Alabama. He was less than pleased at the idea of his daughter's marrying a fellow from "up north." Reluctantly, in 1853 he gave his consent to the marriage.

Eight years later Captain Gorgas made a quick change of loyalties when civil war was seen as looming. He resigned his commission and went to Montgomery a few days before fighting broke out in Charleston Harbor. There his offer of service was gratefully accepted, and he was promoted to the rank of major and placed in charge of Confederate ordnance.

Only an undiluted optimist would have taken such an assignment, for a quick survey of the Confederate military revealed tremendous weaknesses. Plenty of men were eager to fight, but in a battle of any consequence all of them would have had to face an array of heavy Federal guns.

Richmond's Tredegar Iron Works was the only foundry in the South then capable of producing cannon. In order to withstand the big naval guns of Federal warships as well as field artillery of infantry and cavalry units, the South needed cannon, powder, shot, and shells.

When Harpers Ferry Arsenal in Virginia (now West Virginia) fell to the Secessionists, Gorgas saw to it that as many captured guns as possible were put into serviceable condition. At the vast Federal navy yard near Nor-

Josiah Gorgas.
[U.S. Army Military History Institute]

folk, the hasty departure of men in blue yielded what he labeled "a treasure trove of incalculable worth." Workmen had tried to disable scores of big guns, but the damage was quickly repaired. Some of these captured guns took part in nearly every struggle of the Civil War, sometimes turning the tide of battle.

Thanks to Gorgas, Confederate troops began to receive a steady stream of cannon. To make use of them, the Alabama chief of ordnance had to have metal and nitre to manufacture powder. The citizens of Mobile, Charleston, and New Orleans responded to his pleas and donated church bells and lead window weights.

He sent scouts into the deepest caves of the Southeast, where he found enough nitre to begin making gunpowder in quantity. Soon he began importing shiploads of it. At Augusta, Georgia, Gorgas transformed a small Federal arsenal into a mammoth factory that specialized in production of the explosive. Before the conflict ended, the

At what was once a tiny Federal arsenal in Augusta, Georgia, Gorgas created a state-of-the-art powder manufacturing plant.

Augusta powder works was the largest manufacturer of its kind in the Western world.

After 1863 the Alabamian by choice increasingly turned to the use of blockade-runners. Some of the vessels he used brought entire cargoes of ordnance materials; others were filled with cannon, rifles, ammunition, percussion caps, and other essentials. His work was so successful that the man who formerly had worn a uniform of the U.S. Army became a Confederate brigadier general on November 19, 1864.

After Robert E. Lee surrendered at Appomattox Court House, Virginia, Gorgas turned to the only trade he knew well: iron manufacture. Unfortunately, he set up shop in Brierfield rather than Birmingham and soon found himself insolvent.

In this dilemma, Gorgas again changed careers and became an educator. Following his service as head of the junior department at the University of the South in Sewanee, Tennessee, he became president of the institution in 1872.

After six years at Sewanee, the husband of a former Alabama governor's daughter was named president of the University of Alabama. Tuscaloosa welcomed him, and he found life in the city "delightful by every standard."

Illness soon put an end to his capacity to head the fast-growing University of Alabama, so the Pennsylvania native once more found a new vocation. He became a university librarian and spent his remaining years in "a quiet so profound that hectic days of the Civil War seemed to belong to another existence."

At his death in 1883, the man who had followed so many vocations had no idea that the fever that had laid him low in Mexico would shape and direct the life of his firstborn son.

64

Junaluska: American Hero

"Here lie the bodies of the Cherokee chief Juna-luska and Nicie, his wife. Together with his warriors, he saved the life of General Jackson at the Battle of Horse-shoe Bend."

In its opening sentences a bronze historical marker at Robbinsville, North Carolina, gives a capsule account of a nearly forgotten exploit in Alabama. The War of 1812 is not well remembered today, but it dominated American life and thought for three turbulent years.

Still rankled at having been defeated in the American Revolution, British leaders looked for an excuse to send troops back to America. They found it when their war with Napoleon, launched in 1803, escalated nearly a decade later.

Desperate for seamen, the nation boasting one of the most powerful navies of the world began seizing Americans on the high seas. These men were "impressed," or forced to enter British service.

Simultaneously, Britain raised the stakes in the contest for the allegiance of Native Americans. Huge supplies of inexpensive jewelry, alcohol, weapons, and ammunition were used to buy the allegiance of the tribes centered mainly in what is now the Northeast.

The impressment of American sailors and the growing threat of Indian wars gave American leaders an excuse to take action. Motivated in large part by an eagerness to seize British Canada and Spanish-held East and West

Junaluska. [ARTIST'S SKETCH]

Florida, President James Madison and his advisers decided that war was "the only way out of our troubles with Great Britain."

In this mood, they eagerly listened to French diplomats who urged that the infant United States adopt a "nonintercourse" policy toward Britain. Today that would be called economic sanctions, a device still used to weaken or subdue nations regarded as hostile.

Madison, barely five feet tall, raised himself to his full height in November 1811. A special message was sent to Congress recommending that plans be made to prepare for war. Soon the diminutive president learned that his ideas had received overwhelming support—but the lawmakers did little or nothing to prepare for conflict. Having made no significant progress toward recruiting, training, or arming troops, on June 18, 1812, Congress declared war on the former mother country.

Now-forgotten Brownstown, Michigan, was the site of the first armed clash between American and British soldiers with their Indian allies. It took place in November 1812 and launched a series of battles in the northern United States and Canada. York—today known as Toronto—was captured by the Americans in April 1813.

That triumphant victory didn't mean that the war was nearly over or even that the level of fighting would soon be reduced. Instead, the struggle spread like a fire whipped by the wind.

Especially in what was then called the Mississippi Territory, the Indians had long been angry with the white settlers. More and more Americans were appearing in present-day Alabama, always demanding more and more land. Although the tribes made frequent concessions, the whites were never satisfied. Some of them were convinced that gold was sure to be found—and soon—in the hills between modern-day Huntsville, Alabama, and Chattanooga, Tennessee. This notion added greatly to the land fever of the settlers who wanted to be completely rid of those whom they called "pesky redskins."

Among the Indians of the region destined to become Alabama, Red Stick Creeks made up the most warlike faction. Led by a man known to whites as William Weatherford and called Red Eagle by Native Americans, the Red Sticks made secret pacts with Great Britain and then proceeded to wage war on the American settlers.

On August 30, 1813, Red Eagle and his warriors descended upon Fort Mims (or Mimms) not far north of Mobile. When the killing, maiming, and scalping came to an end, only a handful of persons living there were alive. No one knows how many died that day, but many records indicate that there were nearly five hundred deaths.

Since victorious Red Sticks were judged likely to attract new tribal allies, the British threat to the Gulf Coast was now as real as it was in the Northeast. Andrew Jackson, a major general in the Tennessee militia, was placed in charge of launching the Creek War, whose aim was to exterminate tribesmen of the Southeast who were fighting for Great Britain as well as for themselves.

Jackson led his soldiers to Natchez, Mississippi, and prepared to invade Florida. His preparations began prior to the Fort Mims massacre and were delayed significantly when Congress failed to provide funds for supplies for Jackson's army. Suddenly, Congress surprisingly instructed Jackson to dismiss his troops "with the nation's gratitude"—but with no pay, no food, and no transportation home. During the overland march back to Tennessee, Jackson was compared with the toughest tree common in the area and called Old Hickory—a nickname that stuck with him for life.

When news of the Fort Mims massacre reached Washington, Congress quickly changed the orders for Jackson's recall. They instead ordered Jackson to assemble an army and to move immediately against the Creeks of Alabama and Mississippi.

One of Old Hickory's subordinates, Gen. John Coffee, won a victory at Tallasahatchee, near today's Jacksonville. Six days later Jackson scored a minor win at Talladega on November 9, 1813.

Winter was approaching, and the terms of enlistment for many of his men were about to expire. As a result, Old Hickory spent the winter recruiting and training new soldiers and making bold plans to invade the heartland of the Red Sticks in the spring. As an extra precaution, he brought a band of about five hundred Cherokees—traditional enemies of the Creeks—from North Carolina and Georgia to fight under his leadership.

Jackson's tiny army got underway late in February 1814. From captured Indians, Old Hickory learned that his enemies had erected a permanent fortified encampment on a river. At first he was unable to discover whether it lay on the Flint, the Rock, or the Tennessee River.

While pushing forward as rapidly as his men could march, Jackson was informed that he had been promoted to major general of U.S. Volunteers. Then he learned that the Creek encampment was in a protected region called Tohopki or Tohopeka. The Americans knew this area as the Great Horseshoe Bend of the Tallapoosa River, a peninsula more than eighty acres in size and well protected by water.

Once he knew where Red Eagle and his warriors were, Jackson headed southeast toward Dadeville and Lake Martin. At the head of a small body of mounted soldiers and most of the Cherokees, General Coffee was ordered to cross the Tallapoosa River about three miles from the Creek encampment. He was then to surround the Great Horseshoe Bend, eliminating any escape route.

Jackson, who had two small cannon, was confident that he could smash the Creek breastworks, which were five feet high. He was right in that belief, but he failed to note a large group of canoes moored out of his line of vision. Red Eagle had placed the canoes in a spot from which his warriors could use the river to get behind an attacking force and make a surprise assault.

In this situation, a Cherokee warrior named Junaluska jumped into the Tallapoosa and swam across it. At his destination, Junaluska cut the thongs used to tie the Creek canoes to the bank. Swimming very slowly, he pulled the canoes into the swiftest part of the current before turning them loose to drift down the river.

It was for this action that Junaluska was admiringly hailed as "the man who saved the life of Andrew Jackson at Horseshoe Bend." Had the canoes been left in place, there is no way to know how the battle would have ended.

Because the canoes were gone and the escape route blocked, it is believed that substantially more Creeks died on the Tallapoosa than did whites at Fort Mims.

Red Eagle surrenders to Jackson.

With the cream of his fighting force wiped out, Red Eagle retreated into Louisiana and at Buras entered into a treaty with Jackson.

The victory at Horseshoe Bend brought the United States the largest single cession of land ever given by a southern tribe. Some portions of Georgia and nearly half of Alabama were included in the 22 million acres surrendered on August 9, 1814. Soon a domino effect went into motion; no longer supported by the Red Stick Creeks, Spain (an ally of Great Britain) gave up both East and West Florida to the United States.

Today a soldier who shows conspicuous gallantry in battle is likely to be decorated and made a national hero. Perhaps that would have been the case in 1814 had the man who saved the day for Old Hickory been one of his Tennessee Volunteers. Because he was a Cherokee, the exploit of Junaluska received little praise.

Victorious in what were once the Middle Colonies, the British burned Washington a few months after Red Eagle was defeated in Alabama. Old Hickory later sanctioned legislation that forced the Cherokees to cede their lands. When they went to Oklahoma on the Trail of Tears, Junaluska was among them. He is quoted as having said, "If I had known what was going to happen, I would have shot Andy Jackson at Horseshoe Bend."

Hundreds of miles from the Great Smoky Mountains in which he was reared, Junaluska did not lose his fighting spirit. On a dark winter night he slipped out of the Cherokee encampment and walked back to North Carolina.

In a gesture that was highly unusual for the period, North Carolina lawmakers rewarded the Cherokee who was credited with saving the day in the Alabama battle. A special act of the legislature conferred citizenship, $100 in cash, and 337 acres of barren land upon "the man who saved Andrew Jackson's life."

In a tiny cottage erected on land given as a result of valor on the Tallapoosa River, Junaluska died at an age thought to be well over one hundred years. The memorial erected in his honor helps to preserve his memory. In quite different fashion, so does Lake Junaluska Assembly, the conference center of the United Methodists of Alabama and all other southeastern states.

65

Abel D. Streight:
Race Across the State

Union Gen. Ulysses S. Grant realized the strategic importance of Vicksburg, Mississippi, and became obsessed with capturing the vital river port. Of the many expedients he tried, perhaps the most colorful was a Union cavalry raid that was aimed at a vital transportation line.

The Western and Atlantic Railroad, which ran from Atlanta to Chattanooga, was the vital supply line for the Confederate army of Braxton Bragg. Grant reasoned that Bragg would be forced out of Tennessee if he could cut that single-track railroad. Such a move would disrupt Confederate transportation and render Vicksburg much more vulnerable to attack.

It would not be easy to reach the target railroad, however. The line lay deep inside territory firmly held by soldiers in gray. Only an imaginative and daring move, something the enemy would think unlikely, had a chance to succeed.

Whether Grant personally devised the scheme that was put into action in the spring of 1863 is unknown. The plan may have originated with Col. Abel D. Streight of Indiana, who eventually led his opponents in a race across the entire state of Alabama. Regardless of who planned the enterprise, it was approved at the highest levels and got underway on April 22, 1863.

Streight's Independent Provisional Brigade Designed for Special Secret Service moved out of its base in Nash-

*Col. Abel D.
Streight led the
raid as a
mounted infan-
try officer.*
[LIBRARY OF
CONGRESS]

ville, Tennessee. Along with their animals, the troops
traveled from the Tennessee capital to Eastport, Mississippi, by river steamers. Disembarking at the Mississippi-
Alabama state line, they made ready for their dash
through sparsely settled territory in northern Alabama.

To prevent Confederates watching enemy troop movements from discovering Streight's action, a second raid-
ing party was dispatched into Mississippi. This, it was
hoped, would lead any Confederate cavalry toward the
great river, giving Streight's unit an open field for their
trek across Alabama.

Things went well for several days of hard riding. Passing well south of Florence, the Federal raiders reached
Tuscumbia on April 26. From that city they rode through
Russellville, Mount Hope, and Moulton before heading
toward Sand Mountain.

Before they reached Day's Gap, which afforded passage through the hilly terrain, Confederate Gen. Nathan

Bedford Forrest discovered what was happening and started riding hell-for-leather to catch up with Streight. He knew his outfit to be much smaller than Streight's, but he hoped to outmaneuver the Federal raiders.

The soldiers in blue pushed hard all day on April 29 and made camp at the foot of the narrow pass leading to the top of Sand Mountain. They did not know that Forrest and his pursuing force were only four miles behind them that night.

Streight, an infantry officer, was in the unusual position of leading a long-distance mounted raid. Most of his men were volunteers from infantry regiments, but he also had two companies of horsemen. Known as the Middle Tennessee Cavalry, they were natives of Alabama who had enlisted in Union forces. Because some of them knew the countryside well, they led the way in the surprise journey across their home state.

Before Federal units reached the plateau on top of Sand Mountain, they realized that the Confederates were closing in. Streight prepared to ambush his foes by hiding two small pieces of field artillery behind bushes at a point where he thought they could surprise the Confederates.

His trap did not work quite as expected, however. In a fierce fight near the top of the mountain, numerous Federals fell victim to Confederate fire. Sgt. James H. Kierstead of the Seventy-third Indiana Infantry was captured along with several other men who were expected to effect the ambush.

For the next ninety-six hours, the two forces were constantly engaged in small-scale conflicts. Both Streight and Forrest knew that they were engaged in a race with time. If the Federal force managed to reach the vital railroad first, it could severely hamper the Confederate war effort. Forrest pushed his men and horses to the limit of their endurance, determined not to let the rail line suffer damage.

During hand-to-hand fighting on Hog Mountain, the Confederate commander had three horses shot from under him. Each time a dead or severely wounded animal threw him to the ground, Forrest jumped into another saddle and continued his pursuit.

Realizing that he was now too far from Tuscumbia to return to his base, even if he had wished to do so, Streight tried everything he could think of. In addition to devising several ambushes, he burned bridges and tried to block trails by rolling boulders into them.

Close to the Alabama-Georgia state line, Streight's men torched a bridge over Black Creek, whose deep water was colored by decaying vegetation. Had not youthful Emma Sansom come to the aid of Forrest at this point, the Federals might have continued to elude him.

Since the Confederate cavalrymen knew they were greatly outnumbered, they could not dare risk an all-out battle. In a series of skillful maneuvers, Forrest deluded Streight into believing he had thousands of men and dozens of artillery. As a result, the Union leader surrendered at a point about forty miles from the Western and Atlantic railroad line, which was his objective.

Having crossed the entire state of Alabama, victor and vanquished then moved into Georgia. Forrest received a tumultuous ovation from the citizens of the iron-making town of Rome, near the Alabama line, and gave a lengthy interview to George W. Adair of Atlanta.

Streight never got over the embarrassment of yielding sixteen hundred men to a force of only six hundred. Shipped to Richmond's Libby Prison, he was the butt of jokes by other inmates.

Much coarse humor came to focus upon the fact that when planning the raid, Streight chose to mount his men on mules rather than horses. While these animals could transport heavier loads than horses and were able to subsist on coarser food, Streight had reasoned that the sure-footed mules would be more useful than horses in the hilly region he was to cross.

Streight stopped at Libby Prison, rather than the Western and Atlantic Railroad.

He was right in these respects, but he failed to take into account the fact that mules are mean tempered and hard to handle. Worst of all, their constant braying kept the Confederates informed about his location all the way from Mississippi to Georgia.

66

Tecumseh: My Spirit Will Return!

A band of about thirty Shawnee warriors paused at the headwaters of what they believed to be the Chattooga River. After a moment, their leader pointed to the south-southwest, and they resumed their journey.

After crossing Little River and Town Creek, they glimpsed Gunterville Lake in the distance and realized that they were too far north. Two more days brought them near Jones Bluff on the Alabama River, where a band of Creeks had gathered to meet them.

The fame of Tecumseh, leader of the tribesmen from the north, had preceded him. It was generally known that he had formed a confederation of Native Americans in the Great Lakes region and wished to strengthen it by new alliances. Chocktaws and Chickasaws, through whose regions the Shawnee passed on his way to Alabama, refused to listen to him. He was confident, however, that the Red Stick Creeks would be ready to go to war.

Tecumseh received what we would call "a polite and respectful hearing" when he spoke in the region that became Autauga County. He was gravely disappointed, however, that not one warrior signaled eagerness to fight the Americans whom their visitor called the Long Knives. Creeks were not fearful of the swords that the uniformed officers carried at their sides, but they knew arrows were no match for bullets.

*This is the only
portrait of
Tecumseh
believed to be
authentic.*

Unwilling to return to his tribal lands without recruits,
Tecumseh approached Indian agent Benjamin Hawkins
who had called for a great council. Hawkins consented
for the six-foot warrior from the north to attend and address the assembled braves.

They came together at the ancient Creek capital,
Toockabatcha (or Tuckabatche), on the Tallapoosa River
in such numbers that no one could count them. Hawkins
later estimated that when Tecumseh mounted a stump to
speak, he had an audience of about five thousand warriors.

The natives of Alabama were surprised that the man
who had come so far to meet with them had painted his
face black. Numerous eagle feathers were stuck into his
hair, but these were almost commonplace to the Creeks.
They were amazed, however, by the buffalo tails that
hung by deer-hide thongs from Tecumseh's arms and
waist. Herds of buffalo could still be found north of

North Carolina, but they were seldom seen in Alabama except in the most northern hills.

Renowned as a fluent orator, the Shawnee reminded his listeners of white atrocities. "They have taken much of our land and now they want it all," he warned. "Far away, on the Scioto River, Chief Logan of the Mingo tribe returned from hunting and found that Long Knives had been at his camp. Every member of his family lay among the ashes of his wigwam, scalped by white men."

To attentive Creeks the speaker explained, "We are not alone. Redcoats have come across the Great Water to help us. They will give us guns and ammunition when we tell them we are ready to fight with them." He was right in predicting a flare-up of violence; a major conflict did take place soon, known as the War of 1812.

Chief Logan of the Mingo tribe found every member of his family had been killed and scalped by whites.

Having made his speech, Tecumseh was ready to begin his war dance and to invite other warriors to come forward and join him. He was interrupted, however, by a chieftain whom Hawkins and other whites knew as Big Warrior.

Abruptly rising to his feet, the tall Alabamian silently shook his head and turned to leave the council. Enraged, the visitor shouted, "Tuske-uggee-Thlucco, your blood is white! You have listened to my talk, but you do not mean to fight under me. I know the reason; you do not believe the Great Spirit has sent me. My mother was a Creek; we are blood brothers! Why will you not lead your warriors into battle with me?"

Grasping the buffalo tails that dangled from his waist, the Shawnee shook them vigorously and warned, "You will soon know that the Great Spirit himself really did send me. When I get back to Detroit, I will stamp my feet and make the earth tremble. When I have gone to my ancestors, my spirit will return to make life miserable here."

On the long journey back to his tribal homeland, Tecumseh reflected about his many struggles with the Long Knives. At the Wabash River in 1791, according to the calendar of the whites, his opponents were led by Arthur St. Clair, governor of the Northwest Territory. In a fierce battle, St. Clair's troops suffered one of the worst defeats in U.S. military history.

Later the man whose followers called him Mad Anthony Wayne not only trounced his Indian opponents, but in the subsequent treaty they lost vast tracts of land.

Now that William Henry Harrison was governing the Northwest, Tecumseh knew that he would have to go into battle soon. He had just acquired the rank of brigadier general in the British army—the only Native American to be so honored. Yet he feared that without the aid of the Choctaws, Chickasaws, and Creeks, he might suffer defeat.

When he saw that the odds were against him, the brilliant Native American resorted to a ruse. He challenged Harrison to mortal combat one-on-one, suggesting that this form of a duel should decide the outcome of the struggle. But Harrison refused. In the battle of the Thames, about a year after his return from Alabama, the great Shawnee leader was killed.

Months earlier, Creek warriors in and around Toockabatcha had looked at one another in surprise and wonder. On a December day that they judged to be about the time Tecumseh should have reached Detroit, the earth quivered and rolled through much of the Gulf region.

Whites remember this event as the New Madrid, Missouri, earthquake of 1811–12, but in the lore of the Creeks, it is called "the day Tecumseh stamped his feet."

Long after the Native Americans had been forced by Andrew Jackson to give up their tribal lands in Alabama, white settlers in the region had reason to remember Tecumseh's second warning.

When a son was born to the wife of a judge of the Ohio Supreme Court less than a decade after the battle of the Thames, the proud father named him Tecumseh. He did so as a tribute to the man who failed in Alabama but was widely considered to be the most skilled of all Native American military leaders. Relatives and friends abbreviated the name of the white-skinned Tecumseh to "Cump"—a nickname that stuck with him throughout his life.

After young Cump was orphaned, he was informally adopted by wealthy neighbors. They believed that every child should have a proper Christian name, so they called him William, but they never changed his name legally.

In 1863 Cump led three Union armies south from Chattanooga in an effort to smash the Confederate Army of Tennessee. Knowing that he must return north by ship instead of by rail, he considered moving on Mobile.

The tribal name of Tecumseh, center, was given to Tecumseh Sherman of Ohio.

The Confederates, however, thwarted that plan by slowly retreating, and so he eventually found himself near Atlanta. After a series of battles, he turned toward Savannah, instead of Mobile, as the port where he would most likely find plenty of Union warships.

Plundering and looting in a path sixty miles long, Tecumseh Sherman and his men completed their famous—or infamous—March to the Sea. The death and destruction wreaked by the white Tecumseh were far more devastating than any action taken by his namesake.

67

Emma Sansom:
Sunbonnet Heroine

Alabama is the only state in the nation that has heaped honors on a teenage girl for a spur-of-the-moment exploit. The "Sunbonnet Heroine," Emma Sansom, was born in 1847 and may have been the granddaughter of the noted Cherokee leader Joseph Vann. Since she had a dozen older brothers and sisters, Emma could have been self-centered and spoiled as a child, but she was not. Whenever it came her turn to do household chores, she pitched into them with enthusiasm—often singing as she worked.

Life on the farm in Walton County, Georgia, was hard. Red clay that has not been treated with fertilizer is not good soil. When Emma was ten or twelve years old, her father and mother heard that fertile farmland could be had for nearly nothing in Alabama. That led them to strike out for Cherokee County, named for the Native American tribe to which her maternal grandfather is believed to have belonged.

Having crossed the Georgia border into "the land of opportunity," they soon found a good site for a log cabin. That's how Micajah and Lamila Sansom, along with their younger children, came to settle close to Black Creek. Their homestead was on a sloping hillside that later was a part of Alabama City, less than two miles from present-day Gadsden.

Soon Emma was lonely; six of her brothers marched off to fight for the Confederacy and her older sisters mar-

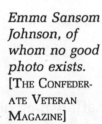

*Emma Sansom
Johnson, of
whom no good
photo exists.*
[The Confeder-
ate Veteran
Magazine]

ried and left home. She enjoyed walking along the bank
of the stream near the cabin, wondering where all the
rushing water in Black Creek was going. In those days
she had no idea that the deep and crooked stream would
give her a special kind of immortality.

One day fifteen-year-old Emma looked up from her
work in the yard and was surprised to see smoke pouring
skyward. From the location of the column of smoke, she
was sure that the bridge over Black Creek was burning.
That meant big trouble, for there were no other usable
bridges within miles.

She called her mother, and the two women raced
toward the bridge to try to put out the fire. They thought
perhaps it had been struck by lightning, but as soon as
they saw it they knew that the fire was not accidental.
Rails pulled from their fence were piled at both ends of
the bridge, having been used as kindling to start the fire,
and they were still burning.

Soon Lamila and Emma spotted men in blue uniforms with muskets and rifles standing at the far side of the bridge. They were Federal soldiers on picket duty. After their comrades had crossed the bridge, they remained to prevent anyone from using it before its charred remnants fell into the water that roared below.

Turning back toward their cabin, Emma and her mother saw more soldiers. This time they were on horseback and wore gray Confederate uniforms. One of them toppled from his saddle seconds after the crack of gunfire was heard from a spot at or near the burning bridge.

"Is there another bridge?" called out a muscular soldier whose shoulder ornaments labeled him as a high-ranking officer.

Lamila shook her head despondently. "There's an old one 'bout two miles downstream," she replied. "But it's fallin' down and ain't safe to use."

As Emma remembered the dramatic moment, the officer then took off his hat and said: "Ladies, do not be alarmed. I am General Forrest. I and my men will protect you from harm."

Almost in the same breath he inquired, "Where are the Yankees?"

"They set the bridge on fire," Lamila explained. "And some of them are standing in line on the far side. If you go down that hill toward the creek, they'll kill you."

Signaling for her daughter to follow her, the farm woman then lifted her skirts and began running toward their cabin and safety. Emma reached the fenced yard first and started to open the gate.

At that instant, she later recalled, Gen. Nathan Bedford Forrest dashed up with a question. "Can you tell me where I can get across that creek?"

Emma told him that there was a trail about two hundred yards above the bridge that their cows used to cross in low water.

Confederate Gen. Nathan Bedford Forrest.

"I think you and your men can get over there," she continued. "And if you'll throw a saddle on my horse I'll take you to the crossing."

Forrest responded, "There's no time to saddle a horse. Get up here behind me."

Lamila, gasping for breath, came up just as her daughter was about to obey Forrest.

"What on earth are you doing, Emma?" she demanded.

Before she could answer, the Confederate general explained, "She's going to show me a ford where I can get my men over in time to catch those Yankees. Don't be uneasy; I'll bring her back safe."

They rode into a field through which a small branch ran, so they were protected by a thick growth of brush along its banks. Nearing the point at which the branch ran into Black Water Creek, Emma said she thought they'd better get off the horse.

Obedient to the girl, the most famous cavalry officer of the Confederacy slipped from his saddle, bent low, and followed her toward the creek.

As she later told the story, rapid action ensued: "A cannon and the other guns were firing fast by this time, as I pointed out to him where to go into the water and out on the other bank, and then we went back toward the cabin. He asked me my name and asked me to give him a lock of my hair."

After the firing stopped, Forrest dashed away on his horse and Emma walked back to her cabin. Before she reached it, she again met the Confederate leader. This time he told her that he had written a note for her and left it on the bureau, and he repeated his request for a lock of her beautiful red hair.

Because the "Sunbonnet Heroine" saved Confederates many hours of riding, they were soon in pursuit of Federal soldiers whom they eventually captured.

A few years later, Emma married Confederate veteran Christopher B. Johnson and went with him to Van Zandt County, Texas. While living there she learned that Union Col. Benjamin H. Grierson had been sent into Mississippi on a raid designed to draw attention away from the men who crossed Black Water Creek. Shortly afterward, Union Col. Abel D. Streight had invaded Alabama and put Tuscumbia to the torch.

Letters traveled slowly and with difficulty in those days, so Emma lost touch with most people she had known in Alabama. Some of them who knew of her exploit remembered her, however, and they paid her way for a trip to Atlanta. At a reunion of Confederate veterans

in the Georgia city, Emma found out that John A. Wyeth
was writing a book about the life of General Forrest.

That's when she pulled out a scrap of paper and gave it
to the author. Written by the Confederate leader more
than thirty years earlier, she explained that it meant so
much to her that she kept it in the family Bible. Hastily
scribbled by a man who had little or no schooling, the
note read:

Hed Quaters in Sadle   *May 2, 1863*
My highest regardes to Miss Ema Sansom for hir gallant
conduct while my forse was skirmishing with the Federals
a cross Black Creek near Gadesden Allabama
                                                    N. B. Forrest
                                                    Brig. Genl

Perhaps because Forrest never learned to spell, the
name of the girl for whom he scribbled a note of thanks
has appeared in several forms.

Years after her encounter with the Confederate general,
Emma was showered with honors. Poet John T. Moore
described her adventure in a ballad with twenty four-line
stanzas. Members of the Alabama legislature voted to reward her with a gold medal and a land grant, but postwar
turmoil prevented her from receiving them.

After Gadsden grew so large that it included what was
once the Sansom homestead, the women of the city commissioned a marble monument of Emma and had it
placed on Broad Street at the entrance to the Coosa River
Bridge. It was erected at a time when the entire United
States included only a few monuments to women of any
age.

Emma's name was placed on a street and a housing
development. Then came the biggest honor of all. The
Emma Sansom High School, erected in Alabama City in
1929, was acquired by Gadsden in 1932 as a result of
annexation.

At that time it included twenty-two rooms and an auditorium. An addition completed in 1942 made the school named for a teenager the site at which thousands of young men and women have earned their diplomas.

Emma Sansom is believed to have been impoverished at the time of her death in Texas. Regardless of how meager her personal belongings may have been, she treasured the note written by the Confederate general and the undying gratitude of Alabamians throughout the state.

68

CSS *Alabama*:
294 Searches

At the vast Liverpool, England, shipyard of Laird and Brothers, an official gave a nod. Workmen removed blocks and cables, and a sleek new ship displacing 1,050 tons slid into the water. Finished as Number 290—the building yard number—moments before its launch, the vessel was christened the *Enrica*. Some who took part in the ceremonies of July 29, 1862, knew that her new name would not last long.

In addition to her launch, cutter, whaleboat, and two lifeboats, the *Enrica* carried several people who had responded to an invitation to a short voyage. They anticipated the trial run down the Mersey River so keenly that many brought along picnic baskets from which the necks of champagne bottles protruded.

To their surprise, a pair of tugs pulled alongside the *Enrica* only minutes after she got underway. An officer who had climbed into the rigging lifted a speaking tube and shouted, "Pleasure ride over; take to the tugs!"

The baffled guests were immediately returned to their point of departure. By the time they reached it, the *Enrica* was out of sight, headed for an obscure inlet on the Welsh coast. There nearly one hundred men waiting on a pier shouted with enthusiasm when her sails were sighted. Soon they surged aboard, one by one, signing the papers that made them members of the ship's crew.

After working her way around the northern tip of Ireland, the brand-new vessel headed for the Azores. In the

Bay of Angra on Terceira Island, she was anchored for only a few minutes before other ships moved alongside. By this time, everyone involved knew that the *Enrica* had managed to slip through a net designed to catch her and would soon become a Confederate raider.

Some of the British seamen who had brought the vessel from its builders to the island threw in their lot with the Confederacy and signed on as able-bodied seamen. A. F. Marmelstien, quartermaster, supervised the transfer of six guns from the *Agrippa* of London. While ammunition, coal, and supplies were being loaded, the steamer *Bahama* arrived with Capt. Raphael Semmes and his officers. During a brief, informal ceremony, the *Enrica* was rechristened. This time, she took the name *Alabama,* in honor of the fourth state to secede from the Union.

The Alabama, *most dreaded of all Confederate raiders.* [LIBRARY OF CONGRESS]

Except for the British subjects who had decided to join the Confederate navy, everyone on the *Alabama* knew the reputation of their commander. Born in Maryland, Semmes entered the U.S. Navy at the age of seventeen. By the time civil war was imminent, he was a commander. He did not hesitate to turn in his commission. Offering his services to the South, which then did not have a single warship, he served as a lighthouse commissioner for a few months.

The packet steamer *Havana* was then converted into the raider *Sumter,* and Semmes was given command. His first capture was just three days later. After being credited with a score of Yankee merchantmen, his ship was in such need of repairs that he put in to Gibraltar. Soon after he anchored, three Union warships appeared and established a tight blockade.

Semmes had no option. He abandoned the *Sumter* and started for home. While en route he received a message saying that he had been made a captain and was immediately to take charge of a British-built vessel to be known as the *Alabama.* In order to reach the rendezvous point, he chartered the *Bahama* and managed to put aboard her two splendid naval guns that he was sure he could put to good use.

Although many documents produced during the Civil War have been lost or destroyed, Semmes's journal for the period from August 20, 1862, to January 4, 1863, was preserved and appears in its entirety in official naval records. According to Semmes, the vessel of which he took command cost £51,716 or $250,305.44. Money for the purchase came from the international banking firm of Fraser, Trenholm, and Company, whose outlay was secured by cotton.

Confederate Secretary of the Navy Stephen R. Mallory sent James D. Bulloch to England with instructions to buy as many ships, heavy guns, rifles, and ammunition as possible. At the same time, Bulloch's opposite number, the U.S. minister to Great Britain, Charles Francis

Capt. Raphael Semmes. [THE CONFEDERATE MUSEUM]

Adams, was instructed to put an end to all British military sales to the Confederacy.

By the time Ship Number 290 was under construction at Liverpool, Adams knew that it was being built for conversion as a raider. Some of his informants found jobs at the dockyard and regularly reported on its progress. Adams then ordered the captain of the heavily armed USS *Tuscarora* to stay close to Liverpool to prevent Number 290 from going to sea. Thus to deceive the U.S. minister and his aides, Bulloch arranged to launch the *Enrica* as though she were headed for a short pleasure cruise.

Having deceived Adams, son of former President John Quincy Adams, Bulloch went with the *Enrica* to the Azores and then returned to England. As he and Semmes parted, he clapped the naval officer on the back and said that he hoped the *Alabama* could come close to matching the record established by the *Sumter*.

Bulloch's wish was one of the largest understatements of the war. The motto of the state of Alabama is "We dare defend our rights." During a period of less than two years, the raider *Alabama* did a lot more than defend—it overhauled, or forced to stop and search, 294 vessels. Of these, 26 were taken captive, 55 were burned, 10 were "released on bond," and a few were impressed into Confederate service.

Since a full load of coal for the two three-hundred-horsepower engines of the *Alabama* weighed 285 tons, Semmes relied largely on her sails. During what he called "the ugly seaways that are so common in the North Atlantic," the raider rolled and tumbled, taking so much water through her top works that Semmes complained of constantly hearing "Pump! Pump! Pump!"

In spite of heavy seas and reliance largely upon the wind, the 211-foot *Alabama* proved to be extremely fast. Since only two of the eight Blakely guns with which she was originally mounted were 68-pounders, Semmes tried to steer clear of warships.

More than any other Confederate vessel, however, the *Alabama* entered everyday language in the North. As her captures mounted, maritime insurance rates soared. Many shipowners tried to place their vessels under foreign registry, hoping thereby to escape capture if stopped by the raider.

Cruising off the coast of Brazil, where he was not expecting to find any Northern warships, Semmes was startled to see the USS *Vanderbilt* steaming toward his vessel. Since the boiler fires of the *Alabama* were seldom permitted to go out, he shouted for his sailors to pour on the coal. Using both sails and engines, he gradually pulled away from the powerful pursuer.

When night fell, the captain of the *Alabama* had her folding smokestack lowered and extinguished the boiler fires. Reversing his course, he boldly sailed directly toward the *Vanderbilt.* With the appearance of his vessel altered so radically, the raider was not recognized when it came within hailing distance.

Captured by the *Alabama* in July 1863, the bark *Conrad* from Philadelphia was unusually seaworthy. It was too fine a vessel to burn, and the capture took place too far from shore to send her into a neutral port.

Quartermaster Marmelstien described what took place after provisions and two brass cannon were transferred to the *Conrad:* "At 5 o'clock p.m. she fired a gun, hoisted the Confederate flag and pendant, the crew manning the rigging and giving three cheers. She was then declared commissioned as the Confederate States' bark *Tuscaloosa.*"

Her name was chosen because the Tuscaloosa River is a major Alabama waterway. Then the Northern vessel converted into a Confederate raider parted company with the *Alabama.*

The U.S. mail steamer *Ariel,* also rated as too good to burn by Semmes, was the site of a ceremony repeated frequently. Her captain, A. G. Jones, agreeing to specific terms, signed a "ransom bond" that read in part: "In consideration of the release of this steamer and its cargo, on behalf of Cornelius Vanderbilt of New York, I make him indebted to the President of the Confederate States of America in the sum of $138,000. This sum is to be paid within thirty days after the conclusion of the present war between the Confederate States and the United States."

Ransom bonds alone amounted to many times the total cost of the *Alabama.* Most of the fifty-five vessels that were burned after being captured were far from a neutral port or were in poor condition.

By May 1864 the raider was in wretched shape herself. She had never been in port long enough to be overhauled properly. So many barnacles were clinging to her bottom that Semmes described his once-splendid vessel as being "like a crippled hunter limping home from a long chase." In desperation, he put into Cherbourg, France, where he hoped to spend a few weeks bringing the *Alabama* back into top sailing condition.

To his chagrin one of the many warships that had been on the hunt for the Confederate craft soon blocked the harbor. Since the USS *Kearsarge* carried enormous 11-inch guns, those of the raider were no match for them. After a long and valiant but futile fight, Semmes saw his beloved ship go down in flames. Picked up by an English vessel, he escaped without serious injury.

The sinking of the Alabama *in French waters.*

Returning home, he fought as an officer of infantry. At his surrender in North Carolina, he indicated his rank as rear admiral and brigadier general.

Eleven years later Charles Francis Adams was called out of retirement to preside over an international commission. Established because the United States blamed Britain for having built raiders for the Confederacy, it convened in Geneva, Switzerland, to ponder the legal case known as the *Alabama* claims.

Italy's king and the emperor of Brazil were members of this tribunal, along with the president of the Swiss Confederation. Under the leadership of the man who let the *Alabama* escape from the trap he had prepared for her, the commission decided to require Great Britain to pay the United States $15.5 million in gold. That decision brought an end to wrangling over how much damage had been done by the *Alabama* and other British-built raiders.

Men now go to sea in craft that may be hundreds of times as large as the vessel commanded by Semmes. Yet as long as naval men continue to have saltwater in their veins, the saga of the vessel that gave new dignity to the name of the state of Alabama will be told and retold around the world.

69

William C. Gorgas: Fever Fighter

Born in Mobile on October 3, 1854, the first-generation Alabamian William C. Gorgas heard a lot about yellow fever while growing up. His father's bout with it during the Mexican War made the boy want to learn more about the mysterious malady that periodically decimated his birthplace.

At age six he went to Richmond with his fighting father and spent four years in the Confederate capital, far from the Gulf Coast he loved. He was a mourner at the funeral of Stonewall Jackson and later went barefoot during winter so some unknown soldier could have a pair of shoes.

Whenever he managed to wheedle powder from his father, he fired his toy cannon in the direction of the nearest Yankee army. When Confederate Gen. Joseph E. Johnston solemnly presented the boy with a powder flask and shot pouch, William volunteered that he had already made up his mind to follow his father into military service.

The disruption of the Civil War made it impossible for young William to get regular schooling, but his father's influence gained him a place at the University of the South in Sewanee, Tennessee, as a special student. He did not graduate and was unable to gain an appointment to West Point. Undeterred, he decided to join the army through a back door.

William C. Gorgas in civilian dress late in life. [LIBRARY OF CONGRESS]

If he couldn't become an ordnance officer like his father, William frequently said, he'd get into a uniform any way he could. Bellevue Medical College in New York City proved to be the entry point he was seeking.

Something in the air was responsible for the malady that caused his father's skin to turn yellow during his recurring bouts with fever, he was told. No one knew the identity of the culprit, but it had been around a long, long time.

On the second voyage of Columbus to the New World, the explorer established the city of Isabella on Santo Domingo. It was soon abandoned because so many settlers turned yellow and died that the settlement named for the Spanish queen was called "the place of sure death."

Two hundred years later and far north of the Caribbean Islands, the largest city among the former English colonies was repeatedly struck. In Philadelphia, Dr. Benjamin Rush wrote in 1703 that the fever caused more than half the city's houses to be closed. Everyone who could afford to do so had fled. Even so, Rush recorded, the noise of death carts "passing slowly over the pavements kept alive anguish and fear in the sick and well every hour of the night."

In his detailed journal the Pennsylvania physician reported the sudden end of an epidemic that took four thousand lives during three months: "On the fifteenth of October it pleased God to alter the state of the air. The

Colonial physician Benjamin Rush believed yellow fever to be caused by contaminated air.

clouds at last dropped health in showers of rain, which continued during the whole day. Appearance of this rain was like a dove with an olive branch in its mouth."

In the struggle with yellow fever, William learned, war was more frequent than peace. That verdict was dramatically underscored in 1878 when Memphis, Tennessee, experienced an estimated eighteen thousand deaths from the malady still thought to be caused by "pestilential air."

Sometimes those fortunate enough to live beyond the range of the yellow terror offered token financial assistance to survivors of epidemics. John Greenleaf Whittier and Henry Wadsworth Longfellow were among many notables who provided autographs for sale in "fever auctions." Eager to put a Longfellow signature into his scrapbook, William made an unsuccessful try for one of them.

After completing his education in what had become the nation's largest city, Lt. William C. Gorgas proudly donned his uniform as a member of the U.S. Army Medical Corps. While he was serving at Fort Brown in Texas, his interest in the strange disease that killed half of those it struck was heightened when he survived a bout with it.

"Glory be!" he exclaimed one day during his recovery. "I'm going to live, and it can't hit me again; I'm now immune!"

His development of immunity to yellow fever proved to be a turning point in his life because he was often assigned to posts where the killer disease was particularly prevalent. He was promoted to captain and then to major, but his life was fairly routine until the United States won the Spanish-American War.

Victory created a dilemma of a special kind; it was necessary for U.S. troops to occupy Havana—notorious for 154 years as a hotbed of yellow fever. Gorgas was named head of sanitation for the city and made dramatic progress in cleaning up its streets and dumps.

Simultaneously, Dr. Walter Reed was working as a medical detective seeking the cause of yellow fever. Although mosquitoes had been suspected for decades, Reed narrowed the field by showing that the disease was transmitted by only one of hundreds of kinds of the biting insects.

Once the *Stegomyia* mosquito, later renamed *Aedes aegypti,* was found to be the carrier, Gorgas attacked its breeding places with a vengeance. He saw the death toll from yellow fever drop in such dramatic fashion that he was rewarded by Congress. A special act of the lawmaking body made the man from Mobile simultaneously a colonel and an assistant surgeon general of the United States.

For years there had been sporadic efforts to cut a canal across the Isthmus of Panama so ships need not go around the tip of South America to make coast-to-coast voyages. Money and manpower poured into the canal project by the French was wasted; yellow fever and malaria made the Canal Zone one of the most notorious pestholes in the Western world.

In 1904 Colonel Gorgas, proudly wearing his new insignia of office and lauded for his cleanup of Havana, was told to make the Canal Zone livable. He knew how to do the job, but when he laid out his plans, some of the men who controlled the purse strings balked. They refused to appropriate the large amount of money needed to rid the zone of mosquitoes, because many of them still doubted that insects were responsible for the disease.

Furious, Gorgas briefly considered leaving the military, but the outbreak of an epidemic persuaded members of the Canal Commission to give him a free hand to spend almost as he pleased. His massive drive to get rid of places where mosquitoes could breed brought yellow fever under control by 1905. Simultaneously, there was a dramatic drop in cases of malaria, which was caused by the bite of infected *Anopheles* mosquitoes.

Theodore Roosevelt, who toured the Canal Zone with the Alabama-born sanitary engineer, returned to the United States praising Gorgas. Soon Gorgas was named to the Canal Commission; then, in rapid succession, he became a brigadier general, surgeon general of the U.S. Army, and major general. Famous throughout the Western world, he was showered with honorary degrees from Harvard, the University of Alabama, Tulane, Brown, the Jefferson Medical College, and many other institutions.

During World War I, his work made it possible to send to Europe a hale and hearty American Expeditionary Force. Among its members, the death rate from illness was an estimated 5 percent of the death rate among Confederate soldiers in the Civil War for whom his father, Josiah Gorgas, had provided guns and ammunition.

Late in life and world famous, Maj. Gen. William C. Gorgas often fingered a framed photograph of Brig. Gen.

Theodore Roosevelt put his influence behind the work of the sanitary engineer from Mobile.

Josiah Gorgas. His joy at having succeeded in following his father into military service without a West Point education was overwhelming. To the man from Mobile, this accomplishment overshadowed the fact that he was credited with having made possible the building of the Panama Canal.

70

Jesse Owens:
Roller-Coaster Gold

Jesse Owens, briefly the focus of world attention, issued a successful book after his career as an athlete ended. Paul G. Neimark, a friend and professional writer, helped get it ready for publication by a New York firm. It received favorable reviews, including an award for best human relations book of 1970.

Part of the success of *Blackthink* stemmed from the basic point of view laid down by a central figure of the 1936 Olympic Games: There is entirely too much racial hatred in the United States. Few would have disputed that conclusion in 1970, but hosts of African Americans were angry when they found that the track star blamed "black extremism" for much of the problem.

Owens wrote that his native state of Alabama, along with the rest of the nation, faced a crisis. As he then saw it, African Americans helped to create the crisis by becoming "loaded-for-bear militants" who went out looking for trouble with whites.

After having pocketed his share of royalties from *Blackthink*, the famous athlete made a complete turnaround. Also produced in collaboration with Neimark, *I Have Changed* was issued in 1972. A brief explanatory note, perhaps a condensation of a letter sent to publishers, laid it on the line. His second book, Owens explained, was not what publishers expected—and was not what *he* had anticipated.

This time he did not chastise black militants; rather, he praised them. Instead of urging racial cooperation as

In Berlin, spectators said that Jesse seemed literally to "fly over hurdles." [THE OHIO STATE UNIVERSITY ARCHIVES]

he had two years earlier, in his second book Owens said—perhaps accurately—that the U.S. racial climate in 1970 was disturbingly similar to that of 1936. While he was conciliatory in tone in 1970, two years later Owens summed up a new set of views in a single sentence: "I don't believe in loving my neighbor."

Since the Olympic great died of cancer in 1980, there's no way to question him about his change of attitude. Perhaps his collaborator saw an opportunity for a new book and persuaded him to go along with the idea. Maybe

Owens was bombarded with barbed criticism from activists of his own race. There's always a chance that he took a look at America and changed his mind.

Whatever the case, totally different books published just two years apart underscore a basic aspect of the life of Jesse Owens. This Alabama-born track-and-field star didn't spend his life on an even keel. His highs were breathtaking in their elevation and speed; his lows hugged the ground along which they crawled.

Henry and Emma Owens chose James Cleveland as the name for their son who was born on September 12, 1913. He didn't receive the name by which he's known until the family went north and a teacher unaccustomed to southern accents slurred his initials—J.C.—into Jesse.

Once conferred on him in a semiofficial way, the adapted name stuck to him for life. Present-day reference works list the accomplishments of Jesse Owens, but James Cleveland Owens is not mentioned.

Jesse's parents were farmers. Although slaves in the South were given their freedom after the Civil War, they had little or nothing else. Along with their white counterparts who were impoverished by the war, former slaves and their descendants became tenant farmers, living and working on land owned by someone else. Many of these folk were unable to pay rent for the land they worked, so they became sharecroppers.

At harvest time the landlord received his share of the crop—often half or more. An amount was also subtracted for anything that might be owed in the way of subsistence during the year. The tenant received what, if any, was left over.

Sharecropping dominated agricultural practices throughout Alabama and the rest of the Deep South until World War II. New jobs created by industrial expansion and the acquisition of small farms by agri-business corporations practically ended all sharecropping.

In many such families, white as well as black, half a dozen family members of all ages worked from sunup to sundown as field hands. There was no way to get ahead under this system.

Some folks used Oakville to designate the area in which Henry Owens and his family worked as sharecroppers. Others called it Danville. Neither community appears on a present-day map of Alabama, however.

Whatever place he lived, James Calhoun—called J.C. by his loved ones—had never known any home except the shack in which he was born. A growing boy in that environment did not consider himself to be a victim of society. He played under a mulberry tree, helped to feed and later to harness the mules, and listened as his father talked about the joys of running.

Plagued by bronchial ailments almost from birth, J.C. was otherwise healthy until age six. Suddenly a painful growth in his left leg enlarged.

"It's got to come out, J.C.," his mother told him one night. Turning to one of her older children she directed, "Get me the butcher knife from the kitchen, then come help me hold this young'un."

His mother's crude surgery excised the growth but left a big hole in J.C.'s left leg. Under the guidance of his father, he exercised regularly and then began to run to strengthen the muscles of his injured leg. Years later he said that the removal of the growth helped him to develop stamina as a runner.

Tennessee Ernie Ford later described sundown in a hopeless situation as leaving an agricultural or industrial worker "another day older and deeper in debt." That's how Henry Owens felt in 1921, so almost on impulse he sold his farming equipment and his five mules and went north to what he thought was the land of opportunity.

He and his family had been in Cleveland, Ohio, for only a few weeks before he wished he could scrape together enough money to go back to Alabama. Since that couldn't be done, he took whatever menial jobs he could find and his wife found part-time work as a cleaning woman. By the time he was twelve, their son, now known as Jesse, often held down three jobs at once. He pumped gas at a filling station (as service stations were then called), shined shoes, and worked at a greenhouse or plant nursery.

Jesse, who'd begun to enjoy running, gained speed and confidence month by month. By the time he was old enough to go to college, Ohio State University scouts were keeping an eye on him. At their insistence, he

From his father, Owens learned to concentrate on running to the exclusion of all other sights and sounds. [THE OHIO STATE UNIVERSITY ARCHIVES]

agreed to enroll as a student with the stipulation that the university would give his father a steady job.

At Ohio State he tied the record for the 100-yard dash and broke the world record for the broad jump by six inches. Inevitably, that performance put him into contention for a place on the U.S. team at the upcoming Olympic Games in Berlin. He arrived in the German capital with $7.40 in his pocket.

Broke as he was, Owens became a celebrity in Germany. He won time after time, then found the eyes of the world focused upon him when Adolph Hitler refused to present four gold medals to the black athlete.

On his return home by way of New York City, the ticker tape showered upon him during a parade in his honor lifted him to a new emotional high. Honors aplenty came to him and his family, though. Ohio State named a new track-and-field facility for him and conferred an honorary doctorate degree upon him. His sister, Gloria, was crowned homecoming queen of the university. In Berlin, civic leaders took down a set of street signs, and in their place erected others that read "Jesse Owens Strasse [Street]."

All of this adulation soon fizzled out when Jesse found himself a world-champion athlete with no job and no prospects. Soaring very high during the years when his name was a household word, Jesse soon learned that admiration seldom translated into economic opportunity. Many people who were born in the 1930s never learned of his Olympic triumphs and his rebuff by Hitler. Difficult as it was to do so, he was forced to live as though he had never gone for the gold.

The celebrity value of his name eventually enabled him to get two books on the high-prestige list of William Morrow and Company. As different as day and night, the volumes that bear the name of a four-time winner of Olympic gold medals clearly reveal that an Alabama sharecropper's son lived a roller-coaster life.

71

Joseph Wheeler: 120 Pounds, Soaking Wet

"We must act quickly and decisively to stop Spanish aggression. If we fail to do so, we are recreant to our pledges to Christianity, to civilization, to humanity, and to Almighty God." Coming from an Alabama congressman with fourteen years of seniority, that challenge created seismic waves in Washington's political circles.

Many in the nation's capital were already wondering how long the nation could watch atrocities in Cuba and do nothing. A lengthy analysis by Joseph Wheeler helped to direct the course of public and official opinion.

Wheeler's challenge made front-page news throughout the nation a few months later when the USS *Maine* blew up in Havana Harbor on February 15, 1898. Although evidence was scanty, it was easy to conclude that Spain was behind the mysterious explosion. Many of Wheeler's fellow lawmakers who had hesitated to take a public stand now jumped on the bandwagon and urged military action.

President William McKinley, who earlier was reluctant to intervene in the Cuban revolution against Spain, drafted a message asking Congress for new authority. He wanted to take steps to end the civil war in Cuba he said in a message on April 11, 1898.

Pushed and prodded by the congressman from Alabama, Congress took just eight days to act favorably on the president's request. With the Spanish-American War

Fightin' Joe excelled at cutting Federal supply lines and wrecking railroads. [LIBRARY OF CONGRESS]

about to become reality, McKinley took another step that astounded the nation. Fully aware that Wheeler had led Confederate cavalry against blue-clad Federals during the Civil War, he made the former Confederate a major general of U.S. Volunteers.

Reared near Augusta, Georgia, by parents who had moved south from Connecticut and then returned to that state, Joseph Wheeler was just sixteen years old when he received an appointment to West Point. He had little contact with the superintendent, Robert E. Lee, but he wrote long letters praising four officers who were among his instructors.

Joseph, as he was then commonly called, did not know that Capt. Fitz-John Porter and Lts. John M. Schofield, Oliver O. Howard, and Alexander M. McCook would later lead Union troops against his countrymen. Although internal conflict was on the horizon at the time of his 1859 graduation, Wheeler was sent to New Mexico to fight Indians. It was in fierce hand-to-hand combat with Native Americans that he came to be called "Fightin' Joe," a nickname that stayed with him for the rest of his life.

Torn between loyalty to Connecticut and Georgia, Lieutenant Wheeler hesitated only briefly before taking off his U.S. Army uniform and becoming a lieutenant of artillery for the Confederacy. While on duty near Pensacola, Florida, he formed such close friendships with a group of Alabamians that he transferred to the Nineteenth Alabama Regiment soon after the battle of First Bull Run in July 1861.

For four full years beginning in April 1861, Fightin' Joe was in the thick of combat. Barely a year after changing uniforms, he so distinguished himself at Shiloh (or Pittsburg Landing) that he was made a brigadier general. For the duration of the war he led cavalry units that were lauded in the South and hated in the North. More than any other Confederate—except Nathan Bedford Forrest—Wheeler excelled at cutting Union supply lines, staging surprise raids, and wrecking railroads.

When William T. Sherman led his Federal armies into Georgia with the hope of crushing the Confederate Army of Tennessee, Wheeler became a chief source of frustration. He fought with special distinction at Ringgold, then distinguished himself anew by outwitting and outfighting the Federal cavalry near Atlanta.

Still living up to his nickname, Wheeler helped to guard the flight of Confederate President Jefferson Davis after the surrender of Lee's Army of Northern Virginia.

Fighting as an infantry officer, Wheeler's leadership at Shiloh made him a brigadier. [THE SOLDIER IN OUR CIVIL WAR]

When captured at war's end, he was sent north to prison in the company of the Confederate chief executive and other notables. On the ship that took him to Fort Delaware and a prison cell, his cabin mate was Alexander H. Stephens, vice president of the Confederacy.

Since the only "crime" with which he was charged was fighting for the region he loved, the Confederate lieutenant general was released after two months of imprisonment. At war's end, like thousands of other veterans, he came close to tears when he saw firsthand the damage that had been done to the South.

After a period of drifting in which he looked for some way to make a living, Wheeler launched a business in New Orleans. Possibly influenced by some of the same men who persuaded him to become colonel of an Alabama unit in Florida, he sold his business and in 1870 moved to Lawrence County, Alabama.

When he reached Alabama, the former Confederate hoped to be a gentleman planter. Within weeks, however, his brother-in-law became involved in an altercation that resulted in the death of a blacksmith. Tom Jones was without funds and desperately in need of a lawyer to defend him. With Jones due to be tried for murder in six months, Wheeler pored over legal volumes for hours every day.

While waiting for the trial to begin, the self-taught Wheeler passed the bar examination and became the attorney for the defendant. He won acquittal for his brother-in-law and so much admiration from his neighbors that they urged him to enter politics.

Fightin' Joe, a Democrat and a war hero who was backed by "the wool hat boys," ran for Congress against William M. Lowe, a Republican and a member of the aristocracy. When the votes were counted, Lowe had 12,365 to Wheeler's 12,408. Wheeler's admirers whooped with joy as he set out for Washington, but the Republican-dominated Congress appointed a committee to investigate the election and awarded the seat to Lowe.

Some beginning politicians would have given up at such a turn of events, but Fightin' Joe was no ordinary aspirant for office. He won the seat by a substantial majority in 1883 and held it until military duties caused him to resign in 1900.

When the Spanish-American War broke out, the Alabama congressman was sixty-one years old. Only five feet five inches tall, he weighed about 120 pounds. He also had a military record of service against the United States, which mitigated against McKinley's naming him a general of U.S. Volunteers. Against the advice of some of his top aides, however, the president yielded to the pleas of Fightin' Joe and ordered him back into military service.

At the head of his men, the brand-new brigadier general reached Cuba without mishap—only to learn that the horses for his and other units had been left behind in Florida. Undaunted, he said that he fought briefly on foot

Destruction of the USS Maine *in an explosion persuaded the United States to go to war with Spain.*

during the Civil War and had not forgotten what he had learned then.

Enlisting the support of a younger officer, General Wheeler and Lt. Col. Theodore Roosevelt outwitted the enemy in the now-forgotten battle of Las Guasimas. That victory made it possible for U.S. troops to reach Santiago, where Roosevelt's Rough Riders fought their way up San Juan Hill on foot. When Spanish forces in Cuba agreed to surrender, Fightin' Joe was on hand for the ceremony.

Now a national rather than a state or regional hero, the Alabamian by choice was made a brigadier general in the U.S. Army. No other high-ranking former Confederate matched his achievement. Hence it is no surprise that the former congressman is one of a very few officers buried in Arlington National Cemetery who wore gray during the Civil War.

72

Tallulah Bankhead: Sque-e-ze Me!

Some now-forgotten marketing genius came up with a radical idea; if the words of a radio advertisement were sung instead of spoken, maybe people would listen. That verdict soon proved to be right, so major advertisers followed suit.

In the years following World War II, practically everybody in the United States realized the importance of this new way of advertising. Shortly thereafter, newspaper headlines everywhere trumpeted the fact that a celebrity was suing for damages over a singing commercial that began:

> I'm Tallulah, the tube of Prell
> And I've got a little something to tell.
> Your hair can be radiant, oh, so easy
> All you've got to do is
> Take me home and sque-e-ze me.

Tallulah Bankhead of Huntington, Alabama, had adamantly refused offers of big fees to endorse commercial products. Without her permission, her name was being exploited for the sake of liquid shampoo. At least, that's what she said when relatives told her of having heard the jingle. Confessing herself to be "furious, absolutely furious, dahling," the actress launched a million-dollar suit.

In 1949 $1 million was big money, so big that Procter and Gamble and the two radio networks involved in the

Tallulah Bankhead wearing the most elegant costume she could find in England. [DOROTHY WILDING PORTRAIT]

suit protested that the name "Tallulah" was generic. Nevertheless, the defendants settled out of court for an undisclosed sum.

Well before it was known that the case would never go to trial, it attracted the attention of two Atlanta college students. "Tallulah Bankhead isn't the only person with that musical name," Mary announced late one afternoon.

"You're absolutely right," her husband nodded. "When I was growing up in Covington, Georgia, I knew a girl named Tallulah Odum."

"That Tallulah was a latecomer. Somewhere in the family records, I'm sure there is a Tallulah Catoosa who grew up soon after the Civil War; she was named for two rivers—not just one."

"You're positive about that?"

"Absolutely positive."

"Terrific! If we can document that early Tallulah, Procter and Gamble will pay our tuition for the next semester—maybe a lot longer."

Family research by the two college students revealed the burial place of a distant relative who had died before they were born. They cranked up their battered old Model A Ford, found a country cemetery, and made rubbings of the tombstone of Tallulah Catoosa. Then they took affidavits from family members who remembered the unusual name.

A packet of records was dispatched to Procter and Gamble by registered mail. Then the hopeful students began checking their mailbox two or three times a day. Long after they had expected to receive a hefty check as reward for information judged valuable to one of the nation's largest corporations, a reply finally appeared in a brown envelope.

It contained a tube of Prell shampoo!

Tallulah Bankhead never remembered a time when she failed to realize that her musical name was unusual—though not unique. She received her river-based name by

way of her grandmother, who went from South Carolina
to Alabama when much of the state bordering on the Gulf
was still undeveloped.

En route to their new home, the emigrants stopped for
a night or two at a then-famous resort. Spectacular Tallulah Falls, Georgia, was created by erosion worked by the
once-mighty Tallulah River. For decades it attracted
many tourists and made headlines when the famous Wal-
lenda walked across the gorge on a tight wire. So when a
little girl came along, the happy Alabama couple decided
to name her for the spot at which they were positive she
was conceived.

A generation later, William Brockman Bankhead lost
his wife, Ada, from an infection developed during child-
birth. Doctors in that day called the too-common malady
"blood poisoning," for which there was no known rem-

*Vacationers pose with the steam locomotive that brought them to Tallu-
lah Falls, Georgia.*

edy. After the young mother was buried, her second daughter was baptized in 1903 with the name Tallulah as a tribute to Will's mother.

The Bankheads of Alabama were prominent in national politics. Members of the family had served in both the House of Representatives and the Senate. Hence Tallulah's father, an attorney, felt a strong pull toward public office.

At the same time, the Huntsville lawyer was strongly attracted to the theater. That may have influenced his decision when Tallulah, reared by two aunts, was fifteen years old.

Without the knowledge of her father, the teenager entered a photo contest in 1918 sponsored by *Picture-Play* magazine, and she won. Elated at the news of her victory, Tallulah was sobered by the realization that an opportunity to act came with a condition. To accept it she would have to leave school and go to New York.

Had Will Bankhead not harbored theatrical ambitions of his own, the future Speaker of the House of Representatives might have refused to let his daughter go "up north" unaccompanied by an adult relative. As it was, he rejoiced at her success, wished her well, and told her to "go and take a big bite out of the Big Apple."

In New York, the girl whose voice was unusually deep and husky made her Broadway debut at the Bijou Theater. Her role in *Squab Farm* fulfilled her obligations to the movie magazine. During the next four years she landed a number of other minor roles, but she reluctantly confessed to her father that she had not yet come close to "setting the woods on fire."

Turning her back on Broadway, the Alabama girl set out for London. She had performed only a few times before she became a favorite topic in the tabloid newspapers for which the British capital is famous.

Her exquisite blonde hair and husky southern drawl demanded attention, but her personal style made her name a household word in the island kingdom. She enjoyed a glamorous lifestyle in Britain in a fashion that few others attempted.

These factors, combined with her native talent, made the Alabama actress the talk of London for eight years. By the time she returned to the United States, newspaper feature writers often dubbed her "the celebrity who makes other celebrities seem tame and mild."

Both on Broadway and in motion pictures, Tallulah scored one triumph after another. Her greatest disappointment came when she did not get the lead role in *Gone with the Wind*.

That failure did not come to her because she did not make an effort for the role. She pulled every string she could, even enlisting the state of Alabama as an enthusiastic backer. Gov. Bibb Graves, the Alabama Public Service Commissioner, and thousands of ordinary folk besieged producer David O. Selznick. In the end, it was younger, green-eyed Vivien Leigh who became Scarlett.

Bankhead turned her enormous energy and enthusiasm into the political arena and in 1948 campaigned for Harry Truman. He showed his appreciation by sending her special tickets admitting her to the reviewing stand at his inauguration. Gossip columnists reported that she was seen there sitting on his lap.

Regardless of what she did or did not do, Tallulah was the stuff of which gossip columns were made. Her many roles on Broadway and in movies had made her face and name familiar to most Americans. Presumably that is why Procter and Gamble decided to settle her suit, although she was not the only or the earliest woman to bear that distinctive name.

As Regina in Lillian Hellman's *The Little Foxes*, the Alabamian took the top award of the New York Drama Critics Circle. Three years later, director Alfred Hitchcock chose the American beauty for one of his most famous productions, *Lifeboat*. This time Tallulah's performance brought her the top award of the New York Film Critics.

Will Bankhead would have been enormously pleased had he lived long enough to know that his daughter's name was a household word. She frequently said that in spite of her pride in being a Bankhead from Alabama she didn't need a surname. "Everybody who's anybody knows Tallulah," she insisted.

"When I was a girl in a convent school," she often said to new friends, "I learned that instead of it's being a liability my name was a great asset. Every school I ever attended was full of Virginias and Susans—but not one of them had another Tallulah!"

PART SEVEN:
Kentucky

Audubon as he appeared when dressed for society, about 1831.
[FREDERICK CRUIKSHANK MINIATURE, AUDUBON MUSEUM, HENDERSON]

73

John James Audubon: Bird Man

Anyone in doubt about the identity of America's most noted wildlife artist has only to visit the Audubon Memorial Museum in Henderson, Kentucky. Memorabilia from and the published work of the naturalist are evidence that John James Audubon has no peer in his field.

Reared in France, the son of a sea captain who was with the fleet that helped the Colonials win the American Revolution, Audubon used the dowry of his wife, Lucy, to establish a business in Louisville. Unfortunately, Ferdinand Rozier, his French partner, spoke only broken English and Audubon was more interested in watching birds than in moving merchandise.

The partners soon came to the conclusion that Louisville was too big and too cosmopolitan for their line of goods. They'd do much better, the two decided, by moving 125 miles down the Ohio River. At Redbanks, the one hundred or so settlers in the community wouldn't want or need much except whiskey, gunpowder, and rough outdoor clothing.

When Audubon and his family landed at what is now Henderson, he was pleased to find an empty log cabin. Describing his reaction to the place, he wrote:

The country around was thinly settled and all purchasable provisions rather scarce; but our neighbors were friendly, and we had brought along our bacon-hams;

our pleasures were those of young people not long married; a single smile from our infant son was, I assure you, more valued by us than all the treasures of a modern Croesus would have been. The woods were amply stocked with game, the river with fish; and now and then the hoarded sweets of the industrious bees were brought from some hollow tree to our little table.

If this sounds as though his new home and place of business were idyllic, that's because it seemed so to him. Rozier could look after their trade while Audubon kept his rifle warm and his fishing line wet.

When required to put time and energy into some form of work that was then common, Audubon proved downright shiftless. Failure did not seem to bother him; he could always drift from one job to another—operator of an inherited lead mine, clerk in a countinghouse (business office), or part-owner of a general store.

Those folk who knew him well—especially women—liked his ways and his appearance so much that they overlooked what seemed to be an incurable case of laziness. Martha Pope, married to a Henderson resident, wrote an ecstatic description of the newcomer who had almost lost his French accent: "Audubon was one of the handsomest men I ever saw. In person he was tall and slender, his blue eyes were an eagle's in brightness, his teeth were white and even, his hair a beautiful chestnut colour, very glossy and curly. His bearing was courteous and refined, simple and unassuming."

Nathaniel Pope may have sensed that it was not a good idea for his wife to spend a lot of time with Audubon. That may be why he invited the self-styled merchant to go with him into the woods and fields, often daily, for weeks at a time.

Much as he hated to lose his hunting and fishing partner, Audubon decided to give up his Henderson business. Maybe he and Rozier would do better in a real city, like St. Louis. So they loaded a keelboat with three hundred barrels of whiskey, gunpowder, and dry goods from the Henderson store.

"Go to it, man," encouraged Pope. "You're too big for this place; you're sure to do well in the city downriver."

It hadn't occurred to the French partners that early winter might be a bad time to float down the river. They drifted for nine weeks before ice drove them aground. Audubon then spent several joyful weeks hunting and fishing with Indians, while his partner sat around a fire brooding.

When spring thaws caused the ice to break, they poled their way upriver to a small settlement, sold their whiskey at an enormous profit, and parted company. Audubon made his way back to Henderson; characteristically, he gave two contradictory accounts of the journey.

To Pope and other friends he bragged that he had tramped 165 miles, mostly through underbrush, in just four days. Later he said that he had paid too much for "a beauty of a horse" on which he rode back in style.

No longer having a stock of merchandise or a partner to look after it, Audubon tried his hand at operating a steam-powered grist and lumber mill. When that venture failed, he was jailed for debt. Released after pleading bankruptcy, he decided that he would try anything except another business venture.

Having started sketching at age fifteen in France, he had developed unusual skill. As a result he was able to sell a few crayon portraits for five dollars apiece. Then he wandered to Cincinnati and found work as a taxidermist. While practicing this trade in 1820, Audubon had a wonderful idea. He had accumulated several bird drawings and decided to publish and sell them.

Audubon worked his way to New Orleans, selling enough pictures—now priced at twenty-five dollars apiece—to keep from starving. In the huge port city he dabbled at painting street signs before he found a patron—a woman, of course.

He spent three hours a day with the woman for more than a week before completing the commissioned nude painting of her. When she accepted the work, she paid him with an excellent hunting gun that he carried for years afterward.

Meanwhile, despairing of ever being supported by her husband, Lucy Audubon had become a teacher and a governess. Returning home after a five-month absence, he tried his hand at teaching music and drawing her pupils. Somehow he scraped together enough money to take his now-thick portfolio of bird drawings to Scotland in search of a skilled engraver. Although Sir Walter Scott raved over Audubon's work, engraver William Lizars gave up after producing only ten plates.

This turn of events sent the painter to London, where he found Robert Havell Jr. Neither man then guessed that their association would last eleven years while Havell turned out plates and Audubon sold subscriptions to the unfinished work. On the day that King George IV agreed to buy a set of prints, called "elephant" because of their huge size, the former ne'er-do-well was sure that he had made his fortune.

Although soon lionized in Great Britain, Audubon attracted no notice in the United States until 1830. Lasting fame came to him years later, when he became recognized as the greatest depicter of North American birds.

That niche would never have been occupied by him had he not found Havell, who transformed his sometimes awkward sketches and paintings into elegant engravings. Reprinted in countless editions, *The Birds of America* still provides a breathtaking experience for a first-time reader.

Lauded though he has been for generations, the artist is not without his critics. Some of them point out that many of his famous plates show birds in positions that they couldn't possibly assume in life. One of the reasons for this is that he frequently sketched dead birds after having wired them into poses that pleased him. Many such specimens he shot himself; some were bought in the markets of New Orleans and other cities.

His artistic success, despite some criticism, failed to bring financial ease to the restless fellow. Although priceless today, the engravings in his oversize book of birds did little more than pay for its production costs during his life.

Widowed, Lucy Audubon turned to New York City where she continued to teach. One of her pupils, George B. Grinnell, developed a passion for the conservation of wildlife and recruited like-minded persons willing to establish a society. How better to honor his teacher, Grinnell reasoned, than to name the conservation society for her husband?

Local Audubon societies were organized as early as 1895; in 1905 a national association was formed. Six years later society members persuaded the New York legislature to adopt the Audubon Act, under whose terms it became illegal to sell the feathers of native wild birds.

How John James Audubon would have wondered and probably laughed had he been on hand to hear New Yorkers talk about conservation! Part of the mystery and charm of this uniquely gifted Kentuckian by choice lies in the fact that he could not qualify for membership in a conservation society.

Headed down the Ohio River from Henderson on a keelboat, Audubon amused himself by firing into flocks of passing birds. He did so, not to put food on the table, but for the fun of seeing some of them drop into the water. On a single day during that voyage, he and his Indian companions killed more than fifty wild swans. They weren't after food; he noted in his journal that the skins of the exotic birds "were intended for the ladies of Europe."

Audubon the immortal artist was also Audubon the mighty hunter! It is not accidental that all of the better-known paintings of him also depict his rifle, his hunting dog, and often his horse.

In this famous portrait a faithful horse stands close to his master. [AMERICAN MUSEUM OF NATURAL HISTORY]

In his Henderson workroom, the walls were dotted with antlers of elks he had stalked and killed, and the floor was partly covered with a panther skin. From Daniel Boone he learned how to kill squirrels without damaging their flesh with bullet wounds. Firing just beneath an animal, the artist could "bark" it from a tree by the impact of a bullet.

Although Audubon often hunted for food, he also shot birds and animals for sheer pleasure. On a Florida expedition he counted it a very poor day when he didn't down at least one hundred birds. When great flocks of passenger pigeons loomed overhead, he liked to fire into them to see how many would fall from a single shot. Once numbered in the millions, these birds were made extinct by hunters like Audubon.

There's considerable doubt that he would be welcomed as a member of the Audubon Society today. Yet his engravings make printed pages seem ready to take flight and soar above the swamp or river or thicket—where in reality the artist would most likely have shot at them.

74

Jefferson Davis: Reluctant President

Kentucky has a record that no other state is likely to equal. Within a period of eight months, two future presidents were born there less than one hundred miles from each other.

Jefferson Davis was born on June 3, 1808, in Christian County—a section that is today Todd County. His prosperous father operated what would now be called a bed and breakfast—two log cabins, one of which offered accommodations for guests.

Although he seldom used it, the future president's full name was Jefferson Finis Davis, perhaps a not-so-subtle hint that Samuel Davis and the former Jane Cook expected to have no other children.

Davis entered Lexington's Transylvania University in 1823 after having studied at other institutions. Influenced by his older brother, Joseph, he had already decided to make a career in military service.

It took a bit of string-pulling to get it, but after a year in Lexington, Davis managed to win an appointment to the U.S. Military Academy. His class ranking at graduation—twenty-three out of thirty-three—might have been higher had he not accumulated numerous demerits for mischievous behavior.

Second Lieutenant Davis began his military career during the Indian wars in the West and then was posted in the East when the noted Sauk warrior Black Hawk led an uprising known as the Black Hawk War of 1832. When

Jefferson Davis, president of the Confederate States of America.
[BRADY STUDIO, LIBRARY OF CONGRESS]

the war ended, Davis accepted Black Hawk's surrender and took him from the Wisconsin Territory to Missouri as a prisoner of war.

As a first lieutenant, Davis led a number of forays into hostile Indian territory before being smitten by Sarah Knox Taylor, daughter of Zachary Taylor, Davis's commanding officer and a future president. They married despite Taylor's objections, but "Knoxie," as Davis called his bride, soon succumbed to a fatal fever after the young couple moved to Mississippi.

The disconsolate twenty-seven-year-old widower wanted completely new surroundings. Hence he resigned his commission and then traveled to Havana, New York, Washington, and his brother's plantation in Mississippi. After a decade as a gentleman farmer he met and married Varina Howell of Natchez.

Only twenty years old at the time of their 1845 marriage, Varina strongly encouraged her husband to go into politics. He won a seat in the U.S. House of Representatives but did not keep it long. Once more, the U.S. Army beckoned to him.

As colonel of a volunteer regiment, Davis led his men to Carmago, Mexico. With Gen. Winfield Scott as its commander, the American army that included Davis clawed its way from Vera Cruz to Mexico City. Back home and not accustomed to his new status as a celebrity, he went to the U.S. Senate and became chairman of its military affairs committee.

His experience in that post made him a natural choice for secretary of war when Democrat Franklin Pierce defeated Scott, a Whig, for the White House. Davis spent only four years as secretary of war, but he made so many changes for the better that he is ranked as one of the ablest men ever to hold that post.

When he took office, the authorized size of the U.S. Army was nearly fourteen thousand officers and men, yet the roster always listed at least four thousand vacancies. When Davis left the War Department, nearly fifteen thousand names on the rolls meant a significant increase in size during four years, an achievement he may have regretted later.

After personal inspection of many coastal fortifications, Davis succeeded in upgrading the ordnance at most. Simultaneously, he introduced new infantry tactics and, against strenuous opposition, moved toward scrapping muskets of the 1812 variety in favor of weapons with rifled barrels.

Strangely, his post at the War Department put him in charge of completing the dome over the U.S. Capitol. His failure to bring it to completion was high on his list of things he most regretted as secretary of war.

Returning to the Senate in 1857, the man born in a state destined to become famous for divided families during the Civil War became an eloquent spokesman for

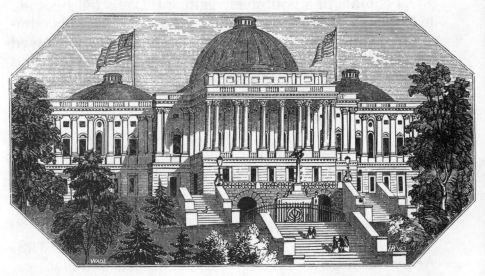

The unfinished U.S. Capitol, a major source of regret by the man who boosted the size of the U.S. Army.

the South. More than any other political leader, he took the place earlier occupied by John C. Calhoun of South Carolina.

After a Kentucky major took his men to Fort Sumter from Fort Moultrie in Charleston Harbor late in 1860, the sectional crisis became acute. Davis, who deplored secession, publicly admitted that South Carolina's withdrawal from the Union created a situation for which there was no remedy except war. Exhausted and half-sick, he made a farewell speech to the Senate on January 21, 1861. Then he set about planning to resume his interrupted life as master of the Mississippi plantation he called Brierfield.

Davis was riding through his fields when he saw a stranger approaching at top speed, waving something in his hand. When the two men came face to face, the messenger from Vicksburg handed over a telegram. Scanning it with disbelief, Brierfield's master learned that, without his knowledge, delegates to the Confederate Provisional Congress in Montgomery, Alabama, had on February 9 elected him president of the Confederate States of America.

Davis had not wanted the job, although he would have gladly accepted appointment as general in chief of the armed forces. When he broke the news to Varina, she studied his face and voice before concluding that he sounded much like "a prisoner who had been condemned to hang at daybreak."

After reluctantly making his way to Montgomery, Davis took the oath of office on February 18. His long and eloquent inaugural address stressed his hope for peace but ended with a solemn challenge to every Confederate: "We have entered upon the career of independence, and it must be inflexibly pursued."

Far too intelligent not to know that the South lacked the resources of money, manpower, and industry found in the North, the native of the Bluegrass State never wavered from faithfulness to his inaugural commitment.

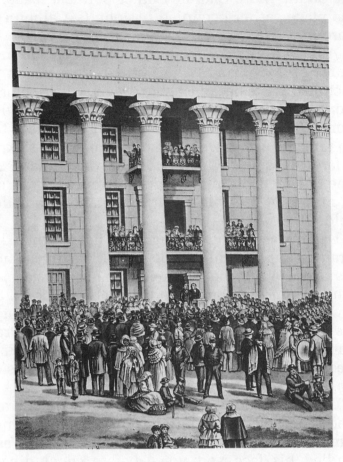

The inauguration of Jefferson Davis at Montgomery, Alabama.

During four years and three months in office, he did everything humanly possible to stem the force of the blue torrents of men who inundated the South.

Perhaps the single most unusual aspect of the career of the president from Kentucky who did not want the post was his 1861 election. The delegates who crowded the convention hall in Montgomery voted unanimously to put into office a man whose inclinations and wishes were not known.

75

Abraham Lincoln: Fate and Cunning

Tom Lincoln, a wandering laborer, could barely afford a one-room log cabin with a breakaway chimney. It was so small, overnight visitors had to sleep on a ledge at the height of the loft.

His son Abraham, born February 12, 1809, in Hardin (later LaRue) County, Kentucky, could not pursue a fancy education. The young Lincoln was lucky to spend a few weeks at a time in what were called "blab schools"— presumably because everyone blabbed at the same time. For his education, he learned a little from Parson Weems's *Life of Washington* and the Bible; after that, he was on his own.

Abraham Lincoln read law, spent some time in the state legislature, and won a single term in the U.S. House of Representatives. Hankering for a seat in the Senate, he challenged his rival candidate, Stephen A. Douglas, to a series of debates. They made his name a little more familiar, but members of the legislature were all set to pick Douglas before the debates started.

With the presidential election of 1860 approaching, Lincoln's wife, the former Mary Todd of Lexington, Kentucky, seems to have been yearning to be mistress of the Executive Mansion in Washington. The Democratic Party was split, with three candidates backed by separate factions of the party. That meant whoever received the Republican nomination was assured the presidency.

Lawyer Lincoln, then living in Springfield, Illinois, had little chance of gaining the nomination. David Davis,

*Abraham Lin-
coln, careworn
by four years of
Civil War.* [NA-
TIONAL ARCHIVES]

an influential Illinois attorney and friend of Lincoln, had
given his word that if the Republican convention would
come to Chicago, his state would not offer a favorite son
as a candidate for the nomination.

When Republicans of the state met for their convention, it turned into a circus. An old fellow appeared on
the floor of the hall with two weather-beaten fence rails.
A placard announcing that they were split by Abraham
Lincoln led to shouts of delight and the promise of "no
favorite son candidate" was abandoned.

In spite of this development, most veteran observers
were sure that the Republican nomination would go to
William H. Seward of New York on the first ballot. It
might have done so had not someone carefully arranged
for the printer to be late in delivering the ballots. That
meant the vote had to be rescheduled.

When the first ballot was delayed overnight, joyful
Seward supporters staged a parade. While they were
celebrating the eventual nomination of Seward, Davis

and other Lincoln backers packed the hall with visitors provided with counterfeit admission passes. They filled the Wigwam—the building erected for the convention— to capacity, and Seward's supporters could not enter when they returned.

In spite of this handicap, the first ballot gave Seward 173 of the 236 votes needed to clinch the nomination. To the surprise of many, Lincoln garnered 102 votes. As preparations were being made for the second ballot, a lot of political maneuvering went on behind the scenes. Lincoln's campaign workers persuaded many delegates to make the man from Kentucky their second choice. Seward picked up just 11 more votes on the second ballot, while Lincoln gained 79.

Seward and some other contenders had been outspoken in their opposition to slavery, the burning issue of

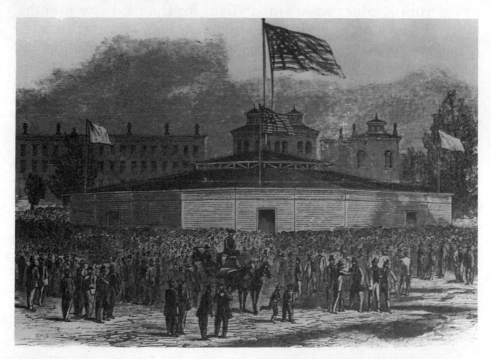

Chicago erected a huge meeting hall, called The Wigwam, for the Republican National Convention of 1860. [Harper's Weekly]

the day. Lincoln had said little about it but did not hesitate to make it clear that he did not believe whites and blacks were equal.

Since the candidate wasn't present at the convention, his campaign manager was free to make all sorts of promises. Before the final vote was taken, he had promised most of the major contenders cabinet positions if Lincoln were elected president. Whether these promises were made with Lincoln's knowledge remains unsure, but they helped to clinch the nomination for him on the third ballot.

No other sudden development on the American political scene was quite so surprising as Lincoln's nomination. A lifelong believer in the work of fate, he was sure that events beyond his control had operated to send him to the Executive Mansion.

Following the advice of veteran campaigners, the man from Kentucky remained silent for the next few months. He gave no interviews and made no speeches, which left the American public largely ignorant of where he stood on key issues.

Republicans, whose youthful party was strongly opposed to slavery, sensed a good chance for victory. They organized Wide Awake clubs in major cities, enlisted Carl Schurz to help deliver the German vote, and worked diligently for their candidate. If he won, it would mean a complete turnover in the vast federal patronage system, with lucrative jobs going to numerous good Republicans.

In 1860 only a small fraction of the population could vote. A white male had to be twenty-one years old and own property or hold a certificate attesting to his military service in order to go to the polls. Women, most free blacks, and all eighteen-year-olds stayed home on election day; it would be years before they would win suffrage.

On the all-important day in November, Democrats divided their votes among Stephen A. Douglas of Illinois, John C. Breckinridge of Kentucky, and John Bell of Tennessee. This meant that none of them gained enough delegates to the Electoral College to win.

At the polls, one American in sixteen checked the name of Abraham Lincoln. This tiny fraction of the population was enough to score a victory. As a result a one-term congressman who had held no elected office for a dozen years captured 59 percent of the votes in the Electoral College.

Unlike his fellow Kentuckian Jefferson Davis, Lincoln was eager to become chief executive, although he did not seem to have a chance. The inscrutable workings of fate and the skill of his campaign manager and aides brought about one of the most bizarre choices of a president in U.S. history.

Knowing that Davis had been inaugurated as president of the Confederate States of America earlier, Lincoln took

Abraham Lincoln on the way to the Capitol to take the oath of office.
[LIBRARY OF CONGRESS]

the oath of office on March 4, 1861, and became the sixteenth president of the United States. En route to his inauguration he repeatedly stressed, "There is no problem that can't quickly and easily be solved."

With eleven states having seceded, he gamely proclaimed himself to be "President of all the people," in the South as well as the North. Soon he issued calls for military volunteers from all 34 states, but this was ignored in the states headed by President Jefferson Davis.

Baffled by the failure of Unionists within the Cotton Belt to countermand resolutions of secession, the man from Kentucky denied that any state had actually withdrawn from the Union. He then put the military might, the economic power, and the industrial muscle of the North to work. For four bloody years, he tried to persuade what he termed "so-called seceded states" to abandon the short-lived nation led by Davis and to return to the Union.

While defeating his fellow Kentuckian, Lincoln radically altered the nature of the United States—perhaps unintentionally. When he took his oath of office, the states in the Union were powerful and semi-independent. In order to defeat the Confederacy, those states had to yield a great deal of their autonomy to Washington. By the time Jefferson Davis fled from Richmond, the federal capital was the power center of the nation.

About 130 years after the assassination of the Kentuckian who became president through fate and cunning, American politics took a new direction. Office seekers began to wage ever more strident campaigns based on promises to return power to the states and reduce the influence of the federal government.

Probably without realizing it, politicians today are increasingly vocal in their zeal to return the United States to a semblance of the condition it was in before Kentucky's second president assumed the mantle of power.

76
Robert Anderson: Hero or Turncoat?

"I thought you said you were due a nice long rest."

"That's right; what makes you think otherwise?" responded Maj. Robert Anderson of the First Artillery, U.S. Army.

"From where I'm sitting I can see the main road. A uniformed messenger just turned into our lane," his wife explained. "Surely they're not going to send you back to some godforsaken hole in the West."

Elizabeth Anderson was partly right. A dispatch from Adj. Gen. Lorenzo Thomas in New York instructed her husband to report to Fort Moultrie in Charleston Harbor—far from the dusty posts of the Indian Territory. Once Anderson had relieved Col. John L. Gardner, he was to take charge of all federal installations in and around the port city.

News of Anderson's new assignment was circulating in Washington by the time the major of artillery was en route during the third week of November 1860. It was generally and correctly assumed that U.S. Secretary of War John B. Floyd was behind the order that took him from the plantation bought by his father, a veteran of the American Revolution.

Floyd was widely accused of having shipped heavy guns to the South during the tension-filled days following the election of Abraham Lincoln. Documentary evidence, however, suggests that the secretary of war did

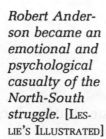

Robert Anderson became an emotional and psychological casualty of the North-South struggle. [LESLIE'S ILLUSTRATED]

nothing of the sort; it would have been impossible to keep such actions secret.

Having general oversight of the personnel under the command of General in Chief Winfield Scott, several factors—not just one—influenced him to pick the Kentuckian to assume command in the South Carolina port.

Because of its location, Fort Moultrie was likely to be an early target of those who began advocating secession as soon as Lincoln became president-elect. The southern grievance was not personal; the anti-slavery stance of the Republican Party placed it in opposition to the Cotton Belt.

Given this delicate situation, Floyd is believed to have reasoned that a native of the South would not inflame the citizens of Charleston. What's more, Anderson had ancestral ties with Virginia and was married to a Georgian whose father was a prominent slaveholder. Few officers of the U.S. Army were considered so likely to lean toward Secessionists as was the major from Kentucky.

Robert Anderson was tormented from the moment he received his orders. Although his ties with the South were numerous and strong, during his thirty-five-year career he had been totally obedient to his superiors in the U.S. Army. If forced to choose between the two conflicting sets of loyalties, he would find himself miserable indeed.

Soon after Anderson reached his new post, the South Carolina legislature moved its sessions from the capital in Columbia to Charleston. It was there on December 20 that the lawmakers of the Palmetto State joyfully passed an ordinance of secession. Believing themselves to have created a small independent republic that would grow rich and powerful from its cotton, South Carolinians prepared to send diplomatic agents to Great Britain and Europe.

Having declared independence, South Carolina didn't intend to tolerate the presence of "foreign agents" who manned a cluster of federal installations in Charleston. At crumbling Fort Moultrie, a relic of the Revolution, Anderson knew that he could not resist an attack of any magnitude.

Ridges of sand provided his chief fortifications, and many of his guns were so old that they might blow up if fired. Over decades, civilian residences had crept closer and closer to the Sullivan's Island installation. Sharpshooters stationed in some of those homes, usually occupied only during the summer, could pick off Anderson's men with impunity.

Frantic messages sent by Anderson to Washington requested and then begged for specific instructions, but none came. In this desperate situation, the West Point graduate weighed alternatives and put loyalty to the U.S. Army first.

Not far from indefensible Fort Moultrie was a splendid U.S. fortification that had never been occupied. Erected on an artificial island built with shiploads of granite, Fort Sumter had been planned to be a coastal defense against European aggression. When the War of 1812 was followed by an interlude of peace, the Charleston fortress was left unfinished. Dozens of big guns remained there, however, and its immense walls had been built to withstand heavy bombardment.

Without authorization, on the evening of December 26, 1860, Anderson led his small command from Moultrie to Sumter. Clearly, he made the move because Sumter was a strong enough haven to shelter his men from hostile fire if it should erupt. In it, they would be safe until the federal government turned the fort over to South Carolina.

Officials of the Palmetto State were furious when they learned what had taken place. In order to show Washington that they meant business, on December 27 the Seces-

During many hours, Confederates on shore poured shot and shell upon Fort Sumter, four miles away.

sionists sent units of the state militia to seize Castle Pinckney, the federal arsenal, and the customs house. This started a ripple effect that led to the seizure of federal installations in every seceded state.

Demanding the immediate evacuation of Fort Sumter, the South Carolinians were met with polite but firm refusals from Anderson. Officials in Washington were in a dither; Anderson's unexpected troop movement elevated Sumter into the most potent of all symbols pointing to the fast-growing sectional divisions.

Under President James Buchanan a feeble attempt to resupply Anderson's command failed. Cadets from The Citadel military academy in Charleston caused the rescue ship *Star of the West* to turn back without accomplishing its mission.

Both in the North and in the South, Fort Sumter became a burning topic of everyday conversation. Many in the North praised Anderson and some managed to send him messages urging him to stay where he was, no matter what might take place.

Throughout the South, especially in places where Anderson's background was known, he was bitterly condemned. His move to Fort Sumter was labeled traitorous, "a sell-out to the enemy." When his name was mentioned anywhere in the eleven states that came together to form the Confederacy, it was typically linked with profanity.

Having reluctantly put duty above love of the Southland in which he was born and reared, Anderson did his best to hold Sumter for the U.S. Army. Provisions became desperately low, and by early April 1861 it was clear that he could maintain his presence only a few more days.

In this situation, Lincoln dispatched a fleet of vessels from New York to restock Sumter with food and other essentials as well as to boost its manpower. It was this action that led the Confederates to fire the first shot of the war.

Anderson's gunners made sporadic attempts to silence the batteries commanded by Gen. P. G. T. Beauregard, but they were outgunned from the start. Though more than three thousand shells were exchanged between the artificial island and the Charleston shore, not a man on either side was killed. With food and water exhausted, the federal forces capitulated.

During surrender ceremonies, an accident during the firing of a one-hundred gun salute killed one of Anderson's men. The Confederates made no attempt to claim the federal garrison as prisoners of war. Instead, Anderson and his men were permitted to board ships that took them to New York and a triumphant welcome. Showered with honors, Anderson was appointed a brigadier general and posted to Kentucky.

Many in the Bluegrass State—perhaps a majority—earnestly tried to remain neutral in the growing North-South controversy. For a time the state had two governors—one a Unionist, the other a Secessionist.

Ordered to recruit men of his native state for Federal service, Anderson faced an uphill battle. Soon he was told secretly to smuggle Federal arms to Unionists in the region that wished to remain neutral. Aided for a time by William T. Sherman, the man who defended Fort Sumter and his officers were put under tremendous emotional strain. Sherman, who didn't fight the battle of divided loyalties, became so frenzied that he was dubbed insane by prominent newspapers.

To soldiers and civilians alike, Anderson was either a gallant hero who risked everything for duty and country or he was a wretched turncoat who sold out Kentucky and the South. Under these circumstances, it is small wonder that his health deteriorated and then failed. He requested light duty, received it, and then resigned—a casualty not of the battlefield, but of conflicting emotions and loyalties.

77

Carry Nation: Hatchet Woman

"Praise the Lord! Peace on earth, goodwill toward men!"

Brandishing a hardware-store tool as she shouted, a sturdily built woman reached the bar and swept the hatchet along the counter. Bottles, decanters, and glasses shattered. Lifting her implement, she hacked deep gashes into the mahogany of the bar surface. Pausing only an instant to look around, she attacked and smashed a cut-glass chandelier before knocking one end of a brass rail loose.

The woman had stormed into the Leavenworth saloon without notice and did not give her name or the purpose of her wrathful visit. Yet men who scrambled to avoid being cut by flying glass knew precisely who she was and why she was there.

By the fall of 1900 Carry Nation was a legend throughout Kansas. Jailed for two months after smashing the elegant Hotel Carey in Wichita, she then stormed through other towns like a cyclone. Although she did no damage to the place, in Topeka she brushed a guard aside and poured five minutes of vitriolic language upon the astonished governor of the state.

No other native Kentuckian became so well known during the first decade of the twentieth century. Born and reared in sparsely populated Garrard County, Nation made headlines wherever she appeared—and no one had any idea where her lightning would strike next.

Her family background offers clues concerning her bizarre behavior, but there are no firm explanations. Mary Moore, her mother, was called "tetched" (unbalanced) by neighbors who did not fancy living close to a woman who believed herself to be Queen Victoria.

Her relatives were sympathetic and tolerant. After all, long before the former Mary Campbell had married planter David Moore, she showed signs of following in her mother's footsteps. James Campbell, who would take a hot toddy any hour of any day, thought he had had one too many the first time his wife asked whether or not the president would be there for dinner. After a dozen episodes, he casually confided to his neighbors that he had ordered that his wife be locked in her room "until she came to her senses."

She never did, despite her awareness that her mate was a blood descendent of a duke of Argyll. Her constant

Carry Nation in her prime.
[KANSAS STATE HISTORICAL SOCIETY]

babbling about not having the proper clothing with which to move among the aristocrats of England seems to have affected her daughter. Carry grew up knowing that her grandmother, her mother, an uncle, and an aunt were "queer," meaning they were eccentrics.

Carry lived with her parents in half a dozen homes by the time she was an adolescent. Except for an emotional conversion experience during a camp meeting, as a girl Carry showed no overt signs of the mental instability that plagued her close relatives. Later, her only child, Charlien, became mentally ill before she was twenty years old.

Smitten with a handsome Union veteran, Dr. Charles Gloyd, Carry married the physician after a very short courtship. Twenty minutes after the wedding, her bridegroom passed out drunk.

Charlien was Carry's only source of comfort, so one day she put the toddler on her arm and walked out of Gloyd's life. He died six months later. The cause of death recorded on his death certificate was "acute alcoholism."

Having drifted to Missouri, the widow Gloyd shunned any man whose breath smelled of alcohol. David Nation, a clergyman who was also an attorney and an editor, seemed a safe bet. Carry married him without looking at his financial situation, however.

Unfortunately, the Reverend Nation turned out to be a drifter who never brought home enough money to feed his family. Determined to stick it out this time, Carry supported the family by running boardinghouses in a series of small Texas towns, then wound up in Kansas.

Haunted by memories of her mother's delusion, and fearful of following her mother's example, she nonetheless experienced what she called "mystical episodes," one after another. Usually she just saw visions, but during one episode she heard the voice of the Lord as clearly as did Moses on Mount Sinai. Like the prophet of old, Carry received a divine commission. An ordinary hatchet that sold for forty cents was just the right instrument to

carry out her mission of getting rid of the liquor that had
sent Charles Gloyd to an early grave.

Unlike her native state in which skilled bourbon makers were regarded as solid citizens, Kansas was bone
dry—at least in theory. A constitutional amendment
adopted in 1880 had made it one of the original prohibition states.

Mulling over the assignment that came to her from on
high, Carry came to a logical conclusion. Since it was
illegal to sell liquor in Kansas, it was the duty of a good
citizen to demolish any and every place where it could
be bought. She designed a sort of uniform, black-and-
white like that of a deaconess, and went to work.

Flailing right and left with her trusty hatchet, in just a
few months the woman with a mission became a legend
throughout Kansas. Satisfied that she had finished her
job in that state, she turned east to Pennsylvania, New
York, and the District of Columbia. On a later triumphant
tour of the West she left hatchet marks on half the bars of
San Francisco.

By this time she was a national and then an international celebrity. At Harvard and Yale, students and
faculty members pelted her with eggs. Bar owners who
learned she was in their city became vigorous in their
resistance to her crusade. She was cut by Bowie knives,
clubbed several times until she dropped her hatchet, and
shot at two or three times.

Frustrated police officials and magistrates did not
know what to do with her once they had her under arrest. Most of the forty or so times she was thrown in jail,
the charge was "disturbing the peace," which carried a
light fine with no time behind bars.

No other American woman, before or since, has
equaled the record of the swashbuckling six-footer
whose earliest years were spent not far from the elegant
city of Lexington. By 1905 Carry Nation's name was a
household word, and many a burly male ran or ducked

At Harvard University the hatchet-swinger received a shower of eggs.

for cover when he saw her coming with a hatchet in her hand.

Was her life guided by the same set of genes that ruled her mother and other relatives whom the courts labeled insane? Possibly, but not positively. She seems to have been greatly influenced by the fact that she was made a widow by the bottle, and in maturity her hatred of alcohol was calculated, not purely emotional.

Yet it was anger, not cold reasoning, that led to one of her most notable exploits. Learning that the famous boxer John L. Sullivan was in New York City, she decided to track him down and make an example of him. She eventually found him, half-drunk, lounging in a Bowery saloon. Some of those who were present that day insisted that Carry slapped Sullivan's face, then swiveled around and minced out in her most feminine fashion.

Perhaps the oddest aspect of the career of this one-of-a-kind Kentuckian was her business skill. She always managed to have enough money to pay her fines and to go on excursions that took her as far away as England.

Carry personally designed and distributed a small pewter replica of her famous hatchet, and it sold by the thousands. Her fame—or notoriety—made her in demand as a speaker, and she quickly learned how to demand and receive fees for her appearances.

She wrote and published tracts, a magazine, and an autobiography that had respectable sales. In a period when a nickel would buy a loaf of first-quality bread, the woman whose roots were in Bluegrass Country earned an average of at least twelve hundred dollars a month for several years. Financially, she was a tremendous success in an era when career women were few in number.

Those who knew her best and who observed her activities most closely agreed that "Carry Nation is crazy like a fox; she makes more money breaking liquor bottles than do a lot of fellows who serve Jack Daniel's all day."

78

Daniel Boone:
His Feet Itched

"You can get a hundred acres, just by signing your name, and there are miles and miles of wild land!"

"Are you sure?" Daniel Boone demanded.

"It's official," responded a friend from Culpeper County, Virginia, who knew that Daniel yearned for a big spread of land. "Now that the British have taken over East Florida, they're anxious for it to be settled by Protestants."

"I might give it a look, if you'll go with me," conceded the thirty-one-year-old who had been living on North Carolina's Yadkin River for a dozen years.

When the Virginian shook his head and explained that he had to get back home, Daniel persuaded his brother Squire to go to Florida with him. In the land of the Seminoles it impressed Squire that there were only a few white hunters.

"You haven't been around much," Daniel told the twenty-one-year-old. "Not many hunters because game is scarce."

Despite this negative assessment, Daniel reputedly made up his mind to settle in the region formerly held by the Spanish. He's said to have given a horse-load of deerskins as a down payment on a piece of land and a cabin in what is now Pensacola. Having promised his wife that he'd be home for Christmas, he and Squire then headed back to North Carolina.

When the winter sun was at the midpoint of its arc on December 25, Boone strode into his cabin. "Kept my promise," he said to Rebeccah. "But won't be here long; we're headed for the swamps!"

Five years younger than her husband, Rebeccah had become a bride at age seventeen. Like nearly all wives of the era, she deferred to her husband. This time, though, she adamantly refused to go to Florida.

Since his early adolescence, Daniel's friends had quipped that his feet itched when he remained in one

Boone, as he looked to an early artist.

place. So he reluctantly gave up the notion of settling in Florida but remained determined not to "rot on a scrawny farm" in North Carolina. Having struck the far South off his list at Rebeccah's insistence, he turned his attention to the West.

More than a decade earlier he had served as a blacksmith and teamster in the military campaign of Gen. Edward Braddock. During the French and Indian War the influence of the British had extended throughout the North American colonies. Most of the fighting took place far to the north, so Daniel acquired little military skill. Yet from one of his companions, professional hunter John Finley, he learned that endless acres of rich land lay in what was then western Virginia.

Remembering Finley's tales, Daniel turned toward the region beyond the Allegheny Mountains after Rebeccah refused to move to Florida with him. He renewed his contact with Finley, recruited him and others, and on May 1, 1769, struck out for the "Kentucke" region of Virginia.

When the party struggled to the top of Cumberland Gap, Boone was awestruck at the vista. "Keep a-goin'," he urged his companions. "There's bound to be level land out there somewhere."

By the time they reached Station Camp Creek, their load of deer hides was getting heavy, so they set up a base. Using it as a center, they explored the countryside for miles in every direction and found so much game that Florida seemed barren by comparison.

Finley, who once had hunted in the region, was surprised to find the Indian village of Es-kip-pa-kith-i-ka no longer in existence. To Boone that seemed a good omen; if settlers should come, they might meet little or no resistance from Native Americans.

Word of Boone's explorations reached Col. Richard Henderson, whose Transylvania Company was a predecessor of today's development corporations. With land available in vast quantities, he persuaded Boone to lead a

party of settlers into the uncharted region. At Boonesborough (now in Kentucky) he began building a fort. Before it was finished he returned to North Carolina for his
family and a band of recruits.

One year later Virginia lawmakers, whose land grant
extended west to the Mississippi River, created Kentucke
County. As captain and later major of the county's militia, Boone was beginning to be a man of importance.

That didn't mean life became easy for him, however.
Along with Betsy and Fanny Callaway, his fourteen-year-
old daughter, Jemima, was captured by Shawnees and
Cherokees and taken to one of their camps. The outlook
was grim, since Jemima's brother James captured earlier,
had been tortured before being killed and slashed to rib-
bons.

Jemima thought one of the Indian leaders looked familiar. Studying his face, she remembered that he was
Hanging Maw, whom she had earlier seen in North Carolina. Since he spoke English well, the girl's terror sub-
sided somewhat as she talked with him. When her Indian captors stopped for the night, two parties of settlers
led by Rebeccah Boone's father slipped up on them and
rescued the girls.

Boone and another search party were less fortunate.
Captured while boiling water to make salt at the Blue
Licks on Licking River, they found white men to be lead-
ing the Shawnees. Two of them were brothers of Simon
Girty, a notorious renegade.

Their captors threw away three hundred bushels of
salt, then forced their prisoners to walk to Detroit by way
of the Little Miami River. After failing to sell Boone and
his companions to the British, the Shawnees took them
to Little Chillicothe, a major encampment on the Miami
River.

One of the captives, an undersized Boonesborough settler, pretended to be simple-minded. Hence his captors
paid little attention to the man they called "Little Shut
His Eyes." Aided by Boone, he escaped and soon re-

turned with well-armed men whose rifles scattered the Shawnees and effected the release of the prisoners.

Although later artists often depicted Boone engaged in bloody hand-to-hand conflict with Indians, he was not a violent man. During his many conflicts with Native Americans, in which he usually triumphed, he never took an enemy's scalp.

The division of Kentucke into three Virginia counties soon led to Boone's elevation to the office of sheriff. Then he was elected to the Virginia General Assembly in 1786, half a dozen years before the Bluegrass State was created.

With the promise of statehood looming for the region he had opened to settlement, Boone's restlessness returned. Kentucky was becoming far too populated, he announced, so he left some of his debts behind and moved to a clearing near the mouth of the Great Kanawha River in what is now West Virginia. After only a decade there, he took his family to the western edge of American civilization, receiving a land grant on Femme Osage Creek in what is now Missouri.

Boone saw Kentucky only once after he had left it for more sparsely settled regions. Tradition has it that when he returned and paid off his debts, he started back to the far West with only fifty cents in his pocket.

His life of adventure captured the imagination of John Filson, who came from what is now Louisville. Intrigued by the backwoodsman, Filson said he used Boone's own words in writing and publishing *The Discovery, Settlement, and Present State of Kentucke.*

Soon avidly read in England, the Filson volume caught the attention of the poet Lord Byron. As a result, one of England's most famous men of letters of the period devoted seven stanzas of his work *Don Juan* to the founder of Kentucky. Lasting world fame followed.

Until the television-spawned Davy Crockett craze in the mid-twentieth century, the builder of Boonesborough was the best known and most admired American frontiersman. Throughout the country, the man who left the

Boone, as depicted by John James Audubon.

Yadkin River for Kentucky rather than for Florida is revered as the founder of the Bluegrass State.

Comparatively few of his ardent admirers remember that the Indian fighter and trailblazer spent his first sixteen years in the Keystone State of Pennsylvania. Had his feet not itched to leave this long-settled and relatively peaceful region, there's no reason to think his name would today be familiar throughout the Western world.

PART EIGHT:
Tennessee

79

Quivering Earth: Reelfoot Lake

On the 16th of December, 1811, about two o'clock in the morning, we were awakened by violent trembling of the earth. It was accompanied by a very awful noise that resembled loud but distant thunder. The whole atmosphere was quickly saturated with sulphurous vapor. The screams of inhabitants, the cries of fowls and beasts of every species, the falling trees, and the roaring of the Mississippi—whose current was retrograde [backward] for a few minutes—formed a scene of horror beyond the power of words to convey.

Writing to Methodist circuit rider Lorenzo Dow, Alexia Bryan of New Madrid, Missouri, gave an objective eyewitness account of the most powerful earthquake recorded in the United States.

At the same time, far to the north, John James Audubon knew he was close to the Tennessee-Kentucky border. Near the Mississippi River and well west of present-day Union City, Tennessee, the naturalist was in search of huge waterfowl that he had been told frequented the area.

Suddenly Audubon's horse gave a terrified whinny and began rolling its eyes. His first thought was that the animal had eaten leaves of a poisonous shrub and was about to die.

Jumping from the saddle, the man destined later to win fame as a painter of birds felt the ground swaying.

Evangelist Lorenzo Dow received a detailed description of events at the epicenter of the 1811 New Madrid earthquake.

"At that instant," he wrote, "all the shrubs and trees began to move from their very roots."

Astonished and for once in his life fearful, Audubon noted, "The ground rose in successive furrows, like the ruffled waters of a lake." Made dizzy by this bewildering experience, he said later that all of his senses "immediately departed." Only a person who has experienced an earthquake can fully understand how he felt that day.

Members of Indian tribes who lived and hunted in the Mississippi Valley had told European explorers that the Great Spirit sometimes stamped his feet and made the earth tremble. Audubon, who earlier had paid little attention to these tales, now remembered them and found them of absorbing interest.

As a boy in France he had heard stories about the earth trembling in Italy, so he discounted the notion of a supernatural cause. "Something about the nature of this wonderful world of ours is at the root of these strange happenings," he said to himself as he turned east and moved away from the river.

European scientists had begun to accumulate an understanding about earthquakes, but that term was not in the vocabulary of ordinary folk. Even those who were considered to be experts had gone on record as saying that North America would never experience a quake. According to them, the continent was far too vast and strong ever to be subjected to a trembling of the earth.

Although Audubon did not know it then, the shock that caused his horse to seem at the point of death shook an area of at least one million square miles. Chimneys were demolished or damaged in Cincinnati and Louisville. China rattled off pantry shelves far to the southeast in Georgia and South Carolina. In Saint Louis the quake was felt so strongly that architects who later designed Union Methodist Church included special protective features in the structure.

On the day when the northwestern tip of Tennessee shook violently, tremors were felt in New Orleans and Detroit. In the District of Columbia, where the federal government had been established only a decade earlier, vibrations were pronounced enough to cause watchmen to ring alarm bells.

Tremors that we now call aftershocks continued for many days. Five weeks after the initial quake, strong vibrations were recorded at Knoxville and Louisville.

Today's experts say that the seismic event centered near New Madrid, Missouri, probably had a magnitude of ten—placing it at the top of the Richter scale by which earthquakes are now measured.

Audubon was at least an hour's ride from the nearest settlement when he felt the earth move under his feet. Most of the section hardest hit was sparsely populated, and the only buildings were log cabins. Pioneers who constructed them from trees conveniently at hand didn't know that they are among the most earthquake-resistant of structures.

Architects took earthquake danger into account when they designed Union Methodist Church in Saint Louis.

Instead of having walls snap and roofs collapse, log cabins "sway with the earth" and seldom suffer earthquake damage except to their breakaway chimneys. Usually constructed of tree limbs and mud, such chimneys were designed to be pulled away from the cabin in the event of fire.

Experts of the U.S. Geological Survey have projected the New Madrid quake upon today's map. According to them, if it took place now, tens of thousands of persons would die and property damage would be many times that suffered in the great San Francisco earthquake and fire.

Its topographical changes were on so vast a scale that they couldn't be accurately measured before the advent of photography from satellites. In 1811 James Ritchie was living close to a stream he called the Pemiseo River, probably a tributary of the Saint Francis in Arkansas and Missouri. After he packed his personal possessions and struck out for central Illinois, he described what he experienced: "For a distance of nearly fifty miles the Pemiseo blew up. Its bed was entirely destroyed. The earth would open in fissures from forty to eighty rods in length and from three to five feet in width. Their depth no one knew, as it was considered foolhardy to try to fathom them."

Large forest trees that stood in the paths of fissures split from bottom to top. Courses of streams changed.

Bottoms of some lakes were pushed upward as much as fifteen feet. Dry land blew up, settled down, and was transformed into lakes of dark, muddy water.

Many immense holes and fissures gradually filled with sand. As a result, they were not noticed a century ago but today are visible in satellite photos.

After the quake, the U.S. government launched its first program of disaster relief. So many farms were ruined in regions of the hardest shock that any owner who could prove his loss was entitled to take possession of 640 acres in the Boon Lick region of western Kentucky.

One effect of the New Madrid quake is so vast that it is a great deal bigger than Arizona's famous meteor crater, believed to have been caused by the impact of a giant meteorite. Tennessee's topographical feature, Reelfoot Lake, created by the runaway Mississippi River, is about twenty miles long and four or five miles wide.

Audubon was close to the place where the ground suddenly began to sink as well as to shake. Although he didn't know it, he was in the middle of migration routes used by almost all known types of North American swimming and wading birds.

Small wonder that the area is today a popular resort that annually attracts visitors from a dozen states. In his diary the naturalist-artist recorded his amazement at seeing the waters of the mighty Mississippi run backward.

He had no idea that the fast-rushing stream was surging into a vast hole created by the earthquake. Now filled with water about fifteen to twenty feet deep, Reelfoot Lake constitutes fifty thousand or so of Tennessee's most interesting acres.

80

Andrew Jackson: Born to Fight!

"Give me your names, boys."

"Robert," replied the older of a bedraggled pair. Pointing to his diminutive brother, he said, "This is Andy."

"All right, all right, but I have to know the name of your pa, and where you both were born," Col. William Davis responded.

"We come from the Waxhaws settlement," Andy volunteered.

"What state? North Carolina or South Carolina?"

"Don't rightly know, mister. Nobody does. But our pa goes by the name of Jackson."

"Then I'm going to enlist both of you Jacksons as South Carolina volunteers."

Pointing to a shed, Davis told the recruits they could draw their muskets from the sergeant in charge. Turning back to Andy, he quipped, "When you've fought a few battles against the British and grown half a foot taller, you'll be as long as your musket, Private Jackson."

"Huh!" snorted the thirteen-year-old. "Don't have to wait for that; I wuz born to fight."

Because of Andy's size, Davis changed his mind and told him to turn in his musket. "You can be a messenger and ride a horse," he promised the heartbroken adolescent who had come to him from his log cabin home.

Serving as a mounted orderly under Davis, Andy Jackson was present at the August 1780 battle of Hanging Rock. At a point about a dozen miles east of North Caro-

General Jackson on his favorite mount, Sam Patch.

lina's Catawba River, Lt. Col. Thomas Sumter took the offensive against redcoats under the command of Sir Banastre Tarleton. There it was almost ridiculously easy for veterans under the professional British soldier to hold their own against ragtag amateurs who made up the Colonial force.

Clinging to the back of his horse, the boy "born to fight" scurried to safety, but six months later he was captured at the home of a cousin. During two or more weeks as a prisoner, he was forced to march forty or so miles to Camden, South Carolina. No food or water was given to him on the trek, so he arrived at the prison camp raging mad.

A British officer soon ordered him to clean his boots, but Andy shook his head and stood motionless. Angry, the redcoat slashed the boy's head and arm with his sword. That incident gave Andrew Jackson scars that he carried with him the rest of his life—along with burning rage at everyone and everything British.

At the conclusion of the American Revolution, Jackson read a little law and won admission to the Tennessee bar before moving to Nashville. Although he had seen only minor action against the British and had no military training, he managed to become a major general of Tennessee Volunteers in 1802. During a dozen years in this capacity his most dramatic fight was waged in defense of his wife, Rachel.

Charles Dickinson, a highly trained marksman, was sure he ran no risk when he made insulting remarks about Rachel Jackson and later about her husband. He was taken by surprise on May 22, 1806, when Gov. Thomas Overton hand-delivered to him a challenge to a duel.

Since authorities in Nashville might have intervened to stop the fight, the men who were at odds with one another decided to ride across the Red River into Kentucky and to meet in a clearing near Harrison's Mill. When they arrived with their seconds, Overton followed

the dueling code and offered Dickinson his choice of two
matched .70-caliber handguns.

Some accounts of the duel say that the opponents
faced one another at the unheard-of distance of eight feet.
Overton, who later stated that they stood twenty-four feet
apart, was probably accurate. Even at that distance, a single one-ounce ball was sufficient to kill a man if properly
delivered.

The morning was very warm, yet Jackson repeatedly
refused to shed his coat that hung loosely over his gaunt
body. Dickinson, who was younger, shorter, and heavier,
had donned a stylish suit of gray and blue. It was appropriate, he said, for a celebration at the dinner he had
arranged for the evening.

When lots were drawn to determine who would issue
commands, fate chose Overton. He guided the duelists to
their positions, then stepped well out of the line of fire
before shouting, "Fire!"

Dickinson snapped his arm upward and fired while
his weapon was still in movement. Since he had often
cut a string stretched at twenty-four feet, he was amazed
to see that his opponent did nothing but place one hand
over his chest.

Taking his time, Jackson slowly lifted his weapon and
squeezed the trigger when it was in position. His shot
passed through Dickinson's stomach, a wound that was
almost instantly mortal.

On the way back to Nashville, Overton noticed that
blood was dripping from one of Jackson's stirrups. Only
then did the duelist admit that Dickinson had "winged"
him somewhere close to his heart.

Examination by a surgeon showed that the bullet was
lodged where attempts to remove it might prove fatal. As
a result, the only president of the United States who
spent time as a prisoner of war carried an American civilian's ball in his chest for thirty-nine years.

Jackson's next fight was not personal. As head of the
state's volunteers he offered to put down the pro-British

*His lanky body, covered with an oversized coat, prob-
ably saved the life of Andrew Jackson, duelist.* [H. B.
HALL ENGRAVING]

Red Stick Creek Indians of Alabama. In that state his last
battle was the most spectacular and significant. At Horseshoe Bend on the Tallapoosa River in March 1814, he all
but exterminated a large band of warriors whose chieftain was Red Eagle.

Spoiling for more and more fights, the man who didn't
know in what state he was born invaded Florida and
soon captured Pensacola. Instead of being a prelude to a
period of tranquillity, this victory led to the most cele-

brated battle of his day. Always eager to meet the British, Jackson knew that a major force was nearing New Orleans. Racing to the largest port on the Gulf of Mexico, he directed hurried fortification of the city.

Since time was limited, he established a virtual military dictatorship and dissolved the Louisiana legislature. Captured deserters from his force were promptly executed, freedom of speech went by the board, and a civilian believed to be stirring up trouble among his troops was arrested and ordered to go before a court-martial.

Dominic A. Hall, a federal judge, thought things were getting out of hand. Hence he issued a writ of habeas corpus designed to gain the release of the prisoner. When Jackson ignored the legal document, Hall found him guilty of contempt of court and fined him one thousand dollars.

Hall's actions were a prelude to the largest land battle fought during the War of 1812. Jackson trounced the British who attacked New Orleans and then learned that his victory was won after the peace treaty had been signed. Citizens of New Orleans treated him as a conquering hero, so he announced that he was ready for new conquests.

Mustered into the U.S. Army, the man born in the Waxhaws became a brigadier and then was promoted to the rank of major general. President James Monroe soon sent him to Florida to subdue the Seminoles, with instructions to stay out of Spanish-held territory.

Predictably, the commander with a white-hot temper expelled the Spanish governor after taking Pensacola for the second time. His scouts reported to him that two Europeans were behind some of the attacks launched by the Seminoles, so he tracked them down. Alexander Arbuthnot and Robert Ambrister produced documents that proved them to be British subjects. That only infuriated Jackson, so he ordered the summary execution of the pair.

A crucial moment in the battle of New Orleans.

Briefly a subject of debate throughout Europe, the executions brought a reprimand from Secretary of War John C. Calhoun. As a result, the Nashville resident began to despise Calhoun almost as much as he did the British.

Once in the Executive Mansion, the first president from the West turned his fighting spirit into civilian rather than military channels. Some cabinet wives were affronted at the idea of being seen in the company of the wife of the secretary of war.

Jackson was a staunch defender of womanhood. He did not fight a duel over the way Peggy Eaton was treated, but he retaliated for treatment of her by making life uncomfortable for many of his top aides and their wives.

The man from Tennessee backed a boost in the tariff on imported goods whose rates were so high that it is still known as the Tariff of Abominations. Resistance to the tariff was universal in the South, but it was Calhoun's state that challenged federal power most stoutly. A Nullification Act passed by lawmakers of the Palmetto State declared that they had the power to make the federal statute null and void.

Nullification, seen in retrospect as a prelude to the Civil War, stirred Jackson into new and vigorous action. He prepared to send troops into Calhoun's state to enforce the law, so a compromise of sorts was reached.

White settlers in Georgia were clamoring for more and more land that belonged to the Cherokees. Since federal troops did not interfere in the dispute, Native Americans saw the size of their domain begin to shrink rapidly. Not satisfied with this victory, Georgians arrested missionaries who lived among the Native Americans.

Eventually the dispute went to the U.S. Supreme Court, whose justices ruled for the Indians on March 30, 1832. "Cherokees may have the court on their side, but we have Andrew Jackson," the losers in the suit proclaimed.

They were right; Jackson ignored the legal decision and put his influence behind a scheme to get rid of the Cherokees altogether. As a result, U.S. Army troops herded most of these Native Americans to Oklahoma during 1838–39.

A fighter to the end of his days, the president incorrectly claimed that his fiscal policies had nothing to do with bringing on the Panic of 1837. This time his contest was with the Bank of the United States, a federal institution. When the president had all government deposits withdrawn, the bank shrunk in size and failed to get its charter renewed.

Old Hickory, who was as tough as the tree from which his nickname was derived, probably spoke without thought when offering to fight the British. Yet long before he was old enough to shave he gave a remarkably accurate capsule summary of his career: Born to fight—as soon as one foe was vanquished, he tackled another.

81

Davy Crockett: Top Entertainer

Quick like a rabbit . . . !

Name the performer who holds the record as the all-time top entertainer born in the Volunteer State.

If you picked Minnie Pearl or Dolly Parton, your aim is good. But to hit the bull's-eye, you'd have had to name a three-term congressman. He had a grin that could charm a cat out of a tree, but the bulk of his entertaining since the days of Andy Jackson has been by proxy.

Davy Crockett first saw the light of day near Limestone Creek in today's Greene County, a bit east of Knoxville. His father, John, was one of the famous Over the Mountain Boys who licked the British in the battle of King's Mountain. That didn't bring prosperity to the Revolutionary War veteran and his family, though.

Davy grew up so poor that he figured he didn't have a thing to lose by running away from home and striking out on his own at age thirteen. Tradition says he wandered around the Northeast for three years, then came back to where his folks were living on the Holston River.

There he found things worse than ever, as if that were possible. His father owed thirty-six dollars to one neighbor and forty dollars to another. At sixteen, Davy began doing farm labor to get his father out of hock, and it took him a solid year to do it.

By that time he was more than casually interested in Polly Findlay and her two cows with calves. He managed

Mighty bear hunter Crockett.

to borrow fifteen dollars, then persuaded Polly to bring
along her livestock and set up housekeeping with him.

By the time he made Polly his wife, Davy was eighteen
or nineteen years old and had a reputation as a sure-shot
hunter. When he tried to make a living off the land, he
soon found that he was a mighty poor farmer.

Blaming his crop failures on worn-out soil, Davy took
off for Lincoln County, near the Alabama state line. By
this time he and Polly had two children, but that didn't
keep him from becoming a soldier.

Following the Fort Mims, Alabama, massacre of white
settlers by Creek Indians, Davy put a musket on his
shoulder and marched off to fight under Andy Jackson.
Glad to be on the winning side at Tullussahatchee in November 1813, he was appalled when he saw the muti-
lated bodies of defeated Creeks afterward.

A sergeant by this time, he followed Jackson to Florida, where he was a scout in the guerrilla war with the

Seminoles. Polly died while he was an Indian fighter, but it didn't take him long to pick out a good-looking widow of a fellow soldier who brought along two more children when she married him.

Like Daniel Boone, he kept looking westward. When he landed in Giles County as a veteran, he was appointed justice of the peace. As a county official, he was a natural choice to become colonel when a militia regiment was organized in his district. That leadership post propelled him into the state legislature, where the work was light and the pay was good for the amount of energy expended.

Once more moving west, he landed close to the place where the Mississippi River is swelled a little by the waters of the Obion. It was great country for a hunter; in a single season Davy racked up a record kill of 105 bears.

There were mighty few settlers in the region; his nearest neighbor was seven miles away. When it came time to pick a man to go to the legislature, a fellow with political experience was a natural choice, so Davy got the post.

Still a drifter at age forty, he tried the stunt Abraham Lincoln pulled when much younger and floated cargo on a raft downriver to New Orleans. When he got back home, broke as ever, somebody joked that with an election coming up he ought to run for Congress.

It sounded like a good idea to Davy, so he entered the race and campaigned throughout the district cracking jokes and swapping tall tales. His victory at the polls transformed him into the Canebrake Congressman who became the laughingstock of Washington when he hit the capital in 1827.

John Quincy Adams made fun of him; that was easy to understand since he was a Yankee from "up east." It was harder to take the ridicule of James K. Polk, who hailed from his part of the country. Flashing his famous grin

"Col. Crockett making a stump speech." [Autobiogra-
phy, 1869 edition]

and embroidering on his tall tales, Davy stuck it out in
Congress in spite of the ridicule.

After two terms he decided that lawmaking was
tougher than bear hunting and put his verdict on paper:
"There's too much talk. Many men seem to be proud they
can say so much about nothing. Their tongues keep
working, whether they have any grist to grind or not.
There are some in Congress who do nothing to earn their
pay but listen day after day. But considering the
speeches, I think they earn every penny, amounting to

eight whole dollars a day—provided they don't go to sleep. It's harder, though, to stay awake than to split gum logs in August."

Congressman Crockett parted with the dominant man of the day despite the fact that Andrew Jackson also hailed from Tennessee. He could not accept Old Hickory's ardent support of a bill to remove Indians east of the Mississippi River to Oklahoma. Voters of his district didn't agree with Davy, so in 1835 they refused to send him back to Congress.

"It's just as well," Davy told his supporters. "I'd rather go to Texas, anyway."

He seems to have gone by way of Little Rock to the vast region where American settlers were fighting with Mexicans. He had hardly hit the ground in Nacogdoches before he swore an oath of allegiance to the provisional government of Texas. Following a fellow from Ohio who had organized a small band of Tennessee Mounted Volunteers, Davy rode into San Antonio on February 3, 1836. There the former congressman fought his way into immortality at the Alamo.

Five years earlier Davy had started to climb the ladder of fame. A New York play called *The Lion of the West* had him thinly disguised as its central character from Tennessee, Nimrod Wildfire. Actor James Hackett, who played the role, had no idea that the 'coonskin cap he wore would become a lasting Crockett trademark.

The success of the play, which Davy attended when the company performed in Washington, spurred the publication of *Davy Crockett's Almanac*. New editions were issued annually for twenty-one years, and during this period they created the mythical Crockett.

In these books he traveled with Mississip, a pet buffalo, and his pipe-smoking bear, Death Hug, and an unnamed hyena. Together the man and his three animal friends dived for pearls in the South Seas, rode lightning flashes to escape tornadoes, and greased the axle of the earth with tallow from a fat bear.

The Canebrake Congressman. [John G. Chapmain painting, University of Texas]

Elevated into national prominence by the play and the
almanacs, in 1834 Davy made a tour in which he was
hailed in Baltimore, Philadelphia, New York, and Boston. As a result some biographers label him as the first
American to make a living by being a celebrity. That verdict is less than accurate; he was a celebrity who died as
dirt poor as he was born.

In 1836 the return of Halley's comet became a central
motif of the Crockett almanac. Andrew Jackson was said
to have commissioned Colonel Crockett to save America

and the planet from harm by the celestial intruder. Davy was reported to have ended the story of his adventure by modestly explaining:

I was appointed by the President to stand on the Alle-ghany Mountains and wring the comet's tail off. I did so, but got my hands most shockingly burnt, and the hair singed off my head so that I was bald.

I div[ed] right into the Waybosh river, and thus saved my best stone blue coat and grass green small clothes. With the help of Bear's grease I have brought out a new crop of hair, but it grows in bights and tuffs like hussuck grass in a meadow, and it keeps in such a snarl that all the teeth will instantly snap out of an ivory comb when brought within ten feet of it.

Published annually for more than a generation, the almanacs served to make the former congressman as well known as the legendary river brawler, Mike Fink.

Gross exaggeration and frontier humor permeate the accounts of adventures usually offered in first-person style. Almanac readers were told that when Crockett arrived in the nation's capital, he casually introduced himself in his own unique fashion:

I'm David Crockett, fresh from the backwoods—half alli-gator and a little touched with snapping turtle. I can wade the Mississippi, leap the Ohio, ride on a streak of lightnin', and slip without a scratch down a honey locust. I can whip my weight in wild cats—and if any gentleman pleases to throw in a ten dollar bill he may add a panther.

Two years before his death at the Alamo, Davy persuaded a Boston publisher to issue his autobiography. He made no secret of the fact that he had help in writing it from Congressman Thomas Chilton of Kentucky. Yet the Crockett book is his own. That makes it a far cry from the epic that bears the name of Daniel Boone but was written by John Filson. Still in print after more than 160 years, the Crockett story has been praised as following the path laid down by Benjamin Franklin's *Autobiography*.

Once the great bear hunter from the Volunteer State became a martyr for the cause of Texas independence, publishers rushed into print with a volume they called *Col. Crockett's Exploits and Adventures in Texas*. The first of many novels about the Alamo, it introduced readers to Thimblerig the gambler and the Bee Hunter—Crockett characters destined to become well known.

A melodrama called *Davy Crockett* made its debut in 1872, and for the next quarter-century ran continuously in the United States and England. It would have gone on much longer had not Frank Mayo, who played Crockett, died after collapsing on stage.

Dustin Farnum recreated and modified the role in a 1916 film, after which Davy retired from public view until he was rediscovered by Walt Disney. Three one-hour television episodes by Disney were combined into a movie that included the song, "The Ballad of David Crockett." To the astonishment of the producers, the ballad became such a hit that ten million records were sold.

That was the beginning of the modern resurrection of the great bear hunter, who was portrayed by Fess Parker in 165 television episodes. In 1960 John Wayne played Crockett in an action-packed movie called *The Alamo*. During the height of popularity of the television series, the price of raccoon tails jumped by 2,000 percent—and still the demand for caps such as Parker wore could not be satisfied. At the University of Hawaii, Margaret J. King wrote a doctoral dissertation on merchandising and other cultural effects of "the Crockett craze."

In person, in print, on stage, in motion pictures, and in television, Davy Crockett has entertained millions for almost two hundred years. Great as some Grand Ole Opry stars are, much time will pass before one of them matches the record of the Canebrake Congressman.

82

Sam Houston: Red Heart

Rebellious adolescents may be more numerous now than ever before, but teenage resistance to family wishes is not new. Today it is fairly easy for an unruly youngster to hightail it to a city and become lost in the crowd. In 1809 the nation was very young and there were few cities—all of them far from Maryville, Tennessee. Given such circumstances, where could a boy from a homestead close to Baker's Creek find refuge if he decided to set out on his own?

Elizabeth Houston, widow of a career militia officer, knew that she had problems with her fifth son. Soon after coming from Virginia to the 420-acre place her husband had bought, she began complaining to her older sons that Sam was too much trouble. They sympathized and tried to tighten the reins, which might have been the worst thing they could have done.

Many Cherokee leaders had mixed blood. For instance, John Ross, Elias Boudinot, and John Ridge were part white, part Indian. Tribesmen living in the region where Sam grew into adolescence treated him like an equal when they talked with him.

That was a far cry from the way his mother and brothers acted toward him, so Sam cultivated his Native American friends. By the time he got ready to leave home for good, no longer speaking to some of his brothers, he had picked out a haven he considered to be just right.

He'd turn his back on his own race and live among the Cherokees!

Already acquainted with Oo-loo-te-ka, who headed a dwindling clan of about three hundred members, Sam Houston appeared at the chieftain's lodge on a sunny fall day. He knew enough Cherokee words to inquire, "Can I stay with you a while?"

Soon after he was welcomed and pointed to a lodge where he could sleep with other adolescents who were eager to become braves. Two or three of Sam's brothers found him and demanded that he return home immediately. When he refused, they became angry. Demands and threats failed to weaken the resolve of the boy already known to be uncommonly stubborn.

Sam made an occasional visit to the merchants of Maryville, where he bought gifts for the Cherokees he now called his brothers. Except for these brief forays, he

Artist's sketch of Houston, dressed for battle.

abandoned white society for the better part of three years.

"Your skin may be white," Oo-loo-te-ka told him on the morning of a ceremonial day, "but your heart is red. I will today adopt you as my son." As soon as the adoption ceremony ended, tribesmen began to call their new member Co-lon-eh.

Some students of Native American languages believe, appropriately, that the name means "the Wanderer." Houston's noted biographer, Marquis James, however, insisted that the name meant "the Raven"—a bird noted for its swift and sure flight.

Regardless of the shades of meaning included in his new name, Co-lon-eh had the time of his life observing and learning Cherokee ways. Back on the farm in Blount County south of Knoxville, he had shown absolutely no interest in attending the nearest school. He could sit for hours pouring over his late father's copy of Homer's *Iliad,* but in a classroom he couldn't be still long enough to write a sentence on the blackboard.

Among his fellow tribesmen, Co-lon-eh was never told to sit still and listen. He was forever on the move, often watching the women making headbands of feathers and then observing others finger-weaving with the inner bark of the mulberry tree.

Sometimes tribal elders devoted entire days to tattooing the young men. When he saw this ceremony in progress, Co-lon-eh found it hard to keep his feet from dancing. Soon he would be old enough to sit motionless, exhibiting no sign of pain, while he got his first tattoo.

Careful observation made him familiar with every detail of the ceremonial preparations. He had not passed into manhood, so he could take no part in the painting of faces and bodies of participants. Yet he learned precisely where to put white clay, how much to use, and whether to move his hand upward or downward in making a stroke with it.

Tattoos were reserved for braves, Cherokees told the boy who was an adopted tribesman.

Among Oo-loo-te-ka's people, hunters observed no age restrictions. As soon as a boy could move silently with a stalking party and run all day in the forest, he was permitted to join the quest for game.

Co-lon-eh's heart raced the first time he saw a deer surrounded and then killed. He became adept at making a swift stroke to impale a fish on a short spear. Using a blowgun made from cane, he missed several birds before scoring his first direct hit with a dart. Already a veteran user of tobacco, he learned to smoke marijuana and to emit puffs as big as those that swirled upward from the mouths and noses of his fellow tribesmen.

His new comrades tried never to let all their fires die out. If all of them were doused by a sudden blowing rain, a tribal elder would bring from his lodge a bow whose string was wrapped around a stout wooden peg. As he whipped the bow from side to side with the peg resting firmly upon seasoned wood, smoke would begin to curl upward, and after many minutes, fresh fire would be created.

On a rainy day in February, Co-lon-eh once extended his hand toward the drill. Shaking his head wordlessly, the tribesman who was custodian of the fire-stick signaled that this vital tool was not for use by boys.

No restrictions applied to participation in the Green Corn Dance, however. This ritual of late spring or early summer was annually denounced by white settlers in brush-arbor camp meetings and from the pulpits of tiny churches that were beginning to dot the countryside.

Questioned years later about his role in the sex-centered ceremonies designed to ensure a full crop of grain, the man formerly known as Co-lon-eh refused to divulge details. In an unguarded moment, however, he summarized his Cherokee years as having been spent largely in "making love and reading the *Iliad*."

There's no doubt that he took the translation of the ancient classic very seriously. When persuaded to pose in Nashville for an itinerant painter in 1831, he dressed himself as his favorite character in Roman history, Marius.

His enjoyment of "making love" exceeded even his avid desire to commit much of the *Iliad* to memory. At the sight of a beckoning adolescent girl who found pleasure without condemnation in a sexual encounter, Co-lon-eh was always ready to toss his battered copy of Homer aside.

Some years later he found the love of his life. Americans who called Oo-loo-te-ka by the name of John Jolly knew that his sister was the common-law wife of a Scottish trader, John Rogers. They had at least two boys and a girl, who was called either Tiana or Diana. Many whites contemptuously referred to the three children as "breeds," meaning half-breeds.

No one knows when Rogers's daughter Tiana entered the life of Co-lon-eh or for how long they were considered by the Cherokees as being mates. Although Oo-loo-

Years after the battle of Horseshoe Bend, this sketch of "Ensign Houston at To-ho-pe-ka on the Tallapoosa River" was approved by the president of the Texas Republic.

te-ka's adopted son later wrote voluminously, he was silent on the subject of his relationship with Tiana.

Houston's reticence in this regard may have stemmed from the fact that Co-lon-eh faded into the background after three years and Sam Houston reappeared. More restless than ever, he joined the militia and was seriously wounded in the battle of Horseshoe Bend while fighting under Andrew Jackson.

Although he went to Congress as Old Hickory's pro-
tégé, Houston differed with his mentor in one important
respect. Violently opposed to the removal of the eastern
Indians to the West, he was for years the most vocal and
influential American friend they had.

This aspect of his career points to the most unusual
aspect of Sam Houston's action-packed career. After
years of toying with the idea, he himself went west into
the Cherokee Nation in Oklahoma. Then he moved south
into what became the Republic of Texas. There the boy
who grew up near Maryville became the only Indian-by-
adoption ever to be elected president of an independent
American republic.

83

Nathan Bedford Forrest: Wizard of the Saddle

Once a major thoroughfare in downtown Atlanta, Forrest Avenue is no more. Motorists who follow its route now drive along Martin Luther King Jr. Boulevard.

Although Atlanta street signs bearing the name of Confederate Gen. Nathan Bedford Forrest are gone, his stature continues to grow. Noted historian Glenn Tucker devoted years to studying the man who was born in 1821 not far from Chapel Hill, Tennessee. Tucker claims that there are valid reasons to believe that "the South might have achieved independence if Forrest's talents had been given earlier and more generous recognition."

That remarkable tribute is based in part on the fact that Forrest won a remarkable victory at Brice's Cross Roads, Mississippi. Annals of the North-South struggle include no comparable exploit. In Mississippi, the Tennessean inflicted on a Union army the most decisive defeat of its sort during the four bloody years in which 623,000 Americans died.

Like Andrew Jackson, Forrest was always ready and sometimes eager to get into a scrap. Early in 1862, he parted company with his superiors when they prepared to surrender Fort Donelson. Leading his men through a gap in the Union lines, he raced to safety and thus to fight again while those he left behind capitulated.

During a period of many months he quarreled repeatedly with Maj. Gen. Braxton Bragg. He refused to fight

Self-taught military genius Nathan Bedford Forrest.

under the command of Maj. Gen. Joseph Wheeler, and he argued with Maj. Gen. Earl Van Dorn.

As a result of an altercation, one of his own lieutenants yanked out a pistol and shot him in the groin. Forrest, who had been twirling a pocket knife, pulled the blade open with his teeth and slashed Andrew W. Gould's midsection.

Informed by a physician that his own wound could prove mortal, Forrest grabbed a pistol before racing to Gould's place of refuge. "I'm a-goin' to kill him before I die!" he cried before delivering a fatal bullet. Shortly after the end of the war, he challenged Judson Kilpatrick, a former U.S. general, to mortal combat.

No other man who wore blue or gray is positively known to have enlisted as a private and to have taken off the uniform of a lieutenant general after Lee's surrender. No other man who fought for the South or for the North almost casually summed up his military career in a single sentence: "I went into the army worth a million and a half dollars, and came out a beggar."

Nath, as some of his early friends called him, was just sixteen when his father's death forced him to become the family breadwinner. He worked as a farm laborer and saved enough money to begin buying and selling a few horses and cows.

Capital accumulated from trading livestock enabled him to dabble in real estate and to become a slave dealer. Big cotton farms bought with profits from these enterprises made him wealthy enough to buy a mansion in Memphis and win election to the city's board of aldermen.

In April 1861 a challenge issued by Abraham Lincoln persuaded Confederates to fire the first shots of the Civil War against Fort Sumter in Charleston Harbor. In reply, the president of the United States called for troops from each of the thirty-four states he claimed still to govern.

Tennessee lawmakers responded to the call for men "to quell the rebellion" by voting for secession, a move that bitterly divided the state. Able-bodied men were forced immediately to choose either the South or the North. As a result, on June 14, 1861, Forrest volunteered for service in Capt. Josiah White's Tennessee Mounted Rifles.

Little is known about White or his command, but the six-foot-two-inch millionaire who enlisted to fight under him as a private was soon cutting a wide swath. A quarrel with White led Forrest to spend much of his fortune equipping an entire battalion, providing his men with horses, and becoming their lieutenant colonel.

From that time forward, Forrest's rise in rank was meteoric. Nine months after putting his battalion in motion, he was a brigadier general. It took him sixteen months to gain the second star that marked him as a major general, but just fourteen months later he became a lieutenant general. Although five of his brothers and two half-brothers also entered Confederate service, their careers were not spectacular.

Forrest was constantly at battle with Union forces and fought in such mammoth struggles as Shiloh and Chickamauga in the state of his birth. Almost casual about frequently hitting the ground when a horse was crippled or killed by a Federal shot, he didn't bother to keep a record of the number of animals he lost. Some biographers claim that no other fighting man in gray or in blue had as many horses "shot from under him."

His reputation was forever tarnished by events that took place three years after he became a soldier. At Fort Pillow, Tennessee, a small Federal force and the gunboat *New Era* threatened to block Confederate navigation on the Mississippi River. From his Jackson, Tennessee, headquarters, Forrest dispatched Brig. Gen. James R.

Imaginative drawing of the Fort Pillow massacre. [HARPER'S WEEKLY]

Chalmers and fifteen hundred men to "remove the canker sore from the river."

About 10:00 A.M. on April 12, 1864, Forrest arrived and took command of an attack that had started at dawn. Soon after the Federal commander refused to surrender at 3:30 P.M., the Confederates overwhelmed their enemies and poured into the little fortress.

For the rest of his life Forrest insisted that the majority of Federal casualties occurred because men who refused to give up were shot while trying to work their way toward the gunboat. Numerous Northern accounts of the bloody day hold that men in blue were shot down in cold blood after having surrendered.

Civil War annals are filled with stories of atrocities. Some of them are based upon actual events, while others were manufactured and placed in newspapers for propaganda purposes. Both sides fought the war of words bitterly, and neither side has an unblemished record.

At Fort Pillow, the alleged massacre of Union fighting men by Confederates was complicated by the ethnic makeup of the garrison commanded by Maj. Lionel F. Booth. His men, almost evenly divided between whites and blacks, didn't die in the same ratio. More than 150 white soldiers survived to surrender, but only 58 blacks were captured. All the rest were mortally wounded or killed.

Outspoken enemies of Abraham Lincoln on the Congressional Joint Committee on the Conduct of the War conducted a formal investigation. They concluded that black soldiers were shot down after having raised their hands in surrender. In addition, the committee charged, some blacks were buried alive and others who were wounded were killed when Confederates set their tents on fire.

Angry denials by Southern spokesmen, then and now, have not settled the question. No one knows exactly what took place after the Confederates stormed into Fort Pillow in overwhelming numbers. A majority of analysts are of the opinion that racial animosity played a role in the high death rate among black Federal soldiers.

William T. Sherman is widely blamed for the burning of Columbia, South Carolina, whether or not he actually issued orders to torch the capital of the Palmetto State. In the same fashion, Forrest is held responsible for the atrocities at Fort Pillow, even though he may not have commanded that they take place.

As if this were not enough to cause present-day African-American leaders to despise him, Forrest was a key leader in the organization of the original Ku Klux Klan. His membership in the secret order was brief, and he soon took a public stand against its violence. That has not prevented some twentieth-century Americans from damning him for the actions of later hate groups that borrowed the group's name.

Nathan Bedford Forrest, among the most colorful and controversial figures of the Civil War, was in many respects a man similar to Andrew Jackson. How greatly his attitudes and actions were influenced by his lack of educational opportunities is anybody's guess. Yet a glance at just one of his communications is revealing.

At a spot he believed to be about twenty miles west of Gadsden, Alabama, the Tennessean dispatched an urgent message to the civic leaders of Rome, Georgia. Unedited, this typical communication from the self-taught military genius who became known as the Wizard of the Saddle reads: "Theirs is a Federal Force of fifteen Hundred cavalry Marching on your place I am pressing them Prepare your selves to Repuls them—they have 2 Mountain Howitsers I wil be clost on them I have kild 300 of their men they air running for their lives."

Glenn Tucker's appraisal of the military leader may be very close to the target. If Forrest had received the benefit of a West Point education, the man from the backwoods of Tennessee might have been even more influential than was Virginia aristocrat Robert E. Lee.

84

Andrew Johnson: Margin of One

May 15, 1868, was fateful. There had been none such in nearly a hundred years of the history of the Government. It was to determine judicially what should constitute "high crimes and misdemeanors in office" on the part of the National Executive [the president]. In a large sense, the independence of the executive office as a co-ordinate branch of the Government was on trial. Conscious that I was at that moment the focus of all eyes, and conscious also of the far-reaching effect, especially upon myself, of the vote I was about to give, I almost literally looked down into my open grave. Friends, position, fortune, everything that makes life desirable to an ambitious man, were about to be swept away by the breath of my mouth, perhaps forever.

Appointed in 1866 to fill an unexpired term in the U.S. Senate, Edmund Ross of Kansas found himself in the national spotlight less than two years later. He would cast the deciding vote in the impeachment trial of President Andrew Johnson, and he was keenly aware of what it might cost him to vote as his conscience directed.

Born near Raleigh, North Carolina, Johnson was only semiliterate when he moved to Greeneville, Tennessee, and began work as a tailor. His wife, Eliza, helped him to master the arts of reading and writing and encouraged him to enter the political arena.

It was easy for the intelligent young tailor to win a place on the town's board of aldermen in 1828. Two years later he became mayor of Greeneville, a post from which he soon jumped to a seat in the Tennessee legislature. By 1843 he had won the first of five terms in the U.S. House of Representatives.

Later governor of the state and then a U.S. senator, he did not support Abraham Lincoln in the election of 1860. Four years later, however, Lincoln picked Johnson as his running mate for a second term.

Lincoln's choice of the only southern senator who did not resign during the secession crisis was deliberate. Having made Johnson military governor of Tennessee in March 1862, Lincoln knew the one-time tailor quite well. He was confident that if Johnson should become vice president, he would back the policies and actions of his chief.

Even more important, perhaps, Lincoln badly needed a southerner on the ticket in 1864. Facing a challenge from Gen. George B. McClellan, who was running on a peace platform, the incumbent president despaired of reelection. In this crisis, Lincoln persuaded Republicans briefly to change their name to the National Union Party. At the same time he took action to assess a "contribution" to the party from every federal officeholder.

These measures, plus the military triumphs of Gen. William Tecumseh Sherman in Georgia, helped Lincoln and Johnson to win a sweeping victory in November 1864. Less than six months later the man from Tennessee became president when John Wilkes Booth assassinated Lincoln.

Washington and the nation were thrown into turmoil by the first assassination of a president. To a hard-core group of Lincoln's congressional opponents, Johnson's upward move seemed to threaten their ability to enforce a program of harsh "reconstruction" upon the defeated South.

Three men were key leaders in opposing nearly anything and everything done by Lincoln's successor. In the House of Representatives, Thaddeus Stevens of Pennsyl-

Andrew Johnson was on record as favoring quick reconciliation with the former Confederate states.

vania had made life difficult for Lincoln; now he resolved to make it impossible for Johnson. In the Senate, Charles Sumner of Massachusetts followed a similar course. In the cabinet, Secretary of War Edwin M. Stanton was ready to stir up trouble in the new president's inner circle.

Especially but not exclusively in the former Confederate states, there was public rejoicing that a man from the South was now the nation's chief executive. Torchlight parades were staged in his honor in some cities, and a publisher hurriedly put together a song sheet that praised the Tennessean many called "an accidental president."

Johnson, who knew which key leaders were eager for his downfall, wanted to follow Lincoln's stated purposes. Hence he did all he could to bring the divided nation together in the immediate postwar months. As soon as Congress went into recess, the president began taking measures designed to ease some of the economic and social problems of the former Confederate states.

An articulate and persuasive speaker, a furious Thaddeus Stevens addressed others who, like him, were known as Radical Republicans. He cried, "If something is not done, the president will be crowned king before the next Congress meets." In New York City, editor Horace Greeley of the most powerful newspaper in the country added his voice to that of Stevens.

When Congress convened in 1867, the Radical Republicans set out "to make Dixie howl" even louder than Sherman had on his March to the Sea. They aimed one new repressive law after another at the South and succeeded in getting many of them passed. Johnson consistently vetoed these measures, sent them back to Congress, and then saw them passed over his veto.

Stevens was probably the mastermind behind a plan to assert the superiority of Congress over the president. Under the terms of the proposed legislation, called the Tenure of Office Bill, Congress informed the president that he could not dismiss anyone whose appointment had been confirmed by the Senate.

Fully aware that his secretary of war was among his most bitter enemies, Johnson sent Stanton a memorandum of dismissal. When it was delivered, the veteran politician ordered his subordinates to remain at their desks and refused to vacate the War Department. Johnson initially tried to get Gen. Ulysses S. Grant to occupy the post he declared to be vacant, but he had to settle for Gen. Lorenzo Thomas.

Johnson's dismissal of Stanton was precisely what his foes in Congress wanted. They cried, "He has wantonly violated the Tenure of Office Act!" A seven-man committee hurriedly put together ten other charges against the president. Collectively, they constituted a bill of impeachment, the first and only such action in U.S. history.

Only congressmen were entitled to vote on the bill of impeachment, and they devoted just two days to consid-

A special committee of seven members prepared the indictment against the president. [BRADY STUDIO, LIBRARY OF CONGRESS]

eration of the measure. On February 24, 1868, they passed it by a vote of 126 to 47. The sergeant-at-arms of the House of Representatives, George T. Brown, then served Johnson with a summons to appear before a high court of impeachment.

The U.S. Constitution stipulates that a court of impeachment shall be made up of U.S. senators sitting in a body; that is, the entire Senate hearing evidence and rendering a verdict. With Republicans holding a majority in the fifty-four-man body, Johnson's foes were sure of a quick conviction that would force him from office. Sen. Benjamin Wade, considered next in line for succession to the presidency, even selected the men he expected to form his cabinet as soon as he took over the Executive Mansion.

On the advice of his attorneys, Johnson stayed away from the trial, which no one could attend without a ticket of admission. Frustrated by increasingly bitter attacks in the newspapers, Johnson began inviting reporters to the Executive Mansion. His sessions with these men, who for the most part supported his views, constituted the first of the White House press conferences.

Salmon P. Chase, chief justice of the U.S. Supreme Court, presided over the trial that began on March 5. To convict the president, thirty-six senators would have to vote against him. Stevens and the Radical Republicans were sure of thirty supporters before the hearings began.

Eleven senators had indicated that they had no intention of impeaching the president. That meant the outcome of the trial would be decided by a dozen undecided senators, all of whom were Republicans. Within two weeks, five of them let it be known that they would vote for conviction.

Testimony against and for the president occupied sixty days, after which the all-important vote was scheduled to be taken on May 12. When it was learned that four of the seven previously undecided senators would support the president, the lawmaking body-jury took a four-day recess.

Johnson's foes hoped to win the support of the remaining undecided senators during the recess and were bitterly disappointed when two of them announced that they would vote for acquittal. This meant that thirty-five lawmakers were pledged to support impeachment and eighteen opposed the measure. With thirty-six votes required for conviction, a man who had kept quiet during the lengthy quarrels would decide the issue.

Edmund Ross let it be known that he was "an earnest opponent of Andrew Johnson" before he arrived in Washington. Once seated in the Senate, he consistently voted for measures proposed by the Radical Republicans. These factors made it appear that he would be in favor of impeachment.

Although he didn't claim to have scholarly knowledge of the U.S. Constitution, Ross was impressed by the argu-

A ticket of admission to the impeachment proceedings. [NATIONAL ARCHIVES]

ments advanced by Johnson and his legal advisers. The Founding Fathers wished the administrative, legislative, and judicial branches of the federal government to be co-equal, they pointed out. That is, George Washington and his contemporaries did not want one branch of the government to be dominant.

Greatly weakening the power of the president while boosting the strength of Congress would defeat the aims of the Founding Fathers, Ross decided. That judgment was strengthened by a stream of hate letters and telegrams from Kansas. As a result, he laid his career on the line and voted against the impeachment of Johnson.

Everyone involved knew that Ross and Ross alone prevented Congress from impeaching the president. Johnson was permitted to remain as the nation's chief executive by the margin of a single vote.

Edmund Ross, a freshman senator, knew the risk he was taking when he cast his decisive ballot. He was not reelected by the voters of Kansas. He gave up all thoughts of a career in politics and soon dropped out of public sight. A few years later, an investigative reporter launched a search for the former senator. He eventually found him in a small New Mexico town, where he was working as a journeyman printer.

Although he had survived impeachment, Johnson was still bitterly opposed by many in Congress, and no significant legislation was enacted during the remainder of his presidency. After a period of rest and retirement in Tennessee, the former president again won election to the Senate and was an active member of that body at his death in 1875.

85

Dutchman's Grade: Carnage on the Home Front

About 7:15 A.M. on July 9, 1918, train number four of the Nashville, Chattanooga and Saint Louis Railroad approached a signal tower about five miles west of the Tennessee capital. Newly created shops at that point promised state-of-the-art maintenance for much of the railroad's heavy equipment.

David C. Kennedy, engineer of the westbound train, blew for his signal "in the customary manner" as he approached the end of a section of double track. Schedules called for the eastbound Memphis express to pass the other train on that section. Since it did not, the express was obviously running late, and that created a dilemma.

If the Memphis express was still twenty to thirty minutes away, Kennedy could proceed safely. But if it was less than twenty minutes away, he would have to wait for it to pass. Ahead of him loomed a ten-mile stretch of single track.

So the engineer's whistle constituted a question in railroad code: "What's the situation? Shall I stop and wait for the Memphis express or go ahead?"

Witnesses later testified that Kennedy's whistle received a clear board, shorthand for "O.K. to proceed; track clear."

Yet before train number four passed through the shop area, a red board dropped in a desperate but futile attempt to convey to Kennedy an order to stop.

The local train from Nashville, made up of the locomotive and cars guided by Kennedy, had slowed to about ten miles per hour as it approached the signal tower. Puffing heavily in order to pull up a long and curving slope locally known as Dutchman's Grade, the engine was out of sight of the signal board when the orders were reversed.

From the opposite direction, passenger train number one from Memphis and Saint Louis had the advantage of gravity. So the crack express was roaring down the grade at more than sixty miles an hour trying to make up for lost time. When the engines collided, both locomotives reared and fell beside the track.

Coaches of the westbound train were lightly built, since they were used only for short runs. Those of the express were heavy-duty ones designed for long runs at high speed. With the locomotives out of the way, the big coaches of the express hit those of the local so hard that they telescoped instantly.

Both locomotives, three baggage cars, and six passenger cars were demolished. Hot coals spewed from engine boilers and started a fire that quickly got out of control.

Practically all the passengers on the local train were workers at the DuPont Old Hickory Powder Plant on the outskirts of Nashville. The haste of the express was partly due to the fact that it carried two hundred men who were coming to aid the U.S. war effort by offering their services at the same plant.

Both engineers, both firemen, and a baggage master were killed on impact. It was hours before anyone had firm information about the number of passengers killed and injured. More than forty of them were known to be pinned beneath a single crumpled car that rescuers were unable to move. Some died quickly, but others continued to cry for help. A few who believed their plight to be hopeless implored police officers to shoot them. Although huge jacks and other heavy equipment sat in railroad yards only a few miles away, by the time rescue workers managed to lift the crushed car, only one of them was still alive.

Willie Tillman, foreman of a crew coming in from Little Rock, somehow emerged from the wreck without a scratch. Although he had only one arm, Tillman managed to get his window down in the seconds in which he sensed that the crash was impending. He jumped out unhurt, did his best to pull survivors from the wreckage, then spent the next three days searching Nashville's improvised morgues for the fifteen members of his crew who perished in the crash.

Several youthful soldiers on the first leg of a trip to the European battle front were aboard. One of them who died, W. M. Winstead, carried an unmailed letter in his pocket.

"War is tough," he had written to his parents, "but things aren't always easy in civilian life. I'm going to be all right. When you hear from me next, I'll be somewhere in France."

Nashville resident Leland Moore was more fortunate. He escaped, he said afterward, because he wanted to hear a funny story that a friend was telling. Other passengers had urged him to go with them to the smoking car, from which no one emerged without serious injury.

An account by one of the first newspaper reporters to reach the scene of the crash read:

> *The scene immediately following the collision is indescribable. Those escaping unhurt or with lesser injuries fled from the spot in a veritable panic. The cornfield on both sides of the track was trampled by many feet, and littered with fragments of iron and wood hurled from the demolished cars. The dead lay here and there, grotesquely sprawling where they fell. The dying moaned appeals for aid or, speechless, rolled their heads from side to side and writhed in agony.*

An estimated crowd of eight thousand curious onlookers flocked to the scene of the catastrophe. Long before noon, the hospitals of Nashville were crowded with 140 injured, while improvised morgues began to overflow within an hour after the first bodies were pulled from the wreckage.

A woman, whose identity no one learned, brought flags and insisted on arranging one near the body of each dead soldier.

Identification of the victims was difficult and sometimes impossible. In the nightmare moments of the wreck, a boiler from an engine toppled against a crushed passenger car and seared many people beyond recognition.

As rapidly as out-of-town passengers could be identified, their bodies were boxed for shipment. At the height of the activity, thirty-eight coffins, stacked like cordwood, stood outside a single funeral parlor.

Unidentified and unclaimed bodies were consigned to representatives of the U.S. government, because all U.S. railroads were then under government operation as a wartime measure. A major factor motivating Congress to order takeover of the nation's rail lines had been the "imperative necessity for efficient and safe operation in this time of national emergency."

Because of the strange position in which the railroads found themselves, the legal consequences of the crash on Dutchman's Grade were without precedent.

President Paten of the Nashville, Chattanooga and Saint Louis Railroad arrived at the scene while bodies were still being taken away. He expressed "deep personal sorrow" before issuing a statement indicating that the railroad had no legal liability since it was being operated by the government.

Formal hearings began on Saturday, July 13.

Rumor had it that engineer Kennedy died with a timetable in his hand, an indication that he recognized the danger but was trying to beat the eastbound train through the section of single track in order to reach a switch at Harding Junction.

Although this evidence was not admitted, a panel of experts and legal advisers ruled that the wreck occurred because crew members of train number four "failed to see signals, or disregarded them."

C. H. Markham, the federally appointed regional director of railroads, issued a formal statement, saying, "It will be the policy of the Government to discourage litigation and to deal directly with injured persons to the end that claimants may receive the broadest benefits without the expense of litigation."

What Markham meant, as events soon showed, was that the government would pay out as little as possible and do everything in its power to discourage claimants.

Many cases were settled "by negotiation" for a few hundred dollars each. In the seventeen cases where victims were never legally identified, survivors received no recompense at all. A few families who hired lawyers and threatened to bring suit against the government settled out of court for sums that ranged as high as five thousand dollars.

Because the nation's attention was gripped by events in Europe, the crash of two trains attracted only a ripple of interest outside Nashville. Some major newspapers ignored the disaster completely. Others carried short stories on inside pages. A few ran page-one accounts on the day after the disaster, then dropped their coverage.

The war that had prompted the government takeover of the nation's railroads in the name of safety and efficiency made the wreck seem unimportant. National attention was so firmly fixed upon events in Europe that the story of the collision was virtually unknown.

Editors considered it vital to run big headlines about the triumph of a president's son: LT. QUENTIN ROOSEVELT BRINGS DOWN HIS FIRST GERMAN PLANE. It was judged important to inform readers that FRENCH SMASH FORWARD A MILE and to reassure them that NO ARMY WILL BE SENT TO RUSSIA.

Headlines of the *Nashville Banner* on July 9, spread across five columns of type on the front page, reported

101 deaths. On the following morning, the *Nashville Tennessean* reported that the death toll had reached 121 (a total later revised downward).

Within transportation circles, however, Dutchman's Grade spurred progress in the adoption of automatic signaling devices. Hand-operated signals, hallowed by years of use, gave way to faster and more accurate ways of communicating with men on moving trains.

Reference books still list the wartime disaster as having taken more lives than any other U.S. train wreck. To an extent unequaled in U.S. history, the obscure and all but forgotten crash near Nashville served to make rail travel safer—just as passengers began to abandon trains in favor of automobiles.

PART NINE:
Mississippi

86

Hernando de Soto: Sunset on the River

Early in May 1541, a hungry and exhausted band of just over five hundred adventurers improvised a camp in order to rest for a few days. The land around them was so heavily forested that their scouts could not make out a landmark in any direction. They believed, however, that they were close to a stream the American Indians called "the Father of Waters," but they were not sure.

Hernando de Soto, the leader, was in his late thirties or early forties. Dozens of artists have imagined what he looked like, but no one knows for sure. No painting, no sketch, and no verbal description of him has survived. His fellow conquistador, Francisco Pizarro, described him as being small; that is the only positive clue as to his appearance.

De Soto and his followers were a ragged and footsore bunch. During their two-year pursuit of treasure greater than that of the Incas of South America they had wandered across much of what is now the southeastern United States.

Some of those in the party left eyewitness accounts that are incomplete but suggestive. According to them, the leader was "a mad man who is perfectly sane." That is, he was consumed by a life-shaping goal by which he expected to eclipse the fame of Hernando Cortés and Pizarro.

Even small delays made de Soto restless and often angry; thus being lost in the woods for a week had turned him into a demon. Long before his men were ready to resume their march, he roared orders that required them to move west.

Stands of pines and oaks gradually diminished in size from an average of more than one hundred feet, and then late one afternoon men at the head of the column began to shout. The trees gave way to underbrush taller than a man's head, but not so dense that movement through it was impossible.

Well before sundown the company of Spanish and Portuguese fortune seekers emerged on a low bluff. At a distance that they estimated to be about five miles, they glimpsed huge flocks of waterfowl. Stretched in a line as far north and as far south as the eye could see, these birds seemed to assure them that the Father of Waters was nearby.

De Soto and his band may have been at or close to Lower Chickasaw Bluff in today's Tunica County in Mis-

Artist's depiction of Hernando de Soto.

sissippi. That is only an informed guess; it is equally possible that they emerged from "the impenetrable forest" close to the tip of Lake Cormorant. Early scholars leaned toward the latter location, a few miles from present-day Walls. Hence the region just southwest of Memphis was named De Soto County.

At the time, the adventurers were probably more interested in an Indian village than in the mighty river. A cluster of huts was surrounded by a wide belt of cultivated fields. That night the ravenous men would feast on maize (orange-yellow Indian corn), beans, squash, and sweet potatoes.

The men who believed themselves to be close to starvation found it easy to take over the village they called Quizquiz. Earlier, they had conquered and plundered hundreds of other such settlements. To their delight, small storage huts elevated above the flood plain by sections of tree trunks proved to be crammed with maize.

When they had left Seville with de Soto, the young and ambitious Spanish and Portuguese nobles would have disdained the idea of finding lodes of maize and sweet potatoes. They expected to return home with all the jewels and precious metals they could transport.

De Soto's father was a minor gentleman, nothing more. Biographer David E. Duncan insists that the family name was simply Soto. Even if he is right, the Anglicized version is firmly embedded in history and is likely to continue to be used in all references to the Spanish explorer.

The elder de Soto either placed a low value upon education or didn't have enough silver to send his son to school. Hernando was capable of scrawling his signature but may have been unable to read and write. His personal observations made during his long journey through what is now North America were dictated to a scribe.

When the eight-hundred-ton *San Christoval* sailed for Cuba in 1538, the flagship was followed by seven large vessels and three smaller ones. Reaching his island destination, de Soto devoted a full year to preparation for conquest of "the northern kingdom of the Incas" that he called Florida.

Few expeditions of the period were so well equipped. Crossbows, swords, lances, neck-collars, handcuffs, and chains for captives were used as ballast for the nine-vessel fleet. Each of the 650 or so men was promised the use of a harquebus, or heavy matchlock gun. Although small by European standards, de Soto's single cannon was calculated to frighten the Incas into submission.

Enough horses were taken along to make it possible for one man out of every six to ride. Herds of young swine crammed into the ships would be driven across the land so the adventurers could frequently have fresh pork. Should the natives try to escape, they would be tracked down by Cuban bloodhounds that de Soto called "war dogs."

No ordinary person could have outfitted such an expedition at his own expense. De Soto, however, was almost casual about the cost of his foray into what he mistakenly believed to be the Incan Empire of the North. In Central and South America—especially in Peru—he had accumulated a fortune so large that he never bothered to estimate his worth.

Many scholars have tried to reconstruct de Soto's route through Florida, Georgia, South Carolina, Tennessee, Alabama, and Mississippi. John Swinton's map, published in 1939, is considered to be one of the most reliable.

According to Swinton, the party of gold-hungry explorers went as far south in Alabama as Mobile, then stayed close to the Tombigbee River and its tributaries for many weeks. When they discovered themselves near the headwaters of streams that emptied into the Gulf of Mexico, they turned west. Soon they entered so dense and vast a forest that they wandered about in it day after day before emerging close to the Father of Waters.

Thirty years earlier, a band of unidentified Spanish sailors had hugged the northern coast of the Gulf for many leagues. They described a spot at which they believed a mighty river emptied into it, but no European had ever crossed the Mississippi far from the Gulf.

Still obsessed with his yearning to eclipse his fellow conquistadors by finding an Inca empire even richer than that of Peru, a weary but optimistic de Soto decided to cross the great river.

More than one hundred of his men had been killed or died of illness, yet to get five hundred men across the Mississippi River was a mammoth undertaking. They not only made the crossing, they pushed far into present-day Arkansas before being trapped by a harsh winter.

By the time the spring thaw came, de Soto realized he would need more men, horses, weapons, and provisions to continue his quest. Hence he moved down the Arkansas River toward the Mississippi, planning to establish a permanent post where small ships could be built. These could be sent to Cuba to bring back needed provisions.

Somewhere close to the mouth of the Arkansas River the seeker of the northern Incas was felled by fever, possibly a severe case of malaria. When nearly delirious, he selected Luis de Moscoso to take command of the expedition. About a year after having crossed the Mississippi River and having returned close to it, de Soto died.

Keenly aware that de Soto had told the Indians that he was sired by the sun and was immortal, Moscoso buried his leader's body. When a chieftain asked about him, the Spaniard responded, "He has ascended to the sun, but will return soon."

After several days, de Soto's body was exhumed. His followers sewed several of their mantles together, then poured buckets of sand into the improvised shroud. On an evening when the Indians were busy with ceremonies, the great explorer's remains were pushed into a hollow live oak log.

This was transported by canoe to the middle of the Mississippi River, and the weight of the sand caused the makeshift casket to swirl rapidly downward in water nineteen fathoms deep. Unaware that the northern Inca

De Soto decides to cross the Mississippi River. [Harper's Encyclopedia of United States History]

kingdom for which he had searched for three years did not exist, de Soto went to the bottom of the river at sunset.

During later generations, the river no other European had crossed before him transported the agricultural and industrial products of mid-America in ever-increasing volume. Although de Soto could not have foreseen it, the value of the goods that floated down the Father of Waters meant that he lay at the bottom of the only thing in North America that had qualities in common with his fabled city of gold.

87

Camel Corps:
Desert Ships

Lt. George B. McClellan strode briskly to the red-brick building that housed the U.S. War Department and opened the door. Once inside, he stared in astonishment. He had led a team of four officers who spent an entire year overseas. Charged with making a study of the latest weapons, tactics, fortifications, and transportation, they had gone from the Crimea to North African deserts.

"Things have changed!" the brilliant young West Point graduate muttered to himself. "There must be nearly a hundred clerks in this place now!"

Introducing himself to the receptionist, he asked to see the secretary of war as soon as possible.

"There's no way he can see you today," he was told. "He's at the Executive Mansion in conference with the president. Try tomorrow afternoon—or the next morning."

"I haven't unpacked my bags," McClellan snapped. "If the secretary is too busy with other matters to give me a few minutes, I'll just leave the last of my reports. They must go directly to him, no one else. Do you understand?"

Nodding comprehension, the receptionist extended his hand to take McClellan's papers but said nothing.

Late that evening the secretary of war, who habitually stayed at his desk until midnight or later, found the last of McClellan's summaries of "Observations in the Crimea and Elsewhere."

After scanning several sections in perfunctory fashion, he came to one entitled "Desert Ships." Suddenly keenly interested, Jefferson Davis read every word about the uses, cost, equipment, and drivers of camels.

For years, U.S. Army officials had been frustrated by the failure of attempts to trace a route through the deserts of the Southwest. Horses and mules typically stood the heat for only a few days; some of them dropped in their tracks within hours after entering the blistering heat.

Before yielding to the pleas of President Franklin Pierce and accepting the War Department portfolio, Davis and others had talked about experimenting with camels. Neither he nor other Americans had any firsthand experience with these animals. It was commonly believed, however, that they stored water in their enormous humps and therefore were widely used in desert areas by the Arabs.

Jefferson Davis
as depicted in
a contemporary
engraving.

Davis, a Kentucky native and West Point graduate, had resigned from the U.S. Army after seven years of hard service. After having purchased Brierfield plantation in Mississippi, not far from the huge spread owned by his brother at Davis Bend, he won a seat in the House of Representatives.

At the outbreak of the Mexican War he joined the outfit headed by Gen. Zachary Taylor, whose daughter had died soon after marrying Davis and journeying to Mississippi. Leading his Mississippi Rifles at the battle of Buena Vista, Davis won high praise from all observers except Gen. Winfield Scott.

Back at Brierfield with his young second wife, Varina, the veteran soldier was presented with a sword of honor. Almost simultaneously, the Mississippi legislature named him to fill an unexpired term in the U.S. Senate. Strongly opposed to the Compromise of 1850, he became the capital's most articulate spokesman for southern causes.

Leaving the Senate in a bid for the governorship of Mississippi, he suffered his only political defeat. That did not dissuade him from stumping in 1852 in support of Franklin Pierce's bid for the presidency. Had the Whig Party not lost 156,000 votes to the Free Soil Party in the 1852 election, Winfield Scott might have become chief executive.

Davis's leadership in the Pierce campaign was so prominent that he felt duty-bound to be in Washington for the inauguration of the man he helped to elect. The president-elect himself hinted that he would like to see this supporter from Mississippi in his cabinet.

Davis would have preferred to have remained at his plantation in Brierfield; he and Varina were expecting a baby soon, and her health was not the best. After several long talks with Pierce, Davis agreed to serve as secretary of war.

More than simply open-minded, the new secretary of war was eager for innovations. That desire was why he

*David D. Porter, who became a U.S. Navy admiral
during the Civil War.*

had sent McClellan and four aides on their expedition
that ended in 1855. By that time, Davis had ordered that
iron rims be placed on the wheels of gun carriages and
had approved the use of rifled muskets that used minié
balls.

On the basis of McClellan's optimistic report, the secretary believed that camels would be helpful in surveying a southern route for a projected transcontinental railroad. Since his department had an annual budget of
nearly twenty million dollars, Davis decided that an ex-

An artist's incorrect sketch showed Camp Verde to house two-humped Bactrian camels that originated in ancient Persia rather than Arabian dromedaries. [U.S. ARMY MILITARY HISTORY INSTITUTE]

penditure of thirty thousand dollars to purchase a few camels would not be regarded as extravagant. Hence he made Lt. David D. Porter a purchasing agent of sorts and sent him to the Middle East to acquire the beasts.

By the time Porter returned in 1856 with thirty-four animals, Davis had done a little more research. He learned that a camel's hump had little to do with storing water and everything he had read seemed to confirm the contention that they were superior to horses and mules for work in deserts.

Porter established a holding area for his camels in Texas, northwest of San Antonio, in what his colleagues jokingly called "a grand camel camp." His herd was more than doubled in size when a second purchasing expedition returned with forty-one additional mean-spirited "ships of the desert."

The men and animals who made up the Camel Corps of the U.S. Army demonstrated that the desert could be mastered. Tested at Camp Verde, the animals from the Near East went for days without water and proved that they could move three or four times as much weight as a horse. Never fully accepted by the soldiers, the half-dozen Arabs who were hired as camel drivers helped to survey a route that was later used, not for a transcontinental railroad, but for the famous U.S. Route 66.

In March 1857, when Davis was again a senator from Mississippi, his successor in the war department office reviewed the Camel Corps and pronounced it a rousing success. John B. Floyd recommended the purchase of an additional thousand animals. His proposal was never implemented, however. The outbreak of the Civil War forced him from office and the animals of the Camel Corps fell into the hands of the Confederates.

Although a few camels were in U.S. Army service for only a half-dozen years, Davis's biographers insist that his grand experiment ranks second only to his presidency of the Confederacy as a memorable achievement by a man who helped to shape the course of the nation.

88

Varina Davis: Convoluted Belle

Varina Howell of Natchez, tall and graceful at the age of seventeen, was reluctant to accompany her parents to a Christmas party. She and her friends had other things they wanted to do, but in 1843 the daughter of a wealthy planter knew that it was useless to oppose her father.

One of the other guests at the party was a relative newcomer, not yet fully accepted by aristocrats of the river. Rumored to be wealthy, the former U.S. Army officer was described as "nearly over his grief" at the death of his wife.

During a brief conversation with her new acquaintance who was twice her age, Varina assessed him carefully. Jefferson Davis cut a good figure and had a fine command of language, she quickly discovered. Somehow, though, he struck her as arrogant and cold, a man who remained aloof while trying to be warm and friendly.

Smitten almost at first sight, Davis pursued Varina relentlessly and eventually gained her consent to marry him. She might not have said yes to his proposal had she known what was taking place between Jefferson and his older brother, Joseph.

As caretaker of the family fortune, Joseph selected a splendid eight-hundred-acre tract and purchased it for Jefferson. Long before Brierfield mansion was ready for occupancy, Joseph drew up and Jefferson signed a document not unusual for the period.

At the time of their marriage, Varina was young enough to be Jefferson Davis's daughter.

No one had ever heard of a prenuptial agreement at that time, but wealthy bridegrooms often prepared wills that stipulated how their property would be distributed upon their death. At the insistence of Joseph, Jefferson directed that not an acre of land would go to Varina if she outlived him.

The early will of Jefferson Davis was a clear omen. As head of the household, he would make all important decisions and would not necessarily consult his wife about them. She was expected to be a dutiful mate who would manage the household, bear children, and keep a smile on her face when she accompanied her husband to social gatherings.

Tension erupted into a quarrel when, without sharing his plans with Varina, Jefferson enlisted in a military unit to fight in the Mexican War. They didn't have a formal separation—such a thing would not have been tolerated in their society—yet they quarreled bitterly. When Jefferson returned a hero and was named to fill a vacancy in the U.S. Senate, he punished his high-spirited young wife by leaving her at Brierfield during his first year in Washington.

A reconciliation, which meant total surrender on the part of Varina, brought her to the capital. As the wife of a senator and then the secretary of war, she entertained frequently. As a result, she formed a relationship that appears strange when seen in retrospect.

Elizabeth Keckley, employed as a household maid, proved to be intelligent and efficient. She and her mistress began a friendship that was terminated when Davis resigned from the Senate and returned to Mississippi. Briefly unemployed, Keckley found another job in the capital. This time she worked for Mary Todd Lincoln and became a trusted adviser to the wartime president.

By the time Keckley was well established in her new post, Varina Davis was presiding as first lady of the Confederacy. Her four years in Richmond were later characterized as "absolutely the worst" she ever experienced. Personal tragedy accounted for many, but not all, of her woes in the Confederate capital.

Shortages developed in the Confederacy almost as soon as the Federal blockade was launched in 1861. By 1863 food was scarce, and the best of it went to the soldiers. The situation produced several organized protests, commonly called "bread riots."

Using shortages of food as an excuse, civilians indulged in widespread looting. Mobile was struck by such a riot, along with Atlanta and Columbia, South Carolina. By far the most serious of these incidents broke out in the Confederate capital early in April 1863.

Some newspaper estimates say that the bread riot in Richmond involved twenty thousand people. Although that estimate is believed inflated, there were so many angry women in the streets that Virginia's governor called out the Public Guard. Tradition has it that Jefferson Davis eventually took charge of the guardsmen and arrested fifty women and about thirty men.

Whatever the cause of the Richmond riot, Varina's sympathies were with the women who said that they had no way to put food on their tables. She agonized over the insoluble problem of securing adequate supplies of flour and other essentials and was gravely offended when her husband stressed that "men in gray must always come first."

Only weeks after the bread riot, she experienced personal tragedy. Earlier, she had objected when her husband decided to name their son after his older brother, Joseph. Varina admitted that the baby bore a striking resemblance to her brother-in-law but told Keckley, "I pray he may soon outgrow the resemblance."

April 30, 1864, was unusually warm. As a result, the windows of the Confederate White House were open and the curtains were fluttering in the breeze. Early in the afternoon four-year-old Joseph sauntered out on a balcony and soon began climbing along its railing. He somehow lost his grip and plunged twenty feet to his death in the brick courtyard below.

Joseph's death gave his mother a bond with a woman she had never met. About one hundred miles away in the Federal capital, William Wallace Lincoln died of typhoid fever soon after his father became president. It was Elizabeth Keckley to whom Mary Todd Lincoln turned for consolation. In Richmond, in the wake of Joseph's death, Keckley's role was assumed by an Irish nursemaid known only as Catherine.

With tragedy having already darkened the lives of the two women whose husbands were contending heads of state, both Varina Davis and Mary Todd Lincoln soon experienced new sorrow.

"It was terrible for that man Booth to shoot Mr. Lincoln," Varina told friends, "but his wife soon knew he could not live. For two solid years, while Jefferson was imprisoned at Fort Monroe, I didn't know from one day

The four Davis children; Joseph sits at the right with little Winnie, "daughter of the Confederacy," standing beside him. [EMBATTLED CONFEDERATES]

to the next whether he'd go to the gallows or be released."

Lincoln's widow, convinced that she was doomed to a life of poverty, made a pitiful and unsuccessful attempt to sell her jewelry and clothing. Significantly, it was Elizabeth Keckley who accompanied her to New York for the enterprise that proved futile.

Varina Davis, reared in wealth, lived in "genteel poverty" after her husband was released from prison. He retreated to the home of a friend in Biloxi, Mississippi, where he spent his final years producing a ponderous and tedious two-volume account of the war, *The Rise and Fall of the Confederate Government*. At no time after leaving Richmond was he able to provide more than the bare necessities for his wife and family.

After Davis's death in 1889, Varina turned her back on the past and moved to New York City. There the strangely convoluted life of the Mississippi belle took yet another turn. She met and soon became a close friend of another widow, Julia Grant, wife of Ulysses S. Grant, the general who had won the war and the eighteenth president of the United States. The widow Grant was relatively affluent from the royalties earned by her husband's memoirs.

Tradition has it that Julia Grant had read an article by Varina, who had turned to writing for newspapers and

Julia Grant.

magazines. When she discovered that the widow of another president was living in a hotel on the Hudson River, Julia went calling. After knocking on Varina's door and giving her name, she was told, "Do come in! I've always wanted to meet you!"

Soon the two former first ladies became fast friends and spent much time together. Frequently Varina accompanied Julia on carriage rides that included a circuit around Grant's tomb.

Since her daughter, Varina Anne ("Winnie"), was already being hailed as "the Daughter of the Confederacy," Varina made few public appearances. Her health began to decline.

At the death of the Mississippi belle who married a domestic tyrant, the son of U. S. Grant took charge of the funeral arrangements. He saw to it that the former first lady of the Confederacy had a military escort when her body was moved from her hotel to a ship headed for Richmond.

Newspapers of the day record that the cortege of Jefferson Davis's widow was accompanied by a military band. The musicians played "Dixie" and "The Bonnie Blue Flag," and Manhattan traffic came to a halt as the Mississippi belle headed toward the vessel that took her to Hollywood Cemetery in the former Confederate capital for burial far from Natchez.

89

Vicksburg:
Forty-Three Days of Siege

"Vicksburg is the key to the Mississippi and maybe the war," said Maj. Gen. U. S. Grant.

Aides who had assembled for their first staff meeting after Grant's appointment as head of the Department of the Tennessee glanced uncertainly at one another. All knew that the river port in Mississippi was important, but few shared their commander's judgment that its conquest was vital to the Union war effort.

Soon they learned that the man now wearing two stars was not seeking their opinions or advice. Rather, he was informing them that he had reached a firm conclusion. According to his reasoning, the two-hundred-foot bluffs on the river side of the city were ideal sites for heavy cannon. Properly manned, Confederate weapons erected at this point could prevent Union warships from going up or down the great river. Forced to move slowly because of a hairpin curve in the river, Grant reasoned, even the finest ironclads would be easy targets at this point.

After a few days in his new post, he launched an overland campaign whose objective was Vicksburg. A tightly coordinated army-navy operation would be essential, he realized. Fresh troops promised by General in Chief Henry W. Halleck would be helpful, but he felt he could not wait for them.

Starting from Bolivar, Tennessee, early in November, the Federal commander planned to reach Jackson via the

Maj. Gen. Ulysses S. Grant.

Mississippi Central Railroad. He soon found that many bridges had to be rebuilt and long sections of tracks had to be repaired. As a result, during a month of movement and fighting against Confederates under Lt. Gen. John C. Pemberton, he did not reach his objective.

Revising his strategic plans, Grant continued to head overland toward Jackson and Vicksburg. Meanwhile he placed Maj. Gen. William T. Sherman at the head of an amphibious force designed to strike their target from the river.

For nine months nearly everything Grant attempted proved futile. In an attempt to reach the city of five thousand by way of the Yazoo River, he directed his men to dig a canal through which his warships might maneuver. Time and time again, the swamps and the weather proved too much for his men. After expending enormous manpower on the canal, it was abandoned.

In desperation, the man who eventually occupied the White House for two terms devised an imaginative but dangerous scheme. He would slowly move his troops southward through the swamps west of the river, using barges and small riverboats. Meanwhile Adm. David D. Porter would try to run his gunboats past the bluffs of Vicksburg in order to ferry Federal units across the Mississippi at a point well below their target. This would enable men in blue to advance toward the city and strike at its relatively unprotected south side.

Incredibly, one of the most daring gambles of the Civil War paid off. Eluding heavy gunfire, Porter managed to get eleven of his twelve ships below Vicksburg with relatively little damage. Grant's men were never able to meet the schedule adopted by their commander, but by the middle of May 1863 they were poised to strike.

Two successive assaults by Federal forces were easily turned back by the Confederate defenders, however. On May 19 one of their battalions suffered casualties of more than 40 percent, and a battle flag riddled with fifty bullet holes hung in shreds. Inside the city, Confederate casualties were only one-fourth that of the attacking Federals.

Three days later, all Union corps commanders put their men in motion against Vicksburg at precisely 10:00 A.M. To the surprise of officers and men in blue who managed to get relatively close to their target, they found that miles of fortifications had been thrown up east of the city. There was no way to take Vicksburg except by means of a protracted siege.

Digging a series of trenches for protection, the Federals gradually moved closer to the city. Soon nearly seventy thousand men were crowded into what some analysts have called "the most elaborate system of trenches before World War I." Including camps and gun emplacements, the works of the attacking forces stretched fully twelve miles in length.

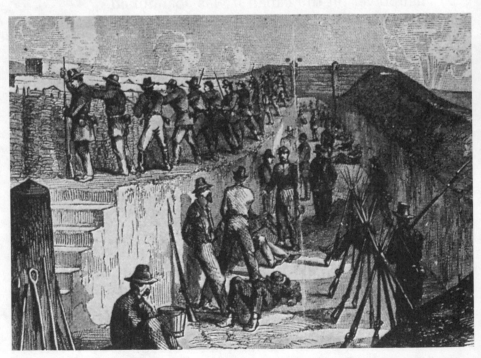

Men of Grant's big army "went underground" in a mammoth maze of trenches. [Century Magazine]

Logically, the Confederate commander in Vicksburg should have surrendered immediately. As well as Grant, he knew that the surrounded city would face increasingly severe privations and eventual starvation.

Yet as soon as shells began falling in the city, civilians and soldiers alike began frantic work with shovels of their own. The soft earth of the hillsides made it relatively easy to scoop out caves that could be buttressed by layers of rock.

Once a squad of fighting men or members of a family were inside one of these improvised "bombproofs," they were safe from gunfire but not from hunger. Some of the more affluent fitted out their bombproofs with tables, chairs, and even carpets.

Soon the food in Vicksburg was reduced to coarse bread made from peas instead of wheat and strange-looking cuts of mule meat. Water supplies became so low that

Defeated Confederates march from Vicksburg.

soldiers were stationed at every well with orders to shoot anyone who tried to use water except for drinking.

After more than a month of total siege, it was obvious to the defenders that they would be forced to give up the city. After preliminary talks, Grant gleefully designated July 4 as the day on which the ceremonies would take place. He did not know that far to the northeast Robert E. Lee's defeated army would be retreating from Gettysburg, Pennsylvania, on that same day.

In Vicksburg, nearly twenty thousand men in gray were paroled; meaning that they swore an oath not to fight again unless and until they were exchanged as prisoners of war. More than any other single achievement, the capture of Vicksburg put Grant on the road to becoming the first lieutenant general since George Washington.

90
The *Sultana*:
Horror on the River

During April 19–20, 1865, the steamer *Sultana* was anchored at the Gravier Street dock in New Orleans. Before noon on April 21 she pulled away, bound up the Mississippi River. About seventy-five prosperous passengers occupied cabins, while deck passengers and the crew of the 719-ton river steamer added up to about two hundred.

Ten hours out of Natchez, engineers spotted boiler trouble. That would mean a stay of several hours, perhaps a day or two, at the nearest port having artisans and equipment needed to make repairs. Vicksburg was immediately chosen as the spot at which the long layover would take place.

Officers aboard the steamer did not know that the city was the debarkation point for soldiers recently released from southern prisons, with thousands pouring in from such places as Andersonville, Georgia, and Cahaba, Alabama.

The former prisoners of war, exuberant at the prospect of going home, set up a camp of sorts four miles from Vicksburg. Camp Fisk, as they termed it, was designed to receive and process about five thousand men.

Some of the lucky ones managed to reach Vicksburg by rail. Others arrived on wheezing little riverboats designed to carry cotton, whose masters were glad to take on anyone who had the money to pay for passage. Hundreds of former prisoners arrived at Camp Fisk by foot.

Rare photograph of the doomed Sultana.

Having reached Jackson by rail and finding they were
likely to be stranded there, they walked the thirty-odd
miles to their destination.

Union Maj. Gen. Napoleon Dana, head of the vast program of prisoner exchange at Vicksburg, encountered
several obstacles in dealing with former Confederate officials. Hence he sent Capt. George A. Williams to Mobile
to negotiate with them and placed Capt. Frederick Speed
in charge of sending the released prisoners upriver.

Most former prisoners were expected to go to Camp
Chase, Ohio, named for the secretary of the treasury. Others were destined for Benton Barracks in Illinois
or smaller places that could be reached by water.
From these posts, they would make their way home
as best they could. Once a former prisoner was properly enrolled, the cost of his transportation northward from Vicksburg was guaranteed by the U.S. government.

Riverboat captains, having heard of the planned ship-
ments of former prisoners, hurried toward Vicksburg
hoping for an unusually profitable voyage. When the
packet *Henry Ames* arrived, her master found that only
about eight hundred men had been processed. He
lingered at the port until more names were entered on
the rolls, staying until he had thirteen hundred veterans
aboard the ship.

Almost before the Vicksburg dockworkers lost sight of
the *Henry Ames*, Capt. Ben Taber's packet *Olive Branch*
pulled into the space just vacated. With river transportation at hand, officers processing the former prisoners ac-
celerated their work, skipping some of the prescribed
questions. By dusk on April 23 the *Henry Ames*, also
loaded to the gunwales, began chugging her way slowly
upstream.

With new contingents of men arriving at Camp Fisk
almost hourly, it was overflowing when the *Sultana* put
into Vicksburg for boiler repairs. Artisans grumbled but
agreed to work around the clock until the steamer was
ready to continue her voyage north.

During the thirty-three hours it took to complete the
boiler repairs, the recently released officers and men became increasingly impatient. Long before the work was
finished, as soon as a man was enrolled, he tried to shove
his way aboard the *Sultana*.

Since the announced time of departure was postponed
at least twice, the vessel was crowded far beyond her
capacity by the time she was ready to leave Vicksburg. So
many men stood shoulder to shoulder on the hurricane
deck that the crew hastily placed stanchions under it so
it would not snap beneath their weight.

The captain of the ship regarded this horde as money
in his pocket, since he received a percentage of each passenger's travel allowance. Several people preserved
records concerning the loading of the vessel, but no two
sets of figures are in agreement.

Shortly after midnight on April 24, the last gangplank was lifted and the men who crowded the decks of the steamer gave a lusty cheer.

When the *Sultana* left Vicksburg and began moving into the current of the river, she was the most heavily loaded vessel ever to sail on the Mississippi up to that time. Her hold was crowded with at least sixty horses and mules and nearly twice as many hogs. Yet this cargo was nothing compared to what the steamer carried in her cabins and on her decks.

About 85 members of the crew were stationed at various points throughout the vessel. Since only 15 cabin passengers had disembarked at Vicksburg, 60 civilians remained aboard. According to official U.S. Army records, 34 officers and 1,832 enlisted men made up the rest of the ship's burden.

Rated to carry a maximum of 376 persons, the *Sultana* groaned from her load of at least three hundred thousand pounds of humans and animals. Members of the crew constantly patrolled the decks, warning the former prisoners not to crowd to one side of the steamer. If they did so, the sailors warned grimly, "She'll tip over in a minute and go down like lead."

The firemen never shut the doors of the furnaces; coal taken aboard for the trip to Cairo, Illinois, was shoveled into them constantly. Inevitably something gave way; no one ever knew whether holes were burned in the sides of the hastily repaired boilers or whether superheated steam built up and exploded.

No lifeboats were aboard, and the boat was equipped with no safety devices except a few cork life belts for the cabin passengers. Hence the sudden explosion of her boilers that ripped the *Sultana* apart meant quick death for hundreds of those who crowded her decks.

When the captain of the USS *Essex* learned of the tragedy, he headed for the watery grave of the river steamer at full speed. Using two boats and a yawl, he was able to

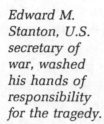

Edward M. Stanton, U.S. secretary of war, washed his hands of responsibility for the tragedy.

pick sixty men and one woman from the water. Bound from Cincinnati to New Orleans, the steamer *Bostonia* rescued nearly one hundred victims of the explosion.

All the rest were ripped apart by red-hot metal from exploding boilers, were crushed by falling timbers, or were plunged into the water. Even those who could swim were unable to master the river's strong current long enough to reach shore.

According to data compiled by the U.S. Customs Service, 1,547 persons, joyfully thinking themselves headed for home, died in two hours. Some records indicate that fatalities were at least 100 more than the officially acknowledged total.

Overloading due to haste and carelessness caused this unparalleled maritime disaster. Not simply on the Mississippi River, but also on the high seas, no comparable death toll has resulted from the sinking of an American ship.

Strangely from today's perspective, the story of so many deaths on the river attracted little media attention in 1865. Because the *Sultana* disaster occurred only days after the assassination of Abraham Lincoln, news accounts of the tragedy were few and short.

Mourning for the first president to be slain and preoccupation with the hunt for the conspirators behind the tragedy caused editors in the North to give only passing attention to the river tragedy.

Speed, who was accused of having accepted bribes to place so many men on the *Sultana,* spent weeks enduring a grueling court-martial. When he was exonerated, the secretary of war said only that he was glad "to see the mess finally settled."

The ship that was vastly overloaded at Vicksburg took more than eight times as many lives as did the Oklahoma City bombing of April 1995.

91

Eudora Welty:
Listen . . . and Look!

Born in Jackson in 1909, by the age of three little Eudora Welty had learned to listen. At almost any hour and in whatever room happened to be convenient, her mother read to her.

Very early, words began to be strongly linked with things they labeled. If she heard the word "saucer," an image would flash on the screen of her imagination. Immediately she would see a piece of white ceramic, nearly but not quite flat—rounded, hard, and designed to be the base on which a cup could sit.

Practically every word that named a thing came to have an identity of its own. When she encountered "moon," a glimpse of a shining round orb came to mind, and she remembered a Concord grape she once held in her mouth before swallowing it whole.

In adolescence she often attended silent movies, whose only words were captions. Now the sight of actions and objects, combined with their names, strengthened the bond between them.

Her mother, Mary Castina, read with a high-pitched West Virginia accent in a cadence that was almost rhythmic. Her father, Christian, had come south to take a position as a junior executive with an insurance company. His Ohio twang was decidedly flatter than that of her mother and lower in tone.

Little Eudora filed the speech patterns of both her mother and her father in the delicate and complex supercomputer inside her head. Then she listened to the speech of her Mississippi-born playmates and noticed emphases, pauses, and intonations distinct from the speech patterns of West Virginia and Ohio.

Years later, reviewers of her short stories and novels consistently lauded her "sensitive handling of the rhythms and nuances of southern speech." According to Welty, she didn't have to work hard at achieving this result; it came naturally and in a special fashion.

When reading silently during childhood, she said, she always listened to and heard the words upon which her eyes fell. This inner voice was human but was not identical to her mother's, her father's, or her playmates'. To her, sounds that no one else heard constituted "the voice of the story or the poem itself."

In the days before kindergartens, little Eudora memorized the alphabet at her mother's knee. By age five, a year before her long-anticipated start to school, she was reading books that had been written for grownups.

At home, Eudora's favorite spot was a child-size chair in the living room, which every member of the family called "the library." It boasted a copy of *Webster's Unabridged Dictionary* and *Compton's Picture Encyclopedia*. Later the *Lincoln Library of Information*, the *Columbia Encyclopedia*, and the *Book of Knowledge* were added to that enchanted room.

At about age six or seven, Eudora was presented with *Our Wonder World*—all ten volumes. She devoured them all but was especially intrigued by volume 5, which included the fairy tales of Hans Christian Andersen and the Grimm brothers, part of *Gulliver's Travels,* and marvelous stories about Saint George and the dragon, King Arthur, and Robin Hood.

Soon the growing girl was delving into the complete works of Mark Twain and Charles Dickens and most of Ring Lardner's stories. As soon as she was old enough to go to it by herself, she became a constant visitor to the library endowed by Andrew Carnegie when the city of

Jackson was rebuilt after the Civil War. It was on the same side of the street as her house, and she only had to walk to the other side of the state capitol to reach it.

If there is such a thing as obsessive reading—total fascination with printed words that automatically conjures up images, sounds, odors, and sensations of touch—young Eudora was afflicted with it. In a fashion quite different from effects produced by many drugs, she was an addict.

Small wonder that, very early, she began practicing putting words together herself. She showed more than usual talent when painting with watercolors, but her real passion was painting with words and evoking sensations from them.

She became a student at the Mississippi State College for Women when the concept of "equal opportunity education" hadn't been conceived. There it was all but inevi-

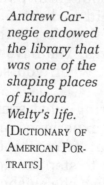

Andrew Carnegie endowed the library that was one of the shaping places of Eudora Welty's life. [DICTIONARY OF AMERICAN PORTRAITS]

table that the girl from Jackson should help to launch a campus literary magazine. She transferred to the University of Wisconsin and after graduation was urged to "study something practical." Hence she attended the Graduate School of Business at Columbia University to prepare for a career in advertising.

It took only a few months at Columbia for her to decide that anything involving persuasive selling was not for her. Back home in Jackson, she wrote briefly for both a local radio station and the *Memphis Commercial Appeal* on a part-time basis.

Suddenly a full-time job presented itself. Within days of hearing about the position, she was one of the publicity agents for Franklin D. Roosevelt's Works Progress Administration. Traveling to all eighty-two counties in the state, she always took along an inexpensive Kodak camera. Film she shot was developed and printed at night in the kitchen of the Jackson home. Long afterward, one hundred of these pictures were put into a volume she called *One Time, One Place: Mississippi in the Depression*.

According to Welty, it was the daily use of a camera that taught her to look as well as to listen as she had learned to do in childhood. It was not enough to point the camera and click the shutter, she said in later life. "The thing to wait on, to reach there in time for, is the moment in which people reveal themselves. You have to be ready; you have to know the moment when you see it."

Still plugging away at her writing during what spare time she had, Welty had a semi-mystical experience one day in Tishomingo County. In a moment of combined listening and looking, she seemed almost to step outside herself. A camera wouldn't quite do what she wished, she realized.

She desperately wanted to understand people more fully. To do so, she must never "point the finger in judgment." Instead, she must strive "to part a curtain, that

Eudora Welty's 1930 photograph of a café window in
Fayette, Mississippi. [MISSISSIPPI DEPARTMENT OF ARCHIVES
AND HISTORY]

invisible shadow that falls between people, the veil of
indifference to each other's presence, each other's wonder, each other's human plight.''

At the age of twenty-seven she reached two plateaus
during a single year. Some of her photographs of ordinary people in Mississippi were exhibited at New York's
Lugene Gallery. Almost simultaneously, *Manuscript*
magazine offered a set of her very own words to readers.
Her short story ''Death of a Traveling Salesman'' peered

into the life of a lonely and frightened shoe salesman who became lost in a sparsely inhabited area of Mississippi.

When the high-prestige Doubleday publishing firm issued a collection of seventeen short stories, it looked as though she had it made. Not quite. During more than twenty-five years, sales of *A Curtain of Green* barely exceeded six thousand copies.

Yet "A Worn Path," one of the stories included in the anthology, brought her the O. Henry Memorial Prize in 1941. Welty's other achievements and awards include the adaptation of *The Robber Bridegroom* for the musical stage by Alfred Uhry and Robert Waldman, the William Dean Howells Medal of the American Academy of Arts and Letters, the gold medal of the National Institute of Arts and Letters, the 1972 Pulitzer Prize for *The Optimist's Daughter*, and five more O. Henry Memorial awards.

Welty has consciously avoided the literary styles made famous by fellow Mississippians Tennessee Williams and William Faulkner. She never, never includes gratuitous violence or raw sex. She deliberately avoided opportunities to portray "the decadent south" of Faulkner.

Both the dream of fabulous riches that gripped Hernando de Soto and the barbarities he practiced while pursuing it are totally foreign to her experience. Unlike Varina Davis, the novelist was not exposed to the tensions of the wartime capital of the Confederacy. She never crawled into a cave to escape Federal shells falling upon besieged Vicksburg.

Spending most of her seemingly sheltered life in the city where she was born, Eudora Welty developed extraordinary abilities to listen and to look and then to put into words what she heard and saw in the lives of everyday Mississippians in ordinary places. As a result, from her red-brick home close to the capitol has emanated a stream of prize-winning stories and novels that are treasured throughout the Western world.